THE HISTORY C
IN THE VILLAGE

". . . the responsive creativity of humans to the love of God is nothing until it discovers itself in the emergence of the concrete reality of the Church.

. . . in stone placed upon stone to build a Church, in wood carved into the fashion of a Cross: in music composed or practised, played or sung: in the doing of certain things upon a particular day, and the giving up of certain things during a particular season: in the fashioning, out of time and care and skill, of something beautiful, and in the maintaining, out of time and care and labour, of the beauty of it: in the gathering and training of others so that they may contribute to, and continue, and enlarge the offering: in the going out to others, so that they may share the offering: in the struggle of brain and pen to find expression and interpretation for the love of God: in the event of worship which celebrates the love of God: in hands stretched out for the receiving of Bread, and in lips raised for the touch of Wine.

Here, at this level of concrete actuality is the response of recognition to the love of God: here is the work of art, the offering of love, which is the Church."

Taken from 'Love's Endeavour, Love's Expense' by W. H. Vanstone, published and copyright 1977 by Darton, Longman and Todd Ltd, London, and used by permission of the publishers.

THE HISTORY OF
ST PETER'S CHURCH
IN THE VILLAGE
OF NEWTON

Drawn by Philip Shaddick

Researched and written by
Susan Rees, Wendy Cope and Edna Davies

Compiled and edited by Susan M. Rees

Published in 2010 by
The Vicar and churchwardens of St Peter's Church, Newton, Swansea.

Available from Susan Rees
01792 405282

ISBN 978-0-9566348-0-1

Front Cover: View of south entrance of St Peter's Church (*Huw Jones*)
Back Cover: Banner of St Peter acquired 1934, believed to have been designed
and made by the Sisters of Kilburn (*Susan Rees*)

Printed and bound in Wales by
Dinefwr Press Ltd.
Rawlings Road, Llandybie
Carmarthenshire, SA18 3YD

Contents

Acknowledgements

Many people have helped in the production of this book and it is a pleasure to record our warm thanks and appreciation to them all. Firstly, we would like to thank the writers of the first *St Peter's Church History and Guide*, 1983, the late Miss G. P. Snow, Mrs Leslie Griffin and Mrs Jean Haines, the editor, whose work was the inspiration. The latter two have also contributed articles in this book. Secondly, we are greatly indebted to a number of persons at public institutions for enabling us to use their resources for research, viz: Mrs Marilyn Jones and staff of Swansea Reference Library and Cambrian Index Project; Bernice Cardy and Gerald Gabb of the Royal Institution of South Wales, Swansea; Kim Collis, and his predecessor Miss S. Beckley, and their staff at the West Glamorgan Archive Service (W.G.A.S.) Swansea; Mr Martin James and Mr Paul Rees of the Representative Body of the Church Wales, Llandaff, Cardiff, for the copy of the Indenture and other help; The National Library of Wales, Aberystwyth.

In Mumbles we would like to thank the Revd Keith Evans, Vicar of All Saints Church, Oystermouth, for graciously permitting us many hours of access to the collection of all the early parish magazines [the *Oystermouth Parish Magazine's* are now stored with W.G.A.S.] and to Mr Bill Barrington, the verger, for his invaluable help as a walking memory of past Mumbles and Newton history; to Carol and John Powell and Kate Elliot Jones of Tŷ Hanes, Mumbles; Mumbles Library; and Revd Howard Long, the Methodist minister.

In Newton, to the Vicar of St Peter's Church for providing free use of the records, registers, and the Inventory which was impeccably recorded by former churchwardens, the late Mr Grahame Sutton, his wife Anne and their son David who took the photographs; to the many parishioners for providing access to photographs and personal memories, giving much other help (too many to name, but many have been acknowledged with the relevant script); and to former clergy of St Peter's: to Bishop David and to his wife, Mrs Rosemary Thomas; the late Ven. Harold E. Williams for a copy of his book *The Parting Mist* and his wife Mrs Joan Williams on the G.F.S.; the late Canon Brunsdon; and former Curates, the Revds. Norman Lea and John Cruse; to Mrs Sue Butler (Brownies); the late Dr F. Davies and his wife Mrs Barbara Davies (History of the 5th Mumbles Scout Group). In the village of Newton, to Paraclete Chapel, including Mr Gary Gregor and Kate Towns for her school project on the history of Paraclete Chapel; to Mrs Val Peters, Mrs Betty

Sivertsen and Miss Diana Smith for their memories of a lifetime of living in Newton, and many other residents who have kindly helped provide information. To the writers of many books and articles for their permission to use their material, they are acknowledged in the bibliography at the back of the book. However, we are particularly grateful to Mr Gerald Gabb who could always be relied on to provide information on a query of local history; to Dr Geoffrey Orrin for his generous help and encouragement at the start of our research. For permission to use their photographs and prints we would like to thank: Mr Harold Grenfell; Mr T. Metheun-Campbell; Mr Richard Morris; Dr David Painting; Mr Philip Shaddick; Diane Thomas; Mr Carl Smith; Mrs Ann Watkins; and to Dr Ronald Austin, Mr David Gwynne, Mr Peter Muxworthy and Mr Ken Reeves for use of old postcards. We are also indebted to Mr Brian Goss for his time in recording the centenary exhibition by digital photography.

We are indebted to the *Austin Bailey Foundation* and the *Trust of J. T. Morgan*, for their generous grants and to the *Gower Society* and *West Glamorgan Archive Service* for their assistance which has greatly helped us towards the printing costs of this book and to them all we express our sincere thanks. Also, to Dinefwr Press, especially to Eddie and David, for their patience and help throughout the printing process.

Most of all, this work would not have been possible without the untiring support and notetaking from the co-writers, and in the early stages of our research from Beryl Banbury. Also, our heartfelt thanks go to our families for their patience and encouragement. A special acknowledgement is made to Ron Austin, the final proof reader, for his painstaking attention to the minutiae of the book and for the time and advice he has generously given. Also, at earlier stages in the book's development, our thanks to Bishop David Thomas and to Colin Rees for their invaluable time and assistance in looking through the script and offering helpful comments; and to the vicar and parishioners of St. Peter's Church for their contributions and encouragement. All these and many others have contributed to the compilation of this work.

Susan, Wendy and Edna

Foreword

From The Right Reverend David Thomas, formerly Provincial Assistant Bishop of the Church in Wales:

I experienced several 'firsts' during a family holiday at Caswell in the late 1940s. One was the sight of an adder slithering along the cliffs; another was my first and only trip round the bay in a duck (amphibious landing craft) left behind by the Americans at the end of the war, and a third was the experience of being taken to a Sunday morning service in St Peter's Church. I have to admit that I found the adder and the duck a lot more interesting than the service! In fact the only thing I can remember about my first visit to St Peter's is that I was struck by how much smaller it was than the church we usually attended. Its great beauty was entirely lost on me at the age of five or six. I might add that, since I am no prophet, it never crossed my mind that, forty or so years later, my family and I would be embarking on almost ten extremely happy years in Newton Vicarage and that, sixty years later, we would be returning to the area in retirement.

For these and for all sorts of other reasons, I am delighted to commend this history of St Peter's Church. I am sure that others will enjoy and benefit from reading it as much as I have. I am sure, too, that they will join me in acknowledging our indebtedness to its authors for the time and trouble they have devoted to it.

*

From the Vicar, The Revd Canon George E. Bennett:

I am delighted that Bishop David has written the Foreword to this excellent history, as I know that he was one of the inspirations for the inception of this labour of love.

As the present incumbent of St Peter's I would like to express my appreciation of all the hard work that the authors have lavished on this history.

In a previous parish of mine, a *Guide* to the church was printed and the Foreword was misprinted as 'Forward'. As we reflect on the achievements of the past, let us go forward together to write our own page to the history of our parish. Thank you for a history which will be much appreciated and frequently consulted in the years to come.

Introduction

When members of the church were preparing for the centennial celebration, in 2003, of the consecration of St Peter's Church, it was recognised that it was an appropriate time to update the history of the church. A small group of us undertook to do the research and this culminated in an exhibition to coincide with the week of the centenary. It was well received and created much interest. After the exhibition, instead of putting all the researched material away in the archives, it was decided to record the information in book form. It has taken awhile for the book to materialise but with the encouragement and help from family and many friends of the church it is a relief to see it at last in print.

As we gathered the information it provided a good opportunity to look back, over more than a century, to the beginnings of the church and to recognise the major milestones. Also, it is a way of acknowledging the contribution of former incumbents and parishioners who have not only helped to lay the foundations but have provided the blocks upon which the church is firmly based today.

The conception of the church in its present form was largely due to an eager young priest, Revd Harold Stepney Williams. He arrived in Mumbles in 1898 and stayed for more than fifty years and it was his vision and tireless energy in fund-raising that created St Peter's Church in 1903. Shortly after his arrival the vicar also founded the *Oystermouth Parish Magazine*. These invaluable records have fortunately been preserved and have formed the basis of our research. It has been interesting to observe the changes in custom and use of language and yet, one hundred years on, there are still some similar activities functioning today.

We have considered it pertinent to include a brief history of Newton village and the school, showing how its inhabitants have been occupied since late Victorian times. We believe they are inextricably linked with the development of the church, for the church couldn't exist without the people. The people of Newton, guided by their pastoral leader, have been the force upon which the church has developed. The various societies and organisations of the church also provided structure and a way of socialising and entertainment, so becoming the heart of the village.

It is hoped this book will have a wide appeal to people of Newton, and beyond, who have had association with the area both in the past as well as the present time, and for those to come in the future.

Susan, Wendy and Edna

*Co writers: Wendy Cope, Edna Davies and Susan Rees
at the 2003 Centenary Exhibition.*

Contributors

SUSAN REES

In 1988 Susan returned to Britain after having lived in New Zealand for a number of years. She was introduced to St Peter's by her husband Colin who had first been married, to the late Heather Lloyd Jones, at the church in 1953 by Harold Stepney Williams. Susan was struck by the simplicity of the church, enhanced by the beauty of the interior furnishings and stained glass windows and was fascinated to discover the story behind these gifts. She soon became actively involved in various aspects of the church and has served on the Parochial Church Council (P.C.C.) for the last ten years. Her curiosity has led to further research which has culminated in the writing of chapters 1-8, 13, 15 and 16.

WENDY COPE

Wendy is a former teacher who has had an interest in local history since her college days. She has been a member of Oystermouth Historical Association from its inception and has been involved in its annual exhibitions at the Ostreme Centre and at Tŷ Hanes, the history centre it ran in Mumbles in the last decade. She has been a parishioner of St Peter's Church since coming to Newton in 1971 and from then on Wendy and her family have been actively involved in many of its organisations. Her husband, Ted, is the secretary of the Churchmen's Club. It was appropriate that she should write chapters 9-12 and 14.

EDNA DAVIES

Although born in Mumbles, Edna (née Harris) has spent most of her adult life, since her marriage, living in Newton. She was educated at Oystermouth School, Swansea High School and Swansea College of Education. Thirty-five years of her teaching career were spent in the old Newton School in Nottage Road and in its replacement school. Consequently, she is well known in Newton and its surroundings, having taught three generations of local residents. Included in her many activities has been a special interest in local history. Edna was well qualified to research and write the last three chapters of the book which cover the story of the Sunday School as well as Newton School and the village of Newton during the last century.

1.

A Brief Historical Background

1. The Old Village of Newton in the late 1800s and early 1900s

High above Mumbles, approached from all sides by steep hills, sits the village of Newton, always referred to as *"Upalong"* by old Mumbles natives. The name Newton is derived from the time, several centuries ago, when it was then a "New Settlement." In the late 1800s and early 1900s – Newton village was a close packed huddle of small cottages, with a few farmhouses, a chapel, a post office, two public houses, and a school which had been licensed for Divine Services. There were also several large residences scattered around, beyond the perimeter of the village. The village was lit by gas from the Swansea Gaslight Co., and supplied with water from the works at Caswell Bay.

Newton Road, Newton, early C20th.   A. R. Way

*The man watching the geese was sitting on a mounting block. The water ran down
a gully at the side of the road. Small bridges crossed the gully in order
to allow dry entry into the houses.*

2. Newton in the Parish of Oystermouth

Newton was a part of the parish of Oystermouth, which, according to Kelly's Directory of 1895, was spread over 2,995 acres and had a population of 3,915 and also contained the hamlets of Blackpill and Norton. The Urban District of Oystermouth was established in 1894 from the Local Board and came within the Gower Union, Swansea County Court District and was part of the West Division of The County of Glamorgan Hundred (i.e. a division of a county, originally supposed to contain a hundred families).

The Parish Church of Oystermouth was All Saints in Mumbles which at the end of the nineteenth century had just received a dynamic young vicar who was to make great changes to the area. His predecessor was Revd D. Secretan Jones who had held the advowson of Oystermouth from 1867 to 1896 and so as Patron he was able to nominate the Revd Harold Stepney Williams to be his successor. The church came within the diocese of St David's, archdeanery of Carmarthen and deanery of East and West Gower.

The population of the parish was rapidly expanding for it had become a desirable place to live once the prospect of it becoming an important industrial suburb was supplanted by its tourist potential.

The Tithe Map of 1845 of the Parish of Oystermouth shows Newton in great detail, giving particulars of every plot, building and field. The reason

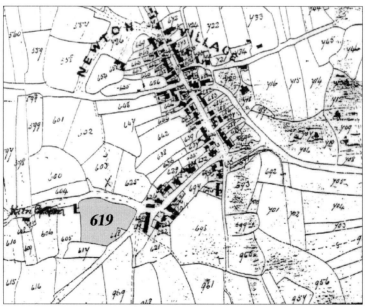

A section of the Oystermouth Tithe Map 1845.
(Courtesy of West Glamorgan Archive Service).
N.B. Plot 619 was to be the site of the new church in Newton.

for the detail lay in the 1836 Act of Parliament, which laid down that the tithes (one tenth of everything produced on the land) could no longer be paid to the Church in hay, corn, eggs, wool or livestock, but had to be in money. The amount depended on the area, and use of each piece of land. A surprisingly large amount of the cliff land was cultivated and on it were two farm houses, *Longland House*, where William Phillips lived and he had 4 acres of fields leading to the beach. The other house was *Cliff House* belonging to David Lloyd and it was in the middle of what is now Langland Golf Course.

It is also noticeable that the area is divided into small plots of land. This may be due to the medieval strip farming methods still evident on parts of Gower. However, tradition has it that many of these plots of land represented the lost stakes of freeholders who had gambled their land away in a game of chance. The games in vogue were either the five-card game or quoits and this accounted for many of the unusual names of the plots, such as Knave's Acre (the knave being the best card in a five-card game). In Greenslade (the valley that terminated in Caswell Bay) was a field peculiarly called "Jack's Shoes' Land." Jack staked a pair of shoes – rare articles in those days – at cards, against the field, and won. By the side of the road from Caswell to Newton was "Tailor's Park", which was staked in a game of quoits. It is recorded that Farmer Richard Wollacott complained to the Oystermouth Urban district Council about a number of youths found gambling on a Sunday in Thistleboon (Thomas, N. L., 1978).

In *Davies West Gower* (Davies 1877) the games mentioned were common in Gower as well as being played in Pembrokeshire and in parts of England and Ireland where they were known under a different name. Davis also goes on to say that several of the common surnames to be found in Gower, such as Kift and Ace, both farming families in Newton, originated from the Flemish race who settled in Gower in the C12th, after the conquest of the region by the Earl of Warwick.

3. The arrival of Christianity to the area

Archaeological evidence suggests that the Newton area has been occupied at least since the early Bronze Age (*c.*1600BC). As far as we know, the Christian faith did not arrive until possibly the 5th century AD, brought in by monastic missionaries and spread by the great saints of the Celtic Church, after whom several local churches are named. The neighbouring church of St Teilo's, Bishopston (Orrin, 1979) is an example, for it is believed to stand on one of the earliest Christian settlements in Wales. According to the ancient *Book of Llandaff*, the church dates back to 480-490 A.D. All Saints, in Mumbles, the mother church of St Peter's, is first recorded in 1141, although evidence has revealed that the

Romans had originally occupied the site around the 4th century AD, after fragments of mosaic pavement were discovered in 1860 during the enlargement of the church (Orrin & Cowley, 1990). It is even thought that there may already have been some form of a Christian church on this site.

There is also evidence that Christianity had been practised in the Newton area in the eleventh century at a nearby site in Caswell Valley, referred to as the Holy Well and dedicated to St Peter. In 1895 excavations of the site nearby revealed another well named after St John, and a chapel and a priest's cell. The foundations were discovered to date from the 13th century and the buildings probably fell into disuse after the Dissolution. Today they are in a ruinous overgrown state, as seen in the photo, but part of the east gable of the chapel is still standing. It has a large square headed window and evidence of a 'squint' or window through which lepers were allowed to view the Sacrament. A survey made by Edward Lhuyd, in 1697, mentions that: *". . . near to these wells standeth an old religious house, but ruinated, and a chapel dedicated to the Virgin Mary, to which place in old time was great resort especially on Lady Day in March, Easter Day in the evening, and on St Peter's Day there was an Ave Maria Bell and such sort of thing . . ."* (Orrin G. R., 1981).

The ruins of Caswell Chapel.
(from *Historic Gower* by Paul R. Davies).

However, it took many more centuries, and the results of several revival movements, before regular worship was practised in the district.

In 1742, Hywel Harris, one of the early giants of the Welsh Calvanistic Methodism movement, visited Gower. He consoled himself, after a visit to Newton, saying: *"many open rebels seem as melted as wax."* Maybe he was preparing the stonyground for the well known evangelist, John Wesley, who visited Newton in 1758, where he preached in a barn. John Wesley recalls in his diary:

"Monday, 28th August – I scarce ever saw such rain in Europe. In one of the main streets the water ran with a stream capable of turning a mill. However, having been appointed to preach at noon in Newton, about 6 miles from Swansea, I was determined not to break my word, though I supposed that but few would attend: but I was mistaken. Such a number came together as no house in the town could contain. A barn was soon prepared; and it pleased God to send gracious rain upon their hearts."

Another evangelist, Lady Diana Barham (1763-1823) of Barham Court, Kent, toured Gower in the early 19th century with a retinue of servants and her secretary. She was an intelligent and very religious woman. She was dismayed at finding *"the darkness of the place and the spiritual destruction of the people"* as she discovered a great dearth of churches and chapels in the area. In fact she was so concerned to

John Wesley, preaching to folk in his home town Crowle.
(Crowle Advertiser special supplement, May 1996).

'bring the light of the gospel' that she returned, nine months later, in 1814 to Fairy Hill in Gower, and began an ardent campaign that greatly contributed to the religious and social development of the area. She died at Fairy Hill in 1823. As a result of her influence and example, several chapels were built for Protestant Dissenters on Gower, including Paraclete Chapel at Newton in 1818. Lady Barham appointed her secretary, Revd William Hammerton (1791-1834), to be Paraclete's first minister. This caused a rift with the Calvinistic Methodists and the chapel becoming Congregational. The manse was built for him in 1820 and he served for 16 years until his death (Hughes, 1962, *Gower*, XV).

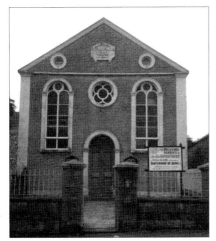

Modernised Paraclete Chapel today.
(The original building is at the back of this rebuild facade).

Revd William Hammerton, 1791-1834.
(From print of portrait, in Paraclete).

In October 1878, Frances Ridley Havergal, a well known hymn writer, came to stay in Newton with her sister, Maria. They stayed at Park Villa (since called Havergal) on Caswell Road, at the end of Caswell Avenue. Frances wrote: *"We have been most graciously guided here . . . and so far as we see at present this arrangement is likely to last our lives[!] for I do not see how anything could suit us better."* For the short time of eight months that she lived in Newton, Frances made a great impression on the village.

She became very involved in the religious life of Newton and preached in the open air, on a grassy bank (now developed in the lower part of the village). She was believed to have played the organ at Newton schoolroom where she was a constant visitor and also worked with the children at nearby Paraclete Chapel. She was well loved by the children, whom she gathered into Temperance Bands and they all signed the Pledge. The month before her death Frances had a visit from Ira Sankey, the American musician, who was on an evangelistic tour with D. L. Moody (Gregor, G., 1997, *Gower*, 48).

Frances died in June 1879, at the early age of 42, of peritonitis. It was noted in the Newton School log book: *"Miss Havergal has died. Her death will be much lamented by the schoolchildren as she took great interest in their spiritual welfare. Fifteen of the children have received Bibles from her, for learning a chapter of Isaiah."*

Memorial plaque outside 'Havergal', erected in 1937.

2.

The Need for a New Church

By the end of the 19th century, church and chapel attendance locally was on the increase. Paraclete Chapel had already been extended with a new wing and gallery and was again enlarged in 1901. The 1851 Census, of religious worship in Wales, recorded that in Newton 130 attended at morning service, 200 at evening service, and 70 children went to Sunday School. To meet the needs of a growing population in Newton, in 1867, a licence was granted to the Revd Montague Earle Welby, Perpetual Curate of Oystermouth Church (1865-1867), to perform Divine Services in Newton school. He was issued the following document:

Connop by Divine Permission Lord Bishop of St David's
To all Christian people to whom these presents are made. Greetings

Whereas we have received in petition of Montague Earle Welby Clerk incumbent of the Parish church of Oystermouth within our Diocese and Jurisdiction, praying that we would grant our licence and authority for the pursuance of Divine Service and the celebration of Holy Sacraments in the schoolroom at Newton which is in the parish of Oystermouth aforesaid NOW KNOW YE that we the said Connop Lord Bishop of St David's taking the prayer into our serious consideration and being desirous of complying with the prayer of the said Petitioner have thought fit to grant and by these presents do hereby grant our full leave licence and authority during our will and pleasure only and revocable by us and our successors as to our and their discretions may seem fit for the performance of Divine service and the Celebration of Holy Sacraments in the said schoolroom according to the Rubic of Churches of England and not otherwise or in any other manner saving always to avail ourselves and our successors our Episcopal rights and dues and also saving and reserving to the Incumbent of Oystermouth aforesaid for the time being all rights profits fees and advantages whatsoever due and of right belonging to him. Given under our seal which in this behalf we used the seventeenth of August in the year of our Lord One thousand eight hundred and sixty seven and in the Twenty-eighth year of our consecration.

In 1883 this need for a church was supported by a report of a commission held to inquire into the **Spiritual Wants of the parishes of the Deanery of Gower East** and recommended: *"Oystermouth – Area 5,914 acres, population 3,915, Church accommodation 750, net value £138 and no house, Clergy – Vicar. At Black Pill, distant about two miles from the Parish Church, there is a school-room, where once a Curate was employed to minister to the spiritual wants of this Parish, and now occasional services are given by a staff of laymen from Swansea, but we recommend that a new Mission Chapel be erected between West Cross and Newton, and a Curate provided."*

When the Revd Montague Earle Welby left Oystermouth in 1867 he had been informed that two churches were to be built at once, one at Langland and one at Blackpill. Another forty years were to pass before this need was realised, for his successor, Revd David Secretan Jones (1867-1898), did not take on this task, although he built himself a house at the top of Newton Road, now called the Manor House, and made improvements at All Saints. When questioned by a reporter of the *Cambrian* newspaper (25/12/1898, p. 5, col. 6), on his retirement, as to what extent the church had grown, Secretan Jones replied: *"I think we should have a church near Langland or Newton. The endowment again is insufficient, being about £80 p.a."* He may not have been dynamic about development but he is remembered for improving the quality of the services at All Saint's Church, and laying firmly the foundations of High Church traditions based on the Oxford movement. The congregation numbers greatly increased. The Oystermouth Vestry Minutes, 20th March, 1882, records *". . . that this meeting is of the opinion that the church services should be conducted at Newton and Blackpill as well as this Parish Church, for which purpose the assistance of a curate is necessary."* This quote suggests that services at Newton were occasional events, until Secretan Jones received his curate. After his arrival, regular Sunday services were held in Newton School causing the school inspector to comment on church furniture taking up space in the room.

By the end of the C19th it was becoming increasingly obvious that there was a growing demand for further churches in the widely scattered parish of Oystermouth. The parish church was not centrally located or large enough to serve the steadily growing population and congregation. Mumbles was rapidly expanding although it never became the industrial suburb envisaged. However, it showed great tourist potential aided by the extension of the railway to Mumbles Head where the new pier was opened in 1898. The population in 1891 was 4,132 and by 1901 it was over 4,800.

In 1898, the Revd Harold S. Williams (1864-1954) arrived at All Saints' Church finding it *"in none too good condition."* He immediately undertook the gigantic task of church extension which continued throughout the forty years of his ministry in the parish. A comment from his curate, Revd Tudor Owen Phillips, is worth recalling: *". . . on my arrival, I was taken for a walk around Oystermouth. Standing on high ground with a commanding view of the Parish, the vicar told me of his plans for enlarging the Parish Church, building a church at Newton, a school and a couple of church halls."*

Sketch of Oystermouth Church, 1889, by David Jones of Wallington.
(Courtesy of Orrin, G. R., and Cowley, F. G., *A History of All Saints' Church, Oystermouth*).

In 1899 the parish magazine quotes a correspondent saying: *"The town was growing, the village is passing away. The church congregation was growing at an alarming rate."* On 19th February, 1899, the church was literally packed. At this time all the best seats in the church were rented by the more wealthy members of the congregation and the poorer members had to sit on forms in less comfortable parts of the church. The Revd H. S. Williams stated: *"In future all seats were to be declared free after the bell stopped ringing to allow for greater occupancy."* (Orrin, & Cowley, 1990).

A couple of comments made by the vicar in the parish magazine, at this time, highlight the problem: *"The church has been excessively crowded this month. On one Sunday morning over a hundred people failed to gain admission and had to go away. There is only one cure for this, a second Church. This, God willing, we are going to build."* (September, 1900). And again, a year later: *"Mumbles has been very full of visitors. The Parish Church at 11 a.m. had a closely packed congregation . . . several were seen unable to find accommodation. When the new church is open it will relieve the congestion."* (September, 1901).

3.

The Site for the New Church

The Revd Harold S. Williams, wasted no time on his arrival in 1898, in addressing the need for a new church, within his parish. He promptly set about fundraising, and, through his Building Committee, in selecting a suitable site at Newton. He kept his parishioners informed of his projects in the parish magazine, by writing as follows: *"A great work lies before us in the coming year. I refer to the erection of the new church for the districts of Newton and Langland. The response to my appeal has been most encouraging; this fact gives me every hope of being able, not only to build the church this year, but also to see it free of debt at the close of the year 1901 D.V."* (January, 1901), and again in March: *"Plans for the new church were passed by the Incorporated Church Building Society. It is hoped that the result will shortly be known."*

The vicar made an application to the Society for granting money towards the cost of a new church. A report in the *Church Builder*, 1901 (*Organ of the Incorporated Church Building Society, London (1862-1915)*, states:

3. – No. 10,255 – OYSTERMOUTH, S. PETER, in the parish of All Saints. Dio. S. David's – The present church accommodation is totally inadequate. The Parish Church is filled morning and evening. In the summer months when there are often 1,000 visitors, hundreds of people have to be turned away. It is very urgent that in a place such as this there should be ample church accommodation. The need of the new church is very pressing. Most of the inhabitants belong to the seafaring and agricultural classes. It is proposed in the first instance to build the chancel, choir and clergy vestries, organ chamber, base of tower, and portion of nave to seat 400 people, at an estimated cost of £5,000. The church when completed will accommodate 634, and is estimated to cost £8,570. All the seats will be free. The S. David's Diocesan Board of the C.B.S. strongly recommend this application for a grant – Applicant, Revd H. S. Williams. Architect, Mr E. Bruce Vaughan, Cardiff. £150 voted for the first portion.

In April, 1901, the vicar reports: *"The difficulty over the site for the new church has been practically settled. There is a choice of two very excellent sites on the Grove Estate at Newton."* The following month in May, 1901, he announces a decision has been made: *"On April 26th an important meeting of the Building Committee was held at Newton School-room. It was decided to build the church on the site which faces the new road running down from Newton Lane to Caswell Road. The church will thus have Caswell Road on its north side, the road running to Langland on its east side and the road running to R. W. Beor's house on the south side. Thus a very convenient and suitable site has, after much tribulation, been secured. It's been decided to advertise for tenders immediately."*

Plot 422 shown on the 1899 O.S. Map, was purchased from the Grove family estate for £200 in 1901. Mr William Robert Grove originally owned several plots in the area which were passed down through generations of his family. The 1845 Tithe Map, depicting Newton Village, shows Lot 619 (see chapter 1) apportioned to Mr William Robert Grove and occupied by Mr Richard Parry, a farmer. The plot, containing 2 rods, was conveyed to the Ecclesiastical Commissioners, by deed, dated 10th of July, 1901, for the building of the new church.

Members of the GROVE family are mentioned in early records of Swansea as portreeves or mayors of the town from 1680 to the first half of C19th. It was through their joint estates that land was amassed in and around Swansea. They are still remembered to this day by a number of roads named after them such as Groves Place, Grove Hill, and Groveland in Swansea, and nearby, Groves Avenue, in Newton.

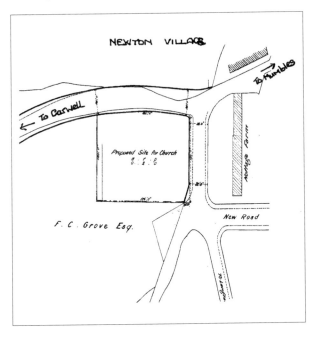

A copy of the Indenture shows that the church was originally to have been called St Barnabas but in 1902 an amendment was made changing the name to St Peter's. Conditions within the Indenture state that it is for the land, mines and minerals excepted. Any damage or subsidence caused to the church must be duly compensated. Other conditions include the construction of a proper boundary wall at least 3'6" high and contribution to half of a roadway, and there was to be no cemetery.

1901 Conveyance of the land on which St Peter's Church is built.

I **Florence Craufurd Grove** *of the Inner Temple Esquire Barrister at law and of the Windham Club St James's Square being under and by virtue of the Will of* **William Robert Grove** *late of the Town of Swansea in the County of Glamorgan Esquire deceased which Will bears date the eleventh day of December One thousand eight hundred and forty four and was on the thirtieth day of July One thousand eight hundred and forty seven with a codicil thereto duly proved in the Prerogative Court of Canterbury and of an indenture bearing date the eighteenth day of December One thousand eight hundred and ninety seven and was expressed to be made between the said* **Florence Craufurd Grove** *and also* **Coleridge Grove** *of Wellington Court Albert Gate London a Major General in Her late Majesty's Army K.B. (now* **Sir Coleridge Grove K.G.B.**) *of the first part the said* **Coleridge Grove** *of the second part* **Herbert Augustus Hills** *of Corby Castle in the County of Cumberland and* **Anna Hills his wife** *of the third part* **The Right Honorable Lord Charles Thomas Montagu Douglas Scott** *of 16 West Halkin Street in the county of London Vice Admiral and K.B of the fourth part* **Francis Richard Round** *of the Colonial Office London Esquire of the fifth part* **John Waller Hills** *of 17 Lincoln's Inn Fields London Solicitor of the sixth part and the said* **Florence Craufurd Grove** *of the seventh part and of the events which have happened seized of the piece of land hereinafter described and expressed to be hereby conveyed for an estate of inheritance in fee simple in possession free from encumbrances subject nevertheless to an* **agreement bearing date the tenth day of July One thousand nine hundred and one** *and expressed to be made between me the said* **Florence Craufurd Grove Esquire** *of the one part and the* **Reverend Harold Stepney Williams** *of the Vicarage Oystermouth in the County of Glamorgan Clerk in Holy Orders of the other part being an Agreement for the sale of the said piece of land hereinafter described for the sum of* **Two Hundred Pounds** *do by these presents as beneficial owners in consideration of the sum of Two Hundred Pounds on or before the execution of these presents paid to the said* **Florence Craufurd Grove** *by the said* **Harold Stepney Williams** *the receipt of which said sum I the said* **Florence Craufurd Grove** *do hereby acknowledge and at the request and by the direction of the said* **Harold Stepney Williams** *testified by his executing these presents grant and convey Title to the said* **Harold Stepney Williams** *according to my estate and interest in the said piece of land hereinafter described do hereby freely and voluntarily and without any valuable consideration give grant and convey and confirm unto the said Ecclesiastical Commissioners for England and their successors All that piece of land containing two roods or thereabouts situate lying and being in Newton in the Parish of Oystermouth in the County of Glamorgan.*

Summary of this document:
The boundaries are described, Mines and Minerals are excepted with compensation for damages, Contractor to build 3'6" high boundary wall also half a roadway, There is to be no cemetery, The church is to be called St Barnabas [but this was later changed to St Peter's].

4.

The New Church Fund

The Revd Harold Williams could not have achieved as much as he did for the extension of the church within his parish, if it hadn't been for his zeal for fund-raising. He firmly believed that it was possible and proved it could be done. During the thirty years of his entire building programme he raised £46,491-12s-2d.

In 1900, soon after the vicar's arrival he launched a New Church Fund (N.C.F.) to raise money for the building of the New Church at Newton. He initiated many schemes so it could be opened 'Free of Debt and without a Bazaar' which was his greatest desire. He first proposed that 5 donors gave £200, 10 donors £100, 10 donors £50, 20 donors £25, and 50 donors £10. He unashamedly contacted the wealthy citizens of Swansea and appealed to all to contribute, printing results month by month in the *Oystermouth Parish Magazine*. Some told him *"You are a great beggar, vicar,"* to which he replied: *"I am afraid I have to plead guilty."* Indeed, he was once mistaken for a beggar when, after wandering around Tewkesbury Abbey, he fell asleep on a bench with his cap in his hand. An old lady dropped two pence into the cap!

Miss Emily Talbot, the wealthy Margam heiress, was one of the first donors and generously donated £300 in the first instance and gave more later. Other well known Swansea names in industry and business followed her: Sir J. T. D. Llewelyn, Messrs. Graham Vivian and Crowe Richardson gave £200; Mr Gilbertson, Mr T. P. Richards of West Cross House and Lady Lyons gave £100; Sir John Jenkins, Sir Robert Morris, and Mrs Clarke Richardson £50; Mr Glynn Vivian £20, and amongst many others there was 'a widow's mite' of £2. The vicar continued to print updates in the *Parish Magazine*, March 1901: *"One little girl in this Parish (it is always the girls who do good things) at Christmas was given a six pence piece to spend. Instead of spending it on herself she put it in her collecting box. Another member of the congregation, unable to come regularly, due to ill health, put her collection money into her box on Sunday morning. We want more of this spirit. Over £3,000 has now been promised to the N.C.F. but £5,000 is much desired so that the church is opened free of debt."*

"We print . . . a complete list of all donations promised to the N.C.F. The total amounts to £3,124-9-3½. Of this, £800 has been paid into the bank. Seeing the building operation soon commencing, it would be well if all would send in amounts promised as soon as possible. All monies should be sent to Mr Fisher of Langland or to the vicar." (May, 1901).

Again, in January 1902 the vicar urges: *"those who have promised donations, please fulfil your promises as soon as possible or else pay by instalments."* He is beginning to sound concerned for he continues to write: *"As the New Church is gradually growing, I need £2,000 yet to accomplish this work. It is a big sum and with the heavy financial responsibilities of the Parish it makes me anxious at times."*

Mr A. Gilbertson, of Glanrhyd, Pontadawe, responded by suggesting he would offer £50 to the fund if nine others would do likewise before the end of March. Those who responded included Mrs Llewelyn Thomas of the Elms, Lord Tredegar, Mr G. Leach and Miss G. Dillwyn Llewelyn, and £50 was given from the estate of the late Mr F. G. Grove who died in 1902. [He was the previous part owner of the land on which the church was built.] During 1902 there were some set backs. Work and fund-raising slowed down and it became apparent the church would not be completed that year. Fortunately, by June, the vicar sounds more optimistic again: *"We are glad the New Church is now going on satisfactorily. The sureties of the contractor are completing the contract. They hope to have the church under cover before the autumn is out. In employing local labour the sureties have given great satisfaction."*

The vicar admits that a great deal of difficulty had to be faced in the erection of the church. He said: *"Let us hope we have faced and overcome the last."* He referred to these problems again in his report at the Consecration Service, at the opening of the church, in November 1903. The church had taken more than a year and a half longer to build, so incurring great expense. He wrote: *"No sooner was one difficulty disposed of than another cropped up."* By mid 1902 he had £4,000 promised and £3,000 had been paid in but he still required another £2,000 to open the church free of debt. In order to encourage his parishioners he eulogises the future building, claiming it will be a credit to the parish; one of the most beautiful churches in the whole district. The design had been universally admired. Sadly, by now it had been accepted that the tower would not be built which he said was: *"a great pity for it would add considerably to the beauty of the building and if a clock were added it would be a benefit to the whole neighbourhood."* In July the vicar sounded more positive. He was pleased to relate that the architect, who had been ill, was better, and the church was now rising rapidly above the ground. He urged his readers to go inside to get an idea of what it was going to be like. 1902 ended with the vicar again urging his flock to make a special effort to see that the church was opened *'Free of Debt and without a Bazaar.'* He spoke trenchantly about bazaars in one of his sermons: *"There is hardly a church anywhere that has not had a Bazaar to aid its fund. The sooner people learn to build their churches out of freewill and self denying offerings the better. This everlasting playing at 'shop' in order to maintain the Master's work is not good for the work, or for ourselves. It deadens the principle that lies at the root of almsgiving. You go to a Bazaar, you spend a certain amount of money, and you receive that value in kind. As a rule, it is a few – namely, the stallholders – who have really to put their hands deeply into their pockets and give, without return . . .What we want in this generation is to teach people to give from* **principle***, from* **conviction***, and* **conscience***."*

The estimated cost of the new church, when completed and furnished, and including the boundary wall, was £6,000 and £1,500 was still needed. In order to achieve this, the vicar launched yet another scheme, proposing that 500 people in the parish took a collecting card and invited friends to join them in collecting all they could. Then they were to bring the card to church on the Opening Day and present it to the bishop at the altar. He urges: *"Let us aim for a collection which will be without parallel in these parts. Have a share. Don't stand aloof and croak about non success. Do your best – you can do no more. Some people do not like asking for money. Who does? If we only perform the duties that are pleasant for us – what thanks to us? None! All shoulders to the wheel. All hands to the rope. Work, Pray and leave in God's hands."* By December, 250 cards had been issued and some reached as far away as Birmingham and London. He continued to try and whip up financial commitment from his parishioners but the returns were slow and by June 1903, he had raised only another £600. He was even bold enough to suggest that the offertory of three parishes in the north of England, where he preached during the summer, be handed over to his Fund. His request was in vain. He wrote: *"Clergy are such money grabbers, aren't they! . . . It is because the laity are even bigger ones . . . poor beggars!"*

In June 1903 Mr Clarke Richardson, of Derwen Fawr, had sent in a second £50, expressing his admiration of the beautiful church that was nearing completion. The parishioners were also busily involved in several fund-raising efforts. Miss Dillwyn Llewelyn, of Caswell Cottage, held a successful open air entertainment in her attractive grounds, and raised £33.1s.8d to which she added a personal donation of £50. Another dramatic entertainment had collected £50 and a sewing party £8.8s. Individuals had also played their part by offering collections from their self denial and Easter boxes and other efforts. However, by the end of the summer 1903, when the work was nearing completion, and bills had to be paid, the vicar still needed £1,200. He also needed donations towards the furnishing of the church. He had to print, several times, a long list of the furnishings required, as he had no response the first time. In August the former owner of the land, General Sir Coleridge Grove (see note, page 30), was in the neighbourhood and paid a visit to the New Church. He expressed his admiration for the building and donated £50.

Just before the opening the vicar wrote: *"The New Church is somewhat grasping just now, but we must put it on its legs and give it a fair start and then it will have to struggle by itself."* He earnestly hoped he was making his last appeal on behalf of the Building Fund. He pleaded with each parishioner, to whom he had sent an envelope, to do their utmost to help produce the £1,200. He asked for the envelopes to be brought to the church on the opening day. He still hoped to raise this final amount so it could be said *"the New Church had been built out of the free-will offerings of the faithful."* He printed a list of all the collectors who had returned their cards. At last, the long awaited day arrived and somewhat with relief, the vicar was pleased to print the near final accounts. The donations received up to the opening of the church amounted to £4,682 and during the services of the week of November 19th, when the church was consecrated, the total collection was £807.4s.8d. He was obviously pleased with the results for he wrote: *"Splendid! Marvellous! Great! The Collectors have done their work well. They have worked vigorously, determinedly, and they have achieved great success. For which thanks be to God."*

Sir William Robert Grove.
(Courtesy of Swansea Museum)

SIR COLERIDGE GROVE (1839-1920), of the Royal Engineers, resided in Knightsbridge. Like his elder brother, FLORENCE CRAUFORD (1838-1902), he had no issue but had inherited the family estate which, in turn, was passed to his nephew, EDWARD HERBERT HILLS, provided he took the name GROVE. The brothers Florence and Coleridge were the sons of the distinguished scientist, SIR WILLIAM ROBERT GROVE, who was famed for his invention of the *Grove Fuel Cell.* He later went on to become a Judge of the Queen's Bench. It is these names which are mentioned in the 1901 Conveyance of their land to Revd Harold Williams for the new church (page 26).

PORTRAITS OF SOME OF THE BENEFACTORS

Sir John Jones Jenkins
(Swansea Museum by G. Gabb)

William Graham Vivian
(Swansea Museum)

John Talbot Llewelyn Bart
(Courtesy of David Painting)

Emily Charlotte Talbot
(Courtesy of Thomas
Methuen-Campbell)

Arthur Gilbertson J. P.
(Courtesy of Richard Morris)

Amy Dillwyn
(Courtesy of David Painting)

Jeremiah Clarke Richardson
(Courtesy of R. Hart
Swansea Museum)

Col. Morgan
(*Jubilee Swansea*, G. Gabb
Swansea Museum)

W. H. Edwards
(*Jubilee Swansea*, G. Gabb
Swansea Museum)

5.

The Building of the Church and its Consecration

The late 19th and the early 20th centuries were an era of church building, for all sorts of reasons, particularly in the urban and suburban areas of England and Wales. The need for a new church in Newton was therefore part of a much wider phenomenon. Eight other churches were built at this time in the rural deanery of Swansea; in Mumbles the parish church, which had already been enlarged twice, now found itself rivalled by no less than six new nonconformist chapels!

In May 1901 the vicar advises his parishioners in the *Parish Magazine* that: *"the plans and specifications for the new church can be viewed at the Vicarage and the architect's office in Cardiff."* He goes on, optimistically, to say that: *"tenders will, in all probability, be in before the end of the month. We hope therefore to see the church started sometime in June and it will take nine to ten months to build. We learn that Mr Bruce Vaughan [Architect] has sent in his design of the New Church to the Academy some weeks ago and that it has been accepted and placed on the walls of the academy."*

The Architect

Edwin Montgomery Bruce Vaughan (1856-1919) commenced his architectural practice in 1881 after being articled to William Douglas Blessley of Cardiff. He specialised in church architecture and became diocesan architect. In all he designed some twenty-eight churches as well as restoring and enlarging several others in Glamorgan, The vast majority of these churches were built in the Early English style.

Orrin (2004) in his book comments: *"St Peter's Church, Newton, Oystermouth, built in the Decorated Gothic style, was an ambitious design for Bruce Vaughan . . . At Newton he had funds to demonstrate his mature architectural ability, which is reflected in the well appointed and finely executed traditional Victorian Church, built in a late Gothic form. Bruce Vaughan's design intended to be carried out in two stages was unfortunately only partially fulfilled since the south-east tower was never built, the structure only reaching the roof."*

Picture taken from The Building News, *Sept. 27th, 1901, p. 417 showing the original design with the proposed tower which, in the event, was not built due to insufficient funds.*

Description of the Design

"Fine, traceried windows. Aisle windows pointed and the clerestory windows square with traceried heads. Tower placed at S.E. angle of nave and rises to a height of 90ft. with a staircase turret giving access to each floor and to the roof and is large enough to contain fine peal of bells. The E. end will be a feature of the church with beautiful, rich, fine, light traceried windows. The site, sloping from west to east considerably, will give loftiness to the whole of the east front, which is nicely broken by the projecting ambulatory, giving access from the priest's vestry on the tower side to the choir vestry. The interior of the church is of the usual form, consisting of a broad nave, with north and south aisles. Nave is 28ft. 4" wide x 82ft. long. Height of the wall plate is 31ft. To the apex of roof it is 48ft. Aisles are each 11ft. 4" wide x 76ft. long. Total inside breadth of church is 56ft., length 119ft. Chancel 25ft. wide, 37ft. long. Church will accommodate 600 persons. Nave and outer aisles will be furnished with chairs while the chancel will be fitted with oak stalls." (Characteristics as printed in the *Parish Magazine*, August 1901).

In 1901 the vicar was disappointed with the slow progress of the building due to a number of setbacks. In the April magazine he reported: *"The delay in proceeding with the building has been most unfortunate. We are glad to say that there is now proud prospect of going ahead . . . Mr Vaughan, the architect, is severely ill."* Again in July 1901 he wrote: *"In response to the advertisements for tenders to erect the new church, the Building Committee received 8 replies. After due consideration, it was decided to accept Messrs A. J. Howells, a Cardiff firm's tender in the sum of £4,758* [actual cost was £5,760]. *Work will commence as soon as legal preliminaries relating to the conveyance of the site are complete."*

The Builders

One of the delays was due to a change of the building contractor A. J. Howells, who was replaced by M. J. Venning & Sons, Building Contractors of Cardiff. They had stood guarantor for the building and it became necessary to honour this undertaking. A local resident recalls her grandfather, Mr J. Venning, who was principal of the building firm, bringing his family, one summer, to Newton while he worked on the church. The architect did not approve of the French slates he had ordered, so Mr Venning used them on houses he built in Roath.

Originally the vicar had announced the official Stone Laying Ceremony to be in the summer, but digging of the foundations did not commence until Tuesday, 30th July, and the first stone was laid on Tuesday, 10th September.

It is recorded in the *Oystermouth Parish Magazine* of September 1901, that: "*While the workers were engaged in digging out the foundations of the new church a bronze coin was found two feet under the surface. It was submitted to Mr Foneford* [of Swansea Museum] *for examination; he dated it 1675.*" Also, the remains of a damaged chisel were found under the present vicarage when the foundations were being laid. It is thought it had been discarded during the building of the church.

*Example of a 1675 coin made of copper and tin
in the reign of King Charles II.*

The Materials

The church is constructed of hammer dressed Quarella sandstone (the name is derived from *charwel* which is Welsh for quarry). It was quarried in Bridgend and was available in three colours. Greenish grey was selected for the church. This type of stone was commonly used for the cut stonework in the more elegant buildings in Wales. An impressive example is to be seen at Margam Orangery (Pers. Com. the late D. Willie, 2007).

The Building News (27th September, 1901, p. 417) comments: "*The characteristic greenish grey colour used at St Peter's makes an unusual contrast with the Bath stone dressings of the columns and arches. It is interesting to note another Swansea church at Landore, being built at the same time, and also designed by Bruce Vaughan, was constructed of the same stone but the contrasting weathering conditions of each testifies to the sea salt in the air at Newton and the industrial influence on the environment at Landore.*"

The Stonemasons

The following local men were known to have been some of the stonemasons who worked on the building of St Peter's: Frederick and Philip Rosser; Fred

Bessant of 2, Whitestone Lane; William Davies, Overland House; S. Phillips, Thistleboon Lane; John Henry Smith 30, Nottage Rd; John Kift of 5, Nottage Road; Thomas Barry 21, Nottage Road and George Howell of 66, Nottage Road (shown in the photograph with moustache).

It is a remarkable fact that most of the families, of the above mentioned men, continued to live in or near the addresses given for the remainder of the century, and some even up to the present day. In the *Parish Magazine*, September 1901, the vicar writes: *"It appears that the Mumbles masons are famed for the excellence of their work. Those who take the trouble to examine the work done on the New Church will find they fully deserve their reputation."*

(Photograph from
Whess come from Boy?
P. Howell).

STONEMASONS BELIEVED TO BE ON THE SITE OF ST PETER'S CHURCH.
(Courtesy of Mr Winston Williams, whose mother's brother, Philip Rosser, is squatting far right of the photograph. He was tragically killed in 1910 after breaking his back in a fall – an occupational hazard).

Laying of the Foundation Stone

At last the vicar was pleased to announce that: *"Miss Talbot, of Margam Abbey, has kindly consented to lay the foundation stone. The Talbots have always been staunch supporters of the Church and generous benefactors. They have built many churches in the Diocese, while every deserving charity receives their liberal support. It is much to be hoped that the parishioners of Oystermouth will do all in their power to attend the stone laying. The Bishop of St David's has expressed his intention of being present."*

Miss Emily Talbot (1840-1918) was the eldest daughter of Christopher Rice Mansel Talbot (1803-1890) and inherited his great fortune and estate on his death. She was described as the richest heiress in Great Britain and was known as a kind, devout and generous gentlewoman, who gave away great sums of money to numerous causes. She was particularly generous to the Church; like other members of her family, Miss Talbot had been inspired by the Oxford Movement in the Church of England (Hughes, 1974). Indeed, Miss Talbot had been the first donor to the New Church Fund and contributed several other generous donations which had already been recorded by the vicar. Unfortunately, when the day arrived, Thursday, 19th September, 1901, she was indisposed so her niece, Mrs Ella Miller, deputised for her and laid the foundation stone. She was the youngest daughter of Emily Talbot's sister, Bertha and would have been a young bride, in her early 20's, at the time she deputed for her aunt Emily. Her aunt liked to involve her many nieces in various official duties.

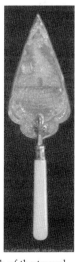

Left: *Mrs. Ella Miller.*

Right: *The trowel bears the inscription: "Presented to Miss Emily C. Talbot on the occasion of her laying the Memorial Stone of St Peter's Church, Oystermouth, 19th September, 1901." It was presented by Mr A. J. Howell, Contractor.*

(Photographs courtesy of Mr Thomas Methuen-Campbell; the photograph of the trowel was taken by Mr Richard Morris).

There was much reporting, both in the press of several papers and in the *Parish Magazine*, of the laying of the foundation stone. The vicar wrote: *"Thursday, September 19th, 1901, will always be regarded in this Parish as a Red Letter Day for it saw inaugurated another house of prayer, this church has been talked about for many years and work has now been commenced and D.V. will be completed in the year."* The *Cambrian* (20th September, 1901) reported: *"At 3 o'clock, the clergy and surpliced choir (conductor Mr Ritson) assembled in the schoolroom close by and walked to the site of the new church singing the processional hymn 'The Church's one Foundation'. Arrived at the site the clergy and others took up a position close to the stone on an improvised platform that was immediately in front of a large marquee which was filled with people. Among those present were the Bishop of Swansea, the Archdeacon of Brecon and numerous local clergy, Mr Graham Vivian, Sir John Jones Jenkins, Miss Ellen Jenkins, Lady Llewelyn, Mr Aeron Thomas MP and Mrs Thomas, Mr and Mrs F. Gilbertson, Mr and Mrs Beor, the Vicar of Oystermouth and Mrs Williams, Revd Secretan Jones, Revd E. Bolney."*

As things turned out, the foundation stone was laid on a day of great sadness both internationally and locally. In the United States, the funeral of the recently assassinated President McKinley was taking place. In Swansea, it was the day of the funeral of Duncan Smith, the archdeacons's son, who had been drowned, and the opening ceremony had to be postponed by an hour for this reason. It spite of these tragedies, there was a large attendance at the stone-laying ceremony and although the weather was stormy, the rain kept off for the occasion. The Archdeacon of Brecon and the Bishop of Swansea led in the devotional part of the service and then Mrs Miller laid the memorial stone saying: *"In the faith of Jesus Christ we place this foundation stone in the name of the Father, and of the Son and of the Holy Ghost."* Short speeches followed the laying of the stone. The Revd Harold Williams expressed regret at Miss Talbot's absence, saying: *"she would have been present, as expected but for the fact, through indisposition, she was unable to come. It was a great disappointment, but they could only hope Miss Talbot would soon recover . . ."*

The Archdeacon Bevan of Brecon heartily congratulated the Revd Harold Williams upon the work he was doing saying: *"Out of the original endowment of the Church at Oystermouth, the Vicar only now received about a shilling a day. They would agree with him that not much Church extension could be carried on upon that sum (Laughter) . . ."* The concluding hymn was 'In the name which Earth and Heaven', and then Sir John Jones Jenkins proposed a hearty vote of thanks to Mrs Miller, saying: *"She laid the stone as good as any Master Mason could have done."* The collection amounted to £82.15s.4d inclusive of a promise from Mr W. H. Edwards, Oxford Street, Swansea.

After the ceremony, a large number of people proceeded to the Langland Bay Hotel, where light refreshments were provided by Sir John Jones Jenkins. The vicar finally thanked Capt. Allen for lending and putting up the flags to decorate the site in preparation for the stone-laying ceremony: *"their labours were appreciated by all. Mr Chapman has taken some excellent photographs of the occasion, so, also has Mr W. H. Lewis of Mumbles."*

The photograph of the official ceremony. The large marquees erected can just be seen on the right and the flags draped over the site, in the middle.

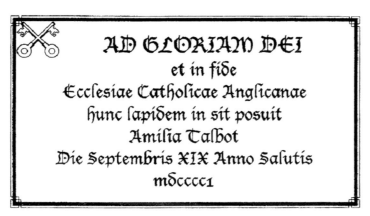

The stone plaque in the bell tower vestry of the church and the translation is: Emily Talbot laid this stone to the Glory of God, and in the faith of the Catholic Anglican Church on the 19th day of September, 1901.

NOTE: [Obviously the stone was engraved before it was known that Miss Emily Talbot was indisposed and was deputised by Mrs Ella Miller, her niece. The inscription's emphasis on the catholicity of the Anglican Church reflects the commitment of Harold Williams and many others (including Miss Talbot herself) to the ideals of the Oxford Movement, otherwise known as the Catholic Revival, in the Church of England].

A Time Capsule bottle was placed beneath the stone and contained current coins of the realm and copies of the *Western Mail*, the *Cambrian* and the *Oystermouth Parish Magazine*.

The Consecration of St Peter's Church

'A fresh inspiration to Christian Progress and activity'
A number of unexpected delays in 1902 meant that it must have been with much relief, as well as pleasure, that the vicar was able at last to announce the date and arrangements for the much awaited and most important day so far. He was able to tell his parishioners that the Bishop of St David's had appointed Thursday, November 19th, 1903, to be the day for the Consecration of St Peter's Church.

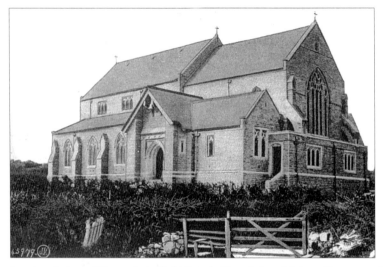

A postcard view of the newly built St Peter's Church from Nottage Farm opposite.
(Courtesy of Geoffrey R. Orrin).

In his October 1903 letter, to the parish, the vicar summarised the efforts over the previous two years, admitting there had been a great many difficulties to overcome. He trusted that: *"the new church would continue in the pattern of its Mother Church, All Saints, which the forefathers had built over 800 years previously, weathering the storms of many a century and bearing witness of their faith and devotion."* He prayed that: *"'the new Temple' would prove in future years to be as much a blessing to the parish as the old one. It would be a new centre of spiritual and moral effort. The consecration of St Peter's Church would be a Red Letter day in the history of the Parish. It ought to be the beginning of a new Church life and effort."*

The vicar set out arrangements for the opening on November 19th, 1903. He printed a list of services to be held throughout the Octave of the Consecration. He anticipated a large number attending, so he advised people to be seated by 10.30 a.m., seats would be reserved for the collectors. The service was to be followed by a public luncheon to be held at the Osborne Hotel, at nearby Rotherslade. Tickets were issued but, it was so crowded that several sittings had to be served in the side rooms.

The *Western Mail*'s description of the opening ceremony states: *"the edifice was crowded. The Bishop, with his chaplain, walked up to the communion table and then, when seated within the rails, the Bishop was presented with the instruments of conveyance for the new church, before the service proceeded."* The music was provided by the newly-formed choir who had been training hard for this auspicious occasion. They were accompanied by an orchestra. They were so good that Revd Welby advised the vicar to use them instead of an organ! The vicar had invited a variety of prominent clergy to preach at the services during the week of the Consecration. He had arranged for the Lord Bishop of St David's to consecrate the church at Matins but, unfortunately, he was indisposed on the day and the Consecration was conducted by the Suffragan Bishop of Swansea (Rt Revd J. Lloyd) to a packed congregation. The day had already started with two Communion Services. Young children were not admitted to the Morning Service (due to limited space) but were encouraged to attend a special Children's Service in the afternoon, and, indeed there was a service for them each day during the following week.

In the evening, at the first Evensong, the Revd John Wakeford, vicar of St Margaret's, Anfield, Liverpool, preached. He was claimed to be one of the most powerful factors in church life, and one of the finest preachers in his city. He often preached on weekdays at a church beside the docks where businessmen clamoured to attend. Other preachers during the week included the Revd W. Neville, vicar of St Mary's, Reading, who was a fluent, earnest and eloquent preacher. Revd M. E. Welby had also been invited to return, forty years after his time at Oystermouth and was quoted to have said: *"Some churches take a long time to build!"* He preached at evensong the following Sunday. He had continued to take a keen interest in the development of St Peter's and had contributed generously to the cost. The Revd F. J. Beck, vicar of Roath, Cardiff, also preached. He was the cousin of the local, distinguished philanthropist, Mr Roger Beck. Several local preachers were invited to take part as well.

The new church, dedicated to St Peter, was endowed with £300, paid for by the suppression of the redundant church of Abergwesin.

6.

The Church Interior and Furnishings and some of the Church Benefactors

Description of the Church Interior

At last, towards the end of 1903, the interior of the church is ready for use. There are three entrances, one on the north side leading through from the porch and is used as the main entrance to the church. The other two are on the south side. The large entrance is approached by a number of steps to a pair of double doors opening into the bell tower vestry – so named, for originally this was where the tower was to be built, (as seen on the drawing on page 33). The other steps, lead to the ambulatory. The well appointed chancel and the nave, with aisles to the north and south side, give the impression of being generously proportioned, as of double squares. The interior walls are made up of the same Quarella Sandstone from the Bridgend quarry as the exterior. This contrasts well with the exposed Bath stone dressings of the arches and on the eight columns, as well as the surrounds of the windows and door quoins (Orrin, 2004).

The chancel has a wagon roof panelled with gilded bosses at the intersections of purlins and common rafters.

E

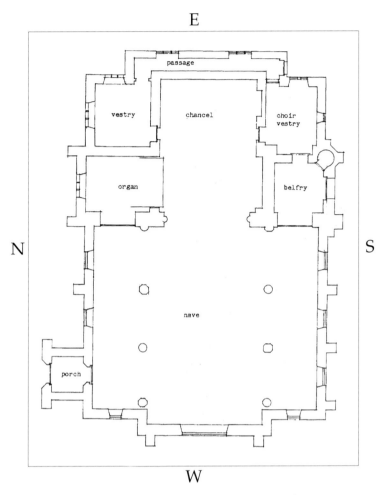

Plan of the interior of the church. Not to scale.

In the **Sanctuary**, on the South side, is a stone **Sedilia** with cinquefoiled arches and credence table with niche (*Sedilia* – seats on the south side of chancel, near the altar, for the use of the clergy).

The nave has open timber hammer-beam roof and the principal rafters are supported on pillar corbels. It is divided from the aisles by arcades of three pointed arches springing from moulded capitals on alternately round and octagonal columns.

The side aisles have a lower level, lean-to, monopitch roof. The choir and clergy vestries lead off from the east end of the south aisle. All three vestries have cement rendered walls and are connected, at the east end, by a project-ing ambulatory, again with cement rendered walls, under a flat roof sheathed in lead.

Decorative Architectural Features

The interior stonework depicts many examples of intricate carving, as on the outside of the church, all in Bath stone, incorporating symbols of flowers, leaves, and birds, as well as figures.

The South doorway leading to the belfry is pure Victorian Gothic style. The pointed arch above double doors has ornamented moulding of vine leaves. There are decorated corbels with Angels on either side of the doorway.

The architrave and frieze above the doorway are decorated with shields embossed with the Cross Keys of St Peter either side with roundels. St Peter is often associated with the symbol of the keys (Matthew 16, v. 19).

The North Porch and Doorway also has a pointed arch and is decorated with ornamental mouldings of vine leaves and grapes. The capitals either side of the entrance door are decorated with acanthus foliage.

The Inner doorway of the North porch has decorated mouldings, around the pointed arch, of acanthus leaves and tablet flowers.

The doorways to the Vicar's Vestry and Choir Vestry have plain architraves above the doors and decorated roundels and bosses of acanthus leaves.

The Inner doorway from belfry to choir vestry has two chubby little cherub heads looking down from either side of the arch.

All the doors are of solid oak with iron decorated hinges and handles befitting of the designs created by the Arts and Crafts Movement, contemporaneous with the building of the church.

Other decorative stone carvings can be seen from the nave. Looking down from either side of the chancel arch are two little angels and at the base of the first arch, either side of the nave, are two heads, that of Christ just above the pulpit, and the head of the Virgin Mary on the opposite side.

At the intersection of the nave arches can be seen different birds and animals amongst the vine decoration. The bases of the chancel arches are of acanthus leaves.

In the vicar's vestry stands a Bath stone fireplace.

[N.B. All the artwork drawn in this and other sections of the chapter is by Diane Thomas].

The scene at the consecration 1903 and the gifts of furnishings received thereafter

One of the first photographs of the interior of the church, taken by M. A. Clare,
just after the organ had been installed in 1907.
(Courtesy of Carl Smith).

When the church was consecrated on November 19th, 1903, it would have seemed very plain and unadorned, almost naked to our eyes accustomed to the present furnishings. Yet, in its simplicity it was described as beautiful and would have seemed very spacious. After several months of repeated requests for contributions towards the furnishing of the new church, the vicar was pleased to write in the September 1903 magazine: *"We are very glad to publish a substantial list of gifts promised to the church."* And later: *"It is encouraging not to appeal in vain but still a few more articles are required before the opening, and then, when the interior is properly furnished, it will be still more beautiful. Everything that goes into the church must be good, thoroughly good – no shoddy articles . . . We can put nothing too good in that sacred house and if God has blessed us with the good things of this world, we should regard it not only as a duty, but a pleasure, to give our wealth to beautify this new Christian Temple . . ."* The vicar also commented: *"that the Newton folk have reasons to be proud of their New Church for it will benefit the parish and will be no small inducement for people to settle there."*

These words are still pertinent today, more than a hundred years later. Each gift, so generously given to the church, represents both a symbol of the donor as well as their love and appreciation of the church, showing how the people and the fabric are intrinsically woven together in its history.

Often gifts have been given in memory of a loved one and it is felt that these should be acknowledged in the following descriptions. The first two large items the church received at its opening are an example of this, both donated as memorials.

The Font was donated by *Mr W. Williams* of the Cliff, who served as the first vicar's churchwarden from 1903 to 1923 and from 1929 until he died in May 1932. The font commemorated his second son, Reginald Gordon Williams, who tragically died on July 6th, 1901, at the age of 17 years after a long illness. The octagonal font in Bath stone has a carved cross on the front face. It rests on four carved iconic style capitals, with pinkish marble columns, possibly of Devonshire marble, and stands on a white marble plinth. The cover is of wood surmounted by a wrought iron cross. In the 1980s the font was removed from its original site by the north door where once a baptistry had been planned for total immersion. It now stands centrally at the back of the nave, under the light of the west window.

The Brass Eagle Lectern was donated by *Mr Sidney Gold* of Glan-y-coed, Newton, in memory of his daughter Noelle Iris Gold who died 20th August, 1900. In 1904 Mr Sidney Gold also donated a platform of solid oak. *"It much improves the appearance of this beautiful lectern,"* wrote the Vicar.

Shortly after the opening came other gifts, both large and small. Three lasting gifts which look as fine today, over one hundred years since they were first donated, are **the Pulpit, the Lychgate and the Organ**. These were all generously donated by *Mr Arthur Gilbertson, 1841-1912,* of Glanrhyd House, Pontardawe, who owned and managed the successful Copper Miners Tinplate Co. Ltd. which he inherited from his father in 1882. Later, he purchased the Glanrhyd Tinplate works and was pioneer of the Basic Steel process. He built other tinplate works at Brynamman and was associated with the building of the Port Talbot Steel works. He was a deeply religious man and an accomplished organist. He built All Saints Church in Pontardawe, as a memorial to his father William, and installed a massive organ and a similar pulpit to the one he donated to St Peter's Church, Newton. He had fourteen children and during the summer he spent time at Bishopston. In 1901-1902 he had Langland Bay House built, but only used it as a weekend and holiday retreat. Successive generations of his family lived there until the 1930s (Davies, 1969, *Gower*, 20).

This photograph, supplied by Dr R. Austin, was found in a Trade Manual CHURCH AND SCHOOL FURNITURE advertising the pulpit for sale, by makers JONES & WILLIS LTD for £120.

The Pulpit donated in 1906 by *Mr Gilbertson* is intricately carved in oak. Revd Harold S. Williams dedicated it on 26th August, 1906.

The octagonal shape seen in both the Pulpit and the Font was one widely used representing the symbol of Jesus unifying God and Man. An octagon is halfway between a circle (God) and a square (Mankind). Just as Jesus was an incarnation of God and man so the octagon mediates between the two. Hopefully, during a sermon, the preacher is communicating the word of God to mortals.

Around the ledge of the pulpit are carved sacred monograms in Greek and Latin letters:

AΩ – Alpha-Omega, the first and last letters of the Greek alphabet, indicating that Christ is beginning and end of all things (Rev. 1. 11).
IHS – Latin transliteration of the Greek letters **IHC** (**IHCOYC**) derived from the spelling of the name **Jesus**.
XP – The Chi(X)-Rho(P) monogram – Stands for Christ (Greek).
INRI – are letters associated with the Crucifixion, placed on a plaque or scroll nailed to the top of the Cross. They stand for: *Iesus Nazarenus Rex Iud orum*, Latin for Jesus of Nazareth, King of the Jews.

The Lychgate was also donated by *Mr Gilbertson* in 1906. The vicar said: *"It was large enough for a carriage to drive through!"* Over the years the lych gate has been repaired a number of times.

The vicar cheekily went on to say, in the same magazine article: *"The church needs an Organ and Chancel Screen."* Mr Gilbertson must have appeared like his fairy godfather, for, in the following year of 1907, he generously donated £600 for the purchase of the **Norman Beard Organ**. The vicar said: *"This is a*

very noble gift, especially when we remember that Mr Gilbertson is only here a few times a year." Sadly, Mr Gilbertson suffered a stroke in 1907 and remained an invalid until his death five years later.

The High Altar and Reredos are both built of oak and were donated by: *Mr and Mrs Livingstone*, in 1919. They were the parents of James Victor Livingstone who died on 23rd February, 1919, aged 13 years and his sister, Sheila Mary Livingstone, who died on 9th March, 1919, aged 6 years. Both children tragically died from the influenza epidemic of 1919, and the inscription is on the reredos to their memory. In 1928 it is recorded that the family lived at Llasyns, Caswell Hill. The **Reredos** is divided into five arched panels. The gilded figure of Christ on the Cross is centrally placed, flanked by figures of the Blessed Virgin and St John on either side. The end niches are for placement of vases.

The Lady Chapel Altar is also built of oak and was the gift of *Mrs Irene Caroline Richardson (1884-1937)*. She was the daughter of the Burgess shipping family, and her husband, Mr Ernald Edward Richardson (1869-1909), was the middle son of John Crow Richardson II, of one of the great copper dynasties which put Swansea on the international map in the mid-19th century. Mr E. E. Richardson tragically died young, like his brothers, at the age of 40, after contracting typhoid on a return journey from Mexico

where he had interests in a mining company.

After his death Mrs Richardson moved to 'Mentone' in Langland Bay, later called *'Tawelfa'* (the house of peace). Mrs Richardson was a deeply religious lady. She formed the *Daisy League* for children and frequently supported the Newton School, and the log-book recorded her giving Religious Instruction. She was very generous to St Peter's and gave, not only of her time and commitment, but also a number of other gifts to the church. In 1912, she dedicated the small window on the west wall, north aisle, depicting St Michael and All Angels. Also, Mrs Richardson gave a house in St Peter's Road, to the church, to be used as a vicarage. Later she provided the surplices for the men and boys in the choir. On December 29th, 1921, she was invited to open the new Church Hall. She eventually moved to another *'Tawelfa'* in Brecon, where she died in 1937.

The **Reredos** behind the Lady Chapel altar was originally constructed of solid oak. It was given in memory of **Miss L. Glascodine** of Langland, by her sisters, and erected in 1933 to mark the occasion of St Peter's becoming a separate parish from Oystermouth. She was a member of the Parochial Church Council (P.C.C.) and was involved in many activities during the early days of the church. Several panels were replaced with fretted wood, when the organ was restored in 2000, to enhance the volume of the music, as the pipes are housed behind it.

The South Aisle Altar is portable and made of veneered wood. It was donated by **Mr Arthur Davies**. It was first used after Canon Brunsdon introduced the idea of having an altar in the centre of the nave, below the chancel steps, so that the vicar is facing his congregation during the celebration of the Holy Communion.

The Woodwork and benefactors

Nearly all of the original wood furniture in the church is of oak. From another of the early photos taken of the interior in 1907 by Mellville A. Clare, it is interesting to note the changes which have occurred in the church over the last hundred years. In the photo can be seen some of the original 250 wooden chairs in the nave, and the litany desk, donated by Mrs Essary, is positioned in the centre of the aisle. The chancel shows that the choir and clergy stalls and the Bishop's chair are already installed. A portable organ is positioned in front of the left hand desk. Note other changes: The high reredos and the dorsal curtains either side of the altar. Light is streaming through the clear glass of the yet undecorated East window. The floor is uncarpeted and the lighting would have been supplied by gas. As yet there is no chancel screen and rood, and the Lady Chapel is still to be instituted. The organ pipes of the newly installed organ are just visible on the left of the photograph.

Thankfully, a large number of Clare's early photographs can still be seen today, many in private collections. His photographs captured all aspects of life in Mumbles and in Gower. They were used to illustrate official guide books and postcards. In 1908 he married Emily Annie Wheeler at St Peter's Church and the couple lived in Nottage Road until 1914 and they ran a shop. By then they had several children who could often be seen in his photos of Newton (Hughes, K., 2004).

One of the earliest photo of the interior of St Peter's.
(Grateful acknowledgement is made to Mr Carl Smith for supplying this
and other photographs by M. A. Clare).

The Chancel Screen is intricately carved in oak and was the gift of **Mrs W. E. Edwards**, of Edgbaston in Birmingham, in memory of her husband. It is inscribed: *"To the glory of God and in loving memory of William Edwards who died March 20th, 1930."*

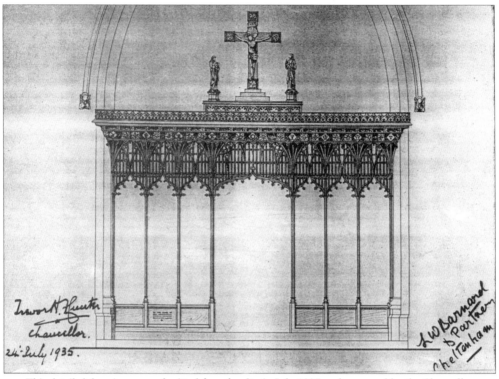

This detailed drawing was submitted for a faculty in July 1935 and approved by the Chancellor, Trevor Hunter. It was dedicated on 13th October, 1935, by the Archdeacon of Gower.
(Kindly supplied by WGAS).

Detail of a section of the frieze below the Rood, drawn by Diane Thomas.

The Rood, the Cross of Christ, above the screen, is flanked by the figures of the Virgin Mary and St John. The symbols of the Passion are clearly displayed on a frieze with a background of grapes and vine leaves (representing the sacrament of wine and the blood of Christ). They are facing the congregation, giving an illustrated reminder of the suffering of Christ.

The South Aisle Screen, in oak, is seen at the front of the south aisle filling the archway to the belfry vestry. It is the parish memorial to the long and devoted ministry of the first vicar, bearing the inscription: *"In grateful memory of WALTER JOHN HICKIN, Vicar of this Parish, 1933-1961"*.

In accordance with the design, seen on the right, submitted by Messrs Williams Clarke (Llandaff) Ltd., a faculty was granted on 19th February, 1962, and it cost £825. It was dedicated at a fitting memorial service on Friday, 12th October, by the Lord Bishop of Swansea and Brecon. Present among the large congregation, who held their vicar in high regard, were his two sisters who faithfully cared for him and also Mr and Mrs Grove, as well as representatives from a number of interests Canon Hickin was involved in throughout the Parish.

Photograph by Harold Grenfell.

The Madonna and Child. The beautiful carved figure is in oak and is to be found in the Lady Chapel. It was donated by **Mrs Davies** in memory of her husband John Walter Davies (1900-1973), "Who loved this church". They lived at the Mount, Langland. He was a stockbroker in Swansea.

The Children's Altar is in the corner of the south aisle and was donated by **Mrs Iris Hunt** in 1933 in memory of her mother, Mrs W. Jenkins.

Many other **wooden gifts** have been given to the church since then, often as memorials and include: four candlesticks donated by **Mrs Winnie Thomas** in 1981 in memory of Evan Thomas (1881-1981) and a Paschal candlestick in oak, donated by **Dr and Mrs Penny** in memory of their son, Simon, who tragically died in a railway accident, in 1987, age 15 years.

Two nave houseling benches donated by the **family of Mrs Phyllys Evans** in her memory are in front of the chairs. There are two others at the back of the church and one in the front of the Lady Chapel.

Two wardens' chairs in oak, each with an indented cross on the back, were donated by the *Carr* family: The 'Vicar's' in memory of Hannah Louise Carr (1833- 1964) and 'The People's' in memory of Edward Charlton Carr (1892-1969).

Two small oak benches, either side of the chancel arch, were given in memory of Garfield and Margaret Toomey. He was churchwarden from 1959-1963.

An Offertory Table was given in memory of Elizabeth and Richard Cottle in 1978.

A large chest of light oak, used for storing altar frontals, located behind the south aisle altar, was given in memory of Felix Basset Jones (1913-1982) by his wife *Phyllis* and daughter *Heather Basset Jones*. There is another old chest, used for frontals in the vestry.

A portable Lectern was given in memory of another church warden, William Werner Sivertsen (1920-1991), and inscribed: "To the Glory of God" by his wife, *Betty Sivertsen*.

There are also a number of other wooden items which include: chest of drawers; and an old tall cabinet with drawers given by *Miss Kirkland* and *Miss D. B. Fry* (November 1964) which had come from a church in Gower. Two Riddel posts surmounted by angels, carved in oak; banner stand for 3 flags; near the entrance are two book cupboards: the first donated by *Mrs Vera Andrews* in 1976 in memory of Francis Brough Andrews, churchwarden from 1957-1963 and the second was donated by members of the *C.W.F.* in 1980; a memorial bookcase with a glass framed cover houses the Book of Remembrance and was given in memory of Mrs F. B. Andrew in 1964. A portable font on an oak stand was donated by *Mr and Mrs W. Williams*; there are several flower stands and one pedestal, one being given in memory of Leslie Raven 1902-1961 and another in memory of Ivan Bruce Carter, 1978; five collection plates [deeper, woven baskets are now used as they are more practical to contain envelopes]; hymn boards, a number of boxes and a magazine holder.

Two recent acquisitions include a plaque of a copper Celtic Cross, now mounted on wood, given by *Archbishop Rowan Williams* on the occasion of his visit on June 21st, 2003, during the church's centenary celebrations; and a clergy board donated by *Adele Bowden* in memory of her parents, Arthur and Elaine Ridgway.

Also, to mark the centenary it was decided to replace the original wood chairs with 250 cushion seated ones. Brass plates were attached on many of the chairs with appropriate inscriptions from the donors. The seat covers in the nave are red and in the Lady Chapel blue. Before the new chairs were positioned it was an appropriate time to refurbish the well worn floor by sanding and sealing it.

A chair and two stools near the chancel step were donated by *Mr and Mrs Viv Howells* in 1998, and in 2000 *Keith and Sue Davies* donated two sedilla stools in the Sanctuary in memory of Harry and Betty Thomas.

Choir Stalls. Following a generous donation, given in 2002, by *Mr David Irving* in memory of his wife Margaret Irving (1925-2002), the choir lecterns were raised and lights were fitted creating a resplendent effect particularly at night.

Photograph courtesy of the late David Irving, taken of the choir stalls after the installation of the new lamps.

Metalwork

Most of the metalwork in the church is brass, depending on a faithful and industrious group of volunteers to keep it in its gleaming state.

After the death of Frances Ridley Havergal a fund was set up in 1897 with the intent of placing a memorial to her, in the 'New Church, Newton', when built. The July 1901 *Oystermouth Parish Magazine* records: *"It has definitely been decided to build a chancel of the church in memory of the late Frances Ridley Havergal . . . her memory is still cherished."* When the church was opened in November 1903 a brass plaque was placed on the south wall in the chancel:

**THIS CHANCEL WAS ERECTED IN THE
GLORY OF GOD**

IN THE MEMORY OF

FRANCES RIDLEY HAVERGAL
WHO DIED AT NEWTON
JUNE 3 1879

"𝔗𝔥𝔢 𝔐𝔢𝔪𝔬𝔯𝔶 𝔬𝔣 𝔱𝔥𝔢 𝔍𝔲𝔰𝔱 𝔦𝔰 𝔅𝔩𝔢𝔰𝔰𝔢𝔡"

An **Aumbry** is on the north side of the chancel wall. It is for the reservation of the Blessed Sacrament and concealed by a small curtain, suspended on a brass rail. There are two **Sanctuary Lamps** – the first, with clear glass, was an anonymous gift in December 1903 for £4. The second, which now hangs over the aumbry, has a red glass shade. It was donated in 1960 by *Mr G. Hazel* in memory of his wife. It cost £33.10 and Mr Hazel also donated £115 for the **Cross, Candlesticks and Vases** to be placed on the altar in the Lady Chapel.

There are two **Processional Brass Crosses** placed either side of the choir stalls in the chancel. One is studded with semi precious stones such as cornelian and mounted on an ebonised wooden staff. The other has a relief cross etched into it and is mounted on an oak staff. It is inscribed "In memory of Albert Edward Stirling Evans, his wife Emily May and son Brian 1980." They were donated by *Betty Sivertsen*, their daughter.

There are also **two pairs of standard Candlesticks** in brass, with barley twist stems and coronet at the top, standing on three carved feet at the base. The collar at the top is studded with semi-precious stones of cornelian and others.

A **Brass Rail to the lectern** was placed in memory of John Budge, a member of the P.C.C., who died in 2002, by his wife *Jean Budge.* They were brass cleaners for many years. **The Communion Rail** was donated by *Mrs Williams* in 1934. It is a brass and oak rail with decorative wrought iron supports which contain coloured shield inserts showing the symbols of the instruments of the Passion as recorded in the gospel of St John 19. There are **two Churchwarden's Wands**, the one for the vicar's warden bears a mounted brass mitre and that for the people's warden bears a brass crown. They were donated by the *choir and sidesmen* **in 1933.** The **Verger's Staff** is shorter, with a brass cross on top. Other pieces of brass include a **Snuffer**, with taper attachment, mounted on an oak staff and a **Gong** surmounted by a cross, plus hammer. A **Votive Candle Stand** in wrought iron was given by the *choir* in memory of one of their members, Sarah Elizabeth Davies, in 1998. The outside **Bell** was donated in 1933 by *Mr and Mrs Gage*. There is also a bell in the chancel, near to the door to the vicar's vestry, donated by *Mrs Judy Powell*.

Altar ornaments and Church Plate

Several ornaments for the altar were presented at the time of the consecration. *Sister Amy*, who was in charge of Thistleboon Orphanage, presented to the church some **precious stones**. It is interesting to note that the colour of each stone has a symbolical significance, e.g. **pearls** were for purity and innocence; **diamonds** for light and joy; **ruby** for divine love, royalty and power. Semi precious stones of **cornelian** and others are to be seen at the base of the **Missal Stand and the Cross** which is studded at each point. Similarly on the altar of the Lady Chapel, **amethysts** are to be seen at the points of the **brass Cross** and the roundel is cross hatched, matching a **pair of candlesticks**. There are other pairs of candlesticks in the church, one pair with an adjuster, donated by *Mrs Thomson*, and four more **vases** which were the gift of the family of *Blanche Edleston* (1876-1955).

The church has an interesting collection of **silver plate** made up of a number of containers used for the consecrated elements of Eucharist to be reverently presented, either from the altar or for private communion for the sick and in the home. Each has been presented to the church over the years in memory of a loved one and is carefully recorded in the inventory.

Textiles, including vestments, frontals, embroidered items, hassocks and banners

Over the years there has been a variety of **vestments** worn as each vicar has been inclined to wear his own. Some of the earlier ones are described here. One of the earliest *copes – a long cloak-like garment, worn by a priest or bishop in ceremonies and at processions* – to be given to the church was that of the first vicar of the parish, Canon Hickin. It was donated by *his sisters*, in August 1961, after his death.

The Cope and Stole of Canon Hickin presented to the church in his memory.

A tribute stated: *"to the many gifts to the church he added his own; now we are happy . . . to acknowledge his last gift that of his own Cope and white Stole. These will be a lasting reminder of his fruitful vicariate."*

The cope is of gold and silver brocade with red hood and the stole is of ivory silk brocade with green, purple and gold embroidery, terminating in ivory fringe lined in gold.

Another valued cope is that which was presented to the Revd Harold E. Williams (1976-1987) by **Mrs May Lalor** in **1982**. It has an interesting history. A parishioner, Mrs Leslie Griffin, writes: *"May Lalor came to Newton from Ireland during Archdeacon H. E. Williams' ministry. It took very little time for her to become part of the community, and to make friends. May was so unassuming in her manner that it took us some time before we realised how gifted a person she was. She was very well read and full of stories about the history and culture of Ireland, which were fascinating to listen to. May noticed that we had begun to embroider cushions for the choir, and asked if we needed any more volunteers, as she had done some work in Ireland. It was soon obvious that her work was of a very high standard indeed. She had brought from Ireland a vestment in very poor condition, given by some Nuns. She told us that she hoped to restore it, and asked the Vicar whether he would accept it as a gift. She kept open house while work was going on – intricate and in gold thread, and we spent many happy hours watching her working. When it was finished, May started looking for more work to do, and the restored frontals bear witness to her work."*

The photograph shows Mrs May Lalor, with Archdeacon Harold E. Williams proudly wearing the cope and stole. (Courtesy of Mrs Ann Watkins, her daughter).

Mrs May Lalor spent much time renovating this magnificent garment from a worn cope which had originally been made in Rome one hundred years before. She had enough material left over to also embroider a stole with gold thread, on ivory silk brocade

A third cope is purple with paler hood and the lettering I.H.S. appliquéd onto it with gold thread tassel. It was the gift of the **Revd J. F. Shaw** in 1995.

Other vestments are defined as:

Chasubles – *a loose, sleeveless, usually ornate, outer vestment worn by a priest celebrating the Eucharist.*

Orphrey – *an ornamental stripe, often embroidered, in the centre of the garment.*

Stole – *a long band of material worn draped over the neck and usually embroidered with three crosses. It is a symbol of humility and an important mark of priesthood.*

58

Maniple – *a strip of material worn wrapped over the left wrist of a priest perform-ing the Eucharist. It is rarely used today.*

Each vestment is worn for different occasions according to its liturgical colour and the season in the church calendar, for example:

1. Green *Chausble* in Iona fabric, with a cruciform *Chi-Rho motif* woven in gold thread. It is accompanied by a green stole and veil with gold line border and a green burse. It matches the more modern green altar frontal. **Green** is the colour of new life and is used when the other colours are not.

2. Ivory coloured silk brocade with a dark blue *Orphrey*. This *Chasuble* is embroidered with lilies and an 'AM' (Ave Maria) motif with ivory brocade stole, burse and veil, with gold edge, to match. These were the gift of *Mr and Mrs Vincent Thomas*. **White** is the colour for purity and innocence. It is the liturgical colour for most major festivals

3. Red silk brocade *Chasuble* with gold Y *Orphrey* with a red Cross pattern. Also, red brocade stole, burse and veil with gold and red fringe in similar design. **Red** is the colour of blood, fire and passion and is the colour used for Pentecost (Whitsun) and for festivals of martyrs.

4. & 5. Two purple silk *Chasubles*, one with a gold cross design embroidered on the back with stole, burse and veil with gold line border to match.

The other has gold Y *Orphrey* and a *stole* in purple brocade with a gold fringe and Cross. This purple *Chasuble* was the gift of *Mr and Mrs Roy Griffin*, in memory of Mrs Leslie Griffins' mother, Mrs Davies. **Purple** is the colour of penance and also represents royalty. It is used during Lent and Advent.

6. An unbleached linen Lenten *Chasuble* with a red pillar *Orphrey*. The *stole* has a Cross in red with red and cream fringe. The *burse, veil and maniples* have a red edge with a Cross design in red. This was the gift of *Messrs R. and E. Heron* in memory of Mrs Kathleen Heron in 1968.

In the 1904 *Parish Magazine* the Revd Harold S. Williams speaks of his delight at receiving: "*. . . some very beautiful stoles . . . which belonged to a notable clergyman and army chaplain, Revd James W. Adams, V.C., who died in October 1903. During his last severe illness he received a letter of sympathy from the King who acknowledged the services rendered to his country.*" He was buried in Ash-well. It is not recorded which of the *stoles* are his. Besides the *stoles* already mentioned there are seven others also in liturgical colours as well as a **black** one used for mourning. An ivory coloured brocade *stole* with gold, green and red embroidery and gold and red fringe was the gift of *Canon James Owen* in 1976. The other *stoles* are red and green, maroon red, and three in green with blue and gold designs.

Shortly after the church was consecrated some **Altar Frontals** were made by a group of ladies, led by *Miss Gwendoline Dillwyn Llewelyn*. In the *Oystermouth Parish Magazine* for July 1904 it is recorded: *"A Sale of Work was held in the Vicarage garden. The proceeds of the sale amounted to £11.14.0d. of this, £7.0.0. was handed over for materials for the green frontal of St Peter's, also on the white lace super frontal. The Vicar wishes it to be known that classes for Church work with a competent teacher will begin in October. They will, of course, have to pay for their lessons and also for the floselle and gold thread that each one uses."*

Miss Gwendoline Dillwyn Llewelyn, 1862-1944, lived nearby at Caswell Cottage. She was the unmarried daughter of Sir John Talbot Dillwyn Llewelyn of Penllergaer. He was the son of John Dillwyn Llewelyn, the pioneer photographer who had inherited the considerable wealth and estates of his maternal grandfather. The family had acquired Caswell Cottage in 1855, and it was used as a seaside residence by future generations of his family until Miss Gwendoline Dillwyn Llewelyn came to live there at the time St Peter's Church was being built. She was a generous donor to the new building fund and a great supporter of the church. Miss Dillwyn Llewelyn decided that the new church should have some beautiful *altar frontals* and offered her help. She engaged an expert, from the Royal College of Church Needlework, to stay with her. Several ladies from Newton went to her

Photograph kindly supplied by
Mr Richard Morris.

home for weekly instruction and formed a 'working party'. Among them were Miss Peel and her two nieces, Miss Violet Peel and Miss Sybil Peel of Sunnyside, Newton Road, and Mrs Mills of Lomey (later Langland Court Hotel).

These ladies had promised to make for the new church the following items: **A Red super frontal and Red and green bookmarkers** made by Mrs Le Boulanger, the Misses Peel, Miss Stratton, Mrs Merriman, Miss M. Morgan, Miss Protheroe, Miss Aitken and Miss Dillwyn Llewelyn.

A Red altar frontal was made by Miss Dillwyn Llewelyn, Mrs Le Boulanger, Misses Steel, and Miss Aitken.

A Red Pulpit fall was made by Miss Dillwyn Llewelyn and Miss Aitken.

The first frontals to be made for St Peter's Church.
Top left – Blue. Top right – Red. Lower left – Green, and lower right – White.

The industrious ladies continued with their work over several years, adding to this beautiful collection of embroidery, and it is a tribute to the skill and dedication that these frontals are still in use in the church today, one hundred years later. More recent working parties have made several repairs to the Green Frontal. In 1972 the fringe was replaced and in 1982 it underwent more structural work. Mrs May Lalor also extended her considerable embroidery skills to a very fine **Gold Frontal** – matching the gold Cope.

A **Lenten Frontal** in red and white was also presented by *Messrs R. and E. Heron*, in memory of Mrs Kathleen Heron, in 1968 at the time they gave the Lenten chasuble **A Green Frontal** with a contemporary embroidered design depicting three sheaves of wheat, was given by *Wyndham Jones* in memory of his wife Elizabeth Martha in 1991. There are now a number of items depicting the wheat motif to match. A **Purple Frontal** for the nave altar, was given by *Canon David Thomas*, former vicar, in memory of his parents John James Absalom (former Bishop of of Swansea and Brecon) and his wife Elizabeth Louise Thomas, in November 1995.

A White Frontal with gold and red contemporary embroidered design of the Cross was given for the nave altar in November 1995 by *Mr Ray Cope* in memory of his wife, Barbara Doreen May. For the **Lady Chapel** a new

Frontal and Dorsal Hangings, in matching patterned blue brocade, were presented by members of the **Mothers' Union and Miss Josephine James** in memory of her mother, Mrs James, who was also a member. This was to match the **Dorsal curtains** which once hung on the East wall, behind and either side of the Altar. They were the gift of the **Misses S. and C. Peel and Mrs Hooker** in 1959. More recently the curtains were removed and the altar pulled forward, so allowing the priest access behind the altar table and to face the congregation as the Communion Sacrament is prepared.

Other works of embroidery include a number of **bookmarks**, all in liturgical colours: green, white, red, purple and dark blue. Four Lenten book marks made of bleached linen, decorated with a red Cross and a red and natural colour fringe, were the gift of **Messrs R. and E. Heron**; and **Mrs Mary Lewis** donated others. There are also four **book covers,** one for each of the Gospels, each of a suitable colour for the Church season. A white linen cover with gold embroidered Cross, Blessing and Holy Spirit designs was given by **Mrs Edna Davies** in memory of her husband, Morgan, in 1996. Three other covers of matching designs, one is red linen and the others in purple and green were the gift of Sheila Griffiths in memory of her friend Irene Mitchie in 1996.

In the *Parish Magazine*, July 1934, we read of a fund-raising effort for new **Hassocks and Cushions**. Mr Vivian donated £10 but another £5 was needed to cover costs. Mrs Leslie Griffin, a parishioner, records the restoration work on the kneelers, from 1966-1970, which was started by the C.W.F. but later many groups were involved. *"Towards the end of Canon Hickin's incumbency, some ladies in the parish worked on five kneelers for the Lady Chapel and on the long Altar kneeler, all of which are still in use today.* [It was a while before any more work was added until Canon Brunsdon's arrival.] *The old kneelers in the rest of the church were found to be deteriorating. However, Mrs Brunsdon suggested that as they were only shabby, instead of replacing them, they should be re-covered in tapestry. Members of the Parish, skilled in embroidery and art, were approached to form a committee. Mrs Devereux who was an art teacher in the village, offered designs, using the symbols of St Peter, i.e. fish, keys and the cockerel. In the meantime, Mrs Brunsdon set an example by embroidering a plain kneeler with a simple figure of a fish, to show how easy it would be for a person unused to this art to do the work. She called this kneeler 'The sprat to catch a mackerel'. It became known as 'Our heirloom', for it encouraged many people to have a go.*

Wool and canvas were ordered in bulk and distributed. The finished work was then handed over to a Committee worker to be fitted onto the kneeler. Many volunteers enjoyed the work so much that they got 'hooked' and came back several times to start another. **Cushions** *were provided for each of the Clergy at their desks, designed with* the emblem of the Church in Wales on a red background. There were also cushions for the Servers, and for the Choir with a lattice pattern on red background.

In the **nave** there are 208 hassocks, all hand embroidered with a red background. As they got more used to the work, people started to 'do their own thing' and many interesting designs can be seen in the church. There is one with the Map of the Dioceses of Wales. Some embroiderers left a signature and a few sewed a memorial on to the underside.

"In the **Lady Chapel** there are thirty-two kneelers all of the same design and embroidered with a blue background. The design shows the face of the Madonna on top and her rose as the border. Most of the work was done by the members of the Mothers' Union. The members of the G.F.S. made another blue hassock with a border of yellow crosses and the lettering G.F.S., in yellow, on the face side."

A Houseling bench Kneeler, also in blue, was given by *Mrs Christie and Mrs Byrde* in 1960. It has a monogram M and a border of yellow flowers.

In the *chancel* a cushion for the Bishop's chair and two litany desks hassocks were specially designed and in the sedilia there are three cushions which have symbolic designs of St Peter. Also, there is a pair of wedding hassocks, depicting doves in flight. Two Communion Rail kneelers embroidered with the symbols of the Eucharist on a red background were presented by *Mrs Heron* in 1959.

All the kneelers were blessed, in batches of 40 as they were finished, by Canon Brunsdon and Archdeacon Williams, and originally placed on the chairs, bringing colour and interest to the church and a testament to the work of the makers.

Banners were more widely used in the church, in earlier days, when there were regular processions and parades of the various groups they represented. The Union Jack, the Welsh National banner, and flags of the 5th Mumbles Scout group in yellow and green, and the 5th Mumbles Beaver Scouts in blue, were housed on a banner stand. These are now in the Scout H.Q. at Picket Mead. **The Banners of St Peter and the Mothers' Union**, were both acquired during the incumbency of Canon Hickin in 1934. A later Mothers' Union banner was given in 1976 in memory of Mrs Marjorie Freeman.

The Banners of the G.F.S. and the Churchwomen's Fellowship were designed and made by *Mrs Marjorie Ganz and helpers*, from 1975-79.

The remaining other items of fabric in the church include, pulpit falls, table cloths, curtains and carpets. The red carpet throughout the church was an anonymous gift in 1970. The deeper red carpet in the Children's Corner and the blue carpet in the Lady Chapel were the gift of *Mrs Gladys Jenkins* in 1973. An embroidered sampler of The Lord's Prayer worked by Mary Ann Hope (1847) was given by *Mrs Mair Hall* in memory of her husband, John Iwan Hall (1921-1994). *Mrs Doreen Hall* has donated two tapestry pictures.

Books and Prints. When the church was first opened in 1903, the *S.P.C.K.* contributed a large number of books which included a Bible for the Lectern, books for the clergy desk and one hundred and twenty Ancient and Modern hymn books. Over the years several versions of the Bible have been introduced and presented as gifts, among them was an Authorised King James version presented by the *parents, teachers and pupils*, of Newton School on July 25th, 1961, in memory of Canon Hickin. It was inscribed: *"A much loved and dear friend of the staff and pupils of Newton School."* Other Bibles presented have been an Authorised Version (ed. John Stirling) in 1954 as a gift *"to the children beginning secondary school education in Monmouthshire."* In 1971 a New English Bible, with Apocrypha, was given by *Mr Brynley Barrington*, and his wife, in memory of baby Adele (born 7.11.1970, died 16.6.1971). In 1981 *Mrs Betty Sivertsen* presented a Good News Bible for the lectern, and fifty others for the use of the congregation, in memory of her family, Mr A. E. Stirling Evans and Mrs Emily Mary, and her brother Brian Stirling Evans. When the Book of Common Prayer was revised, for the Church in Wales in 1984, *Mrs Irene Hodges*, and her children Helen and Paul donated one hundred and sixty-four new ones, in memory of her husband William Jayne Hodges (1895-1953). There is a memorial plaque to him on the North Wall, right of the main entrance. The choice of hymn book has also changed from the Ancient and Modern to a New English Hymnal which is now in use. *Mrs Kirsten Foster* donated thirty copies in 1991 and *Mrs Helen Case* donated twenty copies in 1995 in memory of Philip Gowan Case. Yet another supplementary hymn book has since been donated. In 1998 a Book of Gospels was donated by the *Burgess Family* in memory of Mrs Nesta Burgess.

Other books which have been given as memorials include the Book of Remembrance (cased on the North Wall) in memory of Mrs F. B. Andrews 1964, and a Book of Memorial Gifts, dedicated in memory of Mervyn Montgomery James, October 25th, 1979.

There is also a library in the church. In the vicar's vestry there are a number of ecclesiastical books which have been collected over the years, as well as a collection of past *Parish Magazines*, some recently bound by Revd Dr John Thomas, and copies of the parish registers and Inventory.

There are a number of **prints** around the walls of the church. Among the more recent acquisitions are the following:

1. Brangwyn print given by *Mr Philip Shaddick* in memory of his late wife Isobel. It depicts the seventh station of the Cross.
2. A further set of fourteen Brangwyn prints of the Stations of the Cross were added as a gift from *the Revd Dr John Thomas and his wife*. These were dedicated by Bishop Anthony Pierce, during the Revd Clive Jones' last Confirmation service just before he retired. It was fitting they could be used, shortly after, for the Stations of the Cross services during Holy Week.

7.

The Stained Glass Windows

". . . the silent tutors of unlettered minds"
(the late Prof. D. Ll. T. Jenkins)

There were no stained glass windows in the church for the first ten years. From an early photo of the interior in 1907 taken by M. A. Clare, light is seen streaming through the plain glass of the East window (see chapter 6). There were also no high conifer trees to obliterate the light, as there are today, for they were still young, having just been planted at the consecration.

It is believed the architect envisaged the windows being decorated in late Gothic style with traceried heads and the east end was to be a feature of the church. It was probably with this in mind that the old established firm of C. W. Kempe & Co. were selected, in 1912, to design the first five windows in their characteristic highly decorated style. The church would be graced with their beauty and colourfulness in time for its tenth anniversary.

In the *Oystermouth Parish Magazine*, August 12th, 1912, we read of *"the proposal to put stained glass in three windows of the South wall of the church with subscriptions from the congregation. Cost £65. The work was to be done by C. W. Kempe & Co. Ltd."* A month later, in September: *"All but £20 has been raised. Mr W. J. Rees promises another window."* **Mrs Irene Caroline Richardson** paid for a single light window depicting St Michael, the Archangel, to be placed near where the font originally stood, in the north-west corner of the church. In all five windows were unveiled and dedicated on St Andrew's Day (November 30th, 1912) by the Bishop.

The first five windows were designed and made by **Kempe and Tower**, the firm which evolved from the well known and prolific business started by Charles Eamer Kempe (1834-1907). He was a contemporary of William Morris and Edward Burne Jones and had been influenced by the Gothic Revival architect F. G. Bodley (1827-1907). Both had been trained under the eminent architect Sir George Gilbert Scott. When Charles Kempe died, his nephew Walter Tower (1873-1955) took over the firm, maintaining its high standard and reputation. His mark was a *black tower on a sheaf*, and can be seen in a small cartouche on the lower left hand corner of the windows. An Oystermouth guide described the windows as *"unusually colourful for this firm."* Later they designed the magnificent East window.

The following plan indicates the position of the windows in the church:

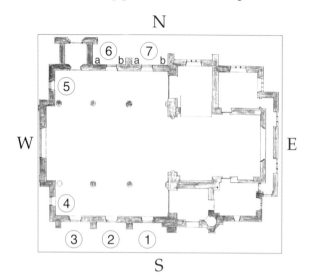

Windows by C. W. Kempe:
1. The Annunciation
2. Adoration of the Shepherds
3. Adoration of the Wisemen
4. St Peter
5. St Michael and All Angels

E. The East Window

Windows by J. Wipple & Co:
6a. Our Lord blessing little children.
  b. St Christopher
7a. St Paul
  b. Child Samuel

W. *Kirkland Window by Celtic Studios*

SOUTH WALL WINDOWS

1. The Annunciation Window
Donated by the *ladies*
of the congregation

D. Sutton.

2. Adoration of the Shepherds
Donated by the *men*
of the congregation

S. Rees.

S. Rees.

3. The Adoration of the Wise Men

This window was the gift of *Mr W. J. Rees*, in memory of his wife, **Mattie**. Mr W. J. Rees was a Swansea Estate Agent, with offices in Druslyn House, Mount Pleasant. The family lived at Park Villa, Caswell Road.

This detail is at the base of the right light.

Harold Grenfell.

WEST WALL

4. St Peter
Donated by the *children* of the congregation

Harold Grenfell.

5. St Michael and All Angels
Donated by *Mrs E. Richardson* (née Burgess, 1884-1937)

Inscription on right window:

"Pray ye for the good estate of Eirene Caroline Richardson at whose charge this window is dedicated to the Greater Glory of God" MCMXII

S. Rees.

EAST WINDOW

At last the Architect's vision *"of a beautiful, rich, fine, light traceried (East) window"* was fulfilled when approval was granted to fill it with stained glass. It was also made by **C. W. Kempe & Co. Ltd.** and was donated by **Mrs W. J. Rees** in July 1921 and is inscribed: *"To the Glory of God and to the memory of William John Rees of Swansea who died 8th October, 1918. This window is the gift of his wife."*

A card was printed, for general distribution, with a description of this memorial window, which read as follows: "The church is dedicated to St Peter. The theme is based on our Lord's words to St Peter, *'Upon this rock I will build my Church,'* and His charge to him to *'feed My Sheep,'* This subject being depicted in the lower part of the three central lights. The remainder of the window represents the Holy Church, with our Lord in the centre crowned and robed as Priest and King, with the Archangels, St Michael and St Gabriel on either side, the former holding the banner and scales, and the latter the staff and lily. Below St Michael are the Blessed Virgin and St John the Baptist, and below St Gabriel are St Stephen (kneeling) and St Paul. In the two extreme outside lights are representative figures of the founders of religious orders, Saints and Martyrs – on the left: St Adrian, St Jerome, St Benedict and St Gregory and on the right: St Catherine, St Thomas Aquinas, St Francis and St Asaph. In the bases of these sidelights are St David and St Augustine. The background of the window is composed of the all-embracing Vine."

East window of St Peter's Church.

The plan (left) was kindly traced by Mr P. Shaddick.

INDEX

1. St Aidan	11. IHS (Greek) Jesus XPS (Latin)
2. St Jerome	12. Our Lord
3. St Benedict	13. Holy holy holy
4. St Gregory	14. Archangel St Michael
5. St David	15. St John the Baptist
6. St Catherine	16. The Blessed Virgin Mary
7. St Thomas Aquinas	17. Archangel St Gabriel
8. St Francis	18. St Paul (kneeling)
9. St Asaph	19. St Stephen (kneeling)
10. St Augustine	

The lower figures 20, 21, 22, 23 in the three central lights are based on our Lord's words to St Peter "Upon this rock I will build my church" and his charge to him "Feed my flock".

EAST WINDOW

Harold Grenfell.

NORTH WALL

In a letter, in the *Oystermouth Parish Magazine*, January 1934, the Revd W. J. Hickin writes: *"In answer to many questions, I may say here, it is expected that two new windows in the North side of the reredos, behind the Lady Chapel Altar, will be put in as early as possible in the New Year."* And again in July he reports: *"I cannot enumerate here all that has been done, but I can say, and want to say, how thankful we all are to those friends of St Peter's who have so generously, and often anonymously, contributed something toward making our church worthy of God."* By October he is able to print a description of the two new windows: *"These windows are fine examples of modern craftsmanship of stained glass. They were designed and carried out in their entirety in the studio of J. Wippell & Co. of Exeter."*

D. Sutton   Harold Grenfell.

a.   b.   a.   b.
   6.   7.

WINDOWS ON NORTH WALL BY J. WIPPLE & Co.

*From working drawings by
J. Wipple & Co showing detail*
(Courtesy of WGAS).

Detail of 6b   (S. Rees)

The left hand light of Window 6a shows **Our Lord blessing little children**. Above Him is to be seen the Holy Ghost, in the form of a dove of Glory out of which fork seven rays, emblematic of the seven gifts of the Spirit. Below in the lozenge is the Symbol of Innocence whilst the white quarries contain the sacred Monogram and Cross.

The inscription reads: *"To The Glory of God and in memory of William Kirkland and Jane Anne his daughter. Their all embracing sympathy brightened the lives of countless fellow creatures."*

The right hand light **6b** shows **St Christopher** carrying the child Christ across the ford. In the distance may be seen the hermit hut and storm clouds of the legend. The fiery cross above is the sign which the Saint avowed to serve. Below is the Sacred Cup of Faith and in the quarries a sword of martyrdom and cross. The tracery contains the three cherubs and the Holy Book inscribed Verbum Die.

7a Window, left hand light shows: St Paul before his conversion on the Damascus road. The Divine Presence symbolised by a Hand issuing from a cloud, and the seven stars are attributes of Our Saviour.

7b Window, right hand light shows: Child Samuel listening to the Word of God. It will be noticed that the boy is dressed in the ephod with its curiously twisted girdle. In continuity with the other window the emblems are Humility, a Cross, Wisdom and a lamp.

7a   Detail photographs by *Harold Grenfell.*   7b

The inscription reads
"To the Glory of God and in memory of James Rendell Dowdall"

THE WEST WINDOW

The west window was the last to have stained glass installed. It is described as having five cinquefoil lights with late decorated style traceried head. It is about 20 feet x 12 feet and is erected about 18 feet above ground level. In the P.C.C. minutes June 16th, 1967, it is recorded: *"The donation of a stained glass window in memory of Miss Kirkland and the Kirkland family was to be given by* **Miss D. B. Fry.**" However, before any work could be carried out, the badly affected stonework, around the area, had to be attended to and was treated with silicones. The stonework repairs were completed in 1968. In the meanwhile the money for the window was lodged in Lloyds Bank on trust. This fine modern window was made at the **Swansea Celtic Studios** to a design by Messrs Howard Martin and Hubert Thomas, their chief designers, taking nearly five months to produce. It was carefully considered by Miss Fry, long term companion of Miss Margaret Kirkland. As Miss Kirkland was the doyenne of the high class Swansea boot and shoe retailers, it was fitting that the patron Saints of Shoe Makers, St Crispin and St Crispinian, were depicted in the design.

St Crispin and St Crispinian were forced to flee from Rome, because of religious persecution, to Gaul where they settled in Soissons. They preached to the people, supporting themselves by shoemaking. The Roman persecutors caught up with them and on the 25th October, in the year 287 A.D., they suffered martyrdom by being cast in a cauldron of boiling lead. Since then the day has been celebrated as the Festival of St Crispin and they became the patron saints of shoe makers.

The theme of the window is that of the Ascension of Christ and the Gift of the Holy Spirit at Pentecost. The background is abstract forming a burst of coloured light and angels around the central figure of Christ and continuing through the symbols of Ascension and Resurrection surrounding the Holy Dove of the Holy Spirit. Under the central figure is the Chi Rho and Chalice. In addition to the Patron Saints there are also the figures of St Patrick – signifying Miss Kirkland's Irish origins – and of St Bridget, who was known for her works of practical charity, as was Miss Kirkland.

This window was dedicated at a special service on September 8th, 1968, by the Bishop of Swansea and Brecon Dr J. J. A. Thomas, and was welcomed by Canon Brunsdon as a valuable contribution to the church.

Miss Margaret Kirkland, with her sister Jane Anne (known as Jennie), managed the boot and shoe manufacturing and retailing business, William Kirkland Ltd., which their widowed father bought in Goat Street, when he came to Swansea in 1905. Together they established a highly successful business which was described as *"one of the best in the trade."* They were sticklers for good workmanship and for Trade Union rates of wages and good conditions of labour, so, deservedly earning their well renowned reputation of excellence. Miss Kirkland was also a firm believer in the value of artistic surroundings in the business house to which the Kirkland establishment bore testimony. The family settled in Groves Avenue, Langland, and called their house Caledon after the town, in County Tyrone, where Mr William Kirkland had been born. He died in 1928 and his daughter Jane Anne, shortly after, in 1931 (Cardy, 2000).

Miss Kirkland donated the St Christopher window on the North wall and dedicated it to their memory. Miss Fry lived with the Kirkland family for many years and was the first woman to work in a newspaper office when she joined the *Daily Leader* in Swansea. She was also one of the first women to drive a motor cycle and car in Swansea. A peep at some of their photos gives an interesting insight into their connections and activities. Judging from the comments in the visitors' book there was always a warm welcome in the home from these cultured and hospitable business women (these books and albums are now lodged in Swansea Museum).

THE NORTH PORCH

(D. Sutton)

In 1977 the **Toomey** family donated this window, in the entrance porch, in memory of "Mr Toomey, son and husband". Mr G. A. Toomey was vicar's warden from 1959-1962.

Key to the West Window (opposite):

The Eagle	**Ascending Christ**	**The Phoenix**
(symbol of Ascension)		(symbol of the Resurrection of Christ)
Disciples – Mary and John		Disciples – Disciples

St Crispin – St Patrick – Chi Rho & Chalice – St Bridget – St Crispinian

THE WEST WINDOW

S. Rees.

8.

The Incumbents and their Assistant Clergy and Church Officers

Ever since its consecration St Peter's Church has been blessed with remark-able and loyal incumbents. For the first 30 years, **1903-1933**, the church stood within the Parish of Oystermouth and was governed from All Saints' Church and served by their vicar and his curates. In 1933 the new Parish of St Peter's, Newton, was formed as defined in the map below.

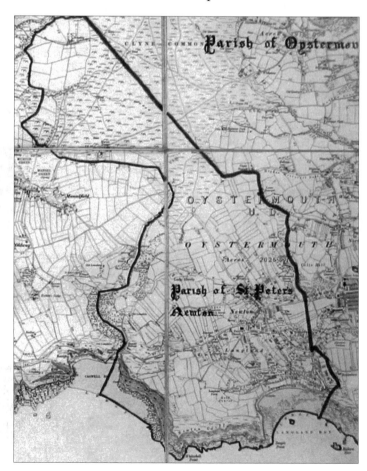

1903-1933:	The Venerable HAROLD STEPNEY WILLIAMS
1933	**FORMATION OF THE NEW PARISH OF ST PETER'S, NEWTON**
1933-1961:	The Revd Canon WALTER JOHN HICKIN
1961-1976:	The Revd Canon T. KENNETH BRUNSDON
1976-1987:	The Venerable HAROLD EDGAR WILLIAMS
1987-1996:	The Revd Canon DAVID THOMAS
1997-2006:	The Revd CLIVE JONES
2006-present:	The Revd Canon GEORGE BENNETT

The Venerable HAROLD STEPNEY WILLIAMS (1864-1954)
Vicar of Oystermouth (1898-1938), Archdeacon of Gower (1923-1954)

Harold Williams was born on March 28th, 1864. He showed an independent and determined spirit from early years. He was forced to interrupt his studies at Cambridge for financial reasons and he worked his way to Australia to spend time as a farm labourer until he was in a position to return home and fulfil his ambition to prepare for ordination.

He graduated from Durham University as a licentiate in theology in 1887 and was ordained deacon at Chester Cathedral on Trinity Sunday 1888 by the great church historian Bishop Stubbs. In 1890 Harold was priested at Llandaff during his second curacy at Tredegar (1889-1892). He married Mary Maud Holland on August 9th, 1892, in Rochester, Kent. In time they had three sons and two daughters. He was to hold three more curacies at Gowerton (1892-93), St Jude's, Swansea (1893-98), and at St John's, Hafod (1898), from where he was invited, by the retiring vicar of All Saints, Oystermouth, The Revd D. Secretan Jones, to succeed him.

The Revd Secretan Jones had held the living at Oystermouth for thirty-one years but due to old age and increasing infirmities was ready to hand over to a younger and more energetic man. Indeed, this is exactly what Harold Williams proved to be. He was described as 'a remarkable son of a remarkable father', who, between them served one hundred and thirty years in the ministry of the church.

The Revd Harold Williams was twenty-eight years old when he was instituted to the living of Oystermouth, at the Bishop's Palace in Abergwili, by the Bishop of St David's on Friday, December 9th, 1898. When he arrived at Oystermouth, he found the church in *"none too good a condition."* The church was also overcrowded and the parish in need of further development if he was to succeed in the work he resolutely set his mind to do. When he was first offered his living at Oystermouth at £87 p.a., without a house, Harold told the Bishop he could not live on that wage. The Bishop replied: *"Go in Faith."* So he went forward in faith and some forty years later he recorded in the *Oystermouth Magazine* that: *"the good people of that day gave me a living wage and I have never wanted since."* His motto was: *"The Lord will provide"* – as he discovered later when he was determined to open the New Church at Newton free of debt and without a bazaar. Shortly after his arrival he inaugurated the *Oystermouth Parish Magazine* as a vehicle of communication between the clergy and the parishioners. He also quickly organised a number of clubs and organisations mostly at All Saints' Church.

Dr Geoffry Orrin describes Harold S. Williams as one of the giants of the church extension movement in the deanery of Gower. His first twenty years as vicar of Oystermouth were immersed in church building programmes. He achieved, through his sheer determination, the results he felt he had been sent to do. He could see the immediate need in his own church for renovation, but it was to wait its turn, as he gave priority to other buildings in the parish first. In 1900 Harold formed a building committee to oversee the erection of the new church at Newton. As soon as he was satisfied this had been achieved and opened nearly free of debt, he addressed his own need for a vicarage which was placed high on his list of priorities. Fortunately for him the Duke of Beaufort, in 1903, gave him a valuable site (valued at £400), ideally situated midway between the parish church and the proposed new one. He and his wife were able to take up residence in June 1904 due to the donation of various grants and some £200 from the parishioners.

This ambitious vicar then turned his attention to other buildings within his parish. In August 1907 Harold Williams published an illustrated pamphlet, entitled *"A Brief record of church work in Oystermouth during the past eight years, 1899-1907."* In it he describes how more than £19,000 had been raised by public subscription for such works. At the time of his death over £60,000 had been raised for church buildings and other church purposes (Orrin, 1990, *Gower*, 41).

Harold revealed himself, through his writings, to have a good sense of humour and he was also a good storyteller. He is quoted to have said he believed Christians should cultivate humour and good fellowship and should lead a life of happiness as opposed to black clothes of a Victorian

Sunday. *"If your face wants to smile, let it."* On his way to St Peter's he passed a local chapel where he saw a board urging all to *"Come and hear Revd . . ."* (a well known preacher of boring repute!) Further down the road he saw another billboard offering a weekly meditation saying: *"Don't worry, it may never happen!"* His editorials in his magazine are full of such humorous observations. He was also a principled man, full of common sense, but he did not suffer fools gladly. He was strongly motivated in seeing things through to completion and was active serving on several local committees.

In 1919 he was appointed Rural Dean of East Gower. It was a busy year for him as he was one of the leaders of the Disestablishment campaign which he felt strongly about. The Welsh Act of 1914, which took effect on 31st March, 1920, separated the four ancient Welsh Dioceses of St Asaph, Bangor, St David's and Llandaff from the Province of Canterbury. The new Province of Wales came into being on 1st April, 1920, and in 1921 he became Prebendary of St David's Cathedral.

The new diocese of Swansea and Brecon was created in 1923 and he was appointed the first Archdeacon of Gower, in the See of Swansea and Brecon, and also Chaplain to its first Bishop, Edward Latham Bevan.

Bishop Bevan with the Canons of the Cathedral Chapter, appointed 1923.
Archdeacon Harold S. Williams stands on the left of the Bishop.

H. S. Williams and his wife and son.
(Photograph provided courtesy
of his late son).

February 1933 was a red-letter month in the history of Oystermouth Parish when the new parish of St Peter's, Newton, was created. For the vicar it must have seemed like the marriage of a daughter as he released his responsibilities. Five years later, at the end of 1938 he resigned his incumbency at Oystermouth after forty years. With the presentation of £500 from his parishioners he built a bungalow at Langland for his retirement. He called it *Yongola* after the sheep station in Australia where he once worked.

He still remained Archdeacon of Gower actively involved in his parish and was driving his car at the age of 84. It is believed that one of his last priestly duties was to give a blessing, at the end of a marriage service, at St Peter's Church. Harold died on St Mathias Day, February 24th, 1954, at the age of eighty-nine years after a brief illness. He will long be remembered for his activity in many aspects of Mumbles life. At the time of his death his successor as vicar of Oystermouth said: *"His Memorial stands for all to see in the building of the parish church, Newton church, the school and hall. He himself would want to be known as a priest who humbly tried to serve God and to do his duty as he saw it."* He was cremated on St David's Day, a week later, and his ashes were interred in a grave in the churchyard of his beloved Oystermouth Church, near the door of the Lady Chapel, during a snowstorm.

CURATES ASSISTING THE REVD HAROLD S. WILLIAMS

Throughout the first thirty years of St Peter's, the vicar was fortunate to be assisted by a succession of curates and priests-in-charge who served St Peter's on his behalf. It seems unlikely that present and future incumbents will be blessed with such a succession. Admittedly, the vicar had a greater need as he eventually had three churches to look after besides All Saints: at Newton, Norton and Blackpill. He also had to attend to three church schools in the parish at Dunns Lane in Mumbles, Newton and Blackpill.

Revd Harold S. Williams with his curates, c.1905.

Revd TUDOR OWEN PHILLIPS, L.Th., Curate 1899-1911. He was the son of the late Dean Phillips of St David's Cathedral and studied at the University of Durham to obtain his degree. He came to All Saints' as curate shortly after the arrival of the new vicar, in 1899. While he worked in Mumbles he lived at 18 Victoria Avenue and at Walters Crescent. The vicar wrote: *"He comes with good credentials – a good type of a healthy minded, athletic Christian, and will doubtless exercise a good influence over young men . . ."*

Soon after his arrival he records being taken around the parish by his vicar who told him of his plans to enlarge the parish church and build a new church at Newton as well as a school and a couple of church halls. He remained working within the Oyster-mouth Parish for ten years. References are often made in the *Parish Magazine* to his conducting services in the schoolroom at Newton and attending many meetings, as well as supporting the large Sunday School. In 1911 he moved to a living at Haverfordwest and he was succeeded by Latimer Davies at Oystermouth Church.

Revd ARTHUR BURROWS, Curate 1901-1903. He lived at Summerfield, Newton and looked after the Newton parishioners, taking services in Newton schoolroom. He became Superintendent of Newton Sunday School and stayed for three years before moving on to *"an excellent appointment in Kent."*

Revd W. LLEWELYN THOMAS, M.A.(Oxon.), Curate 1903-1907. He was educated at Christ College Brecon and Keble College Oxford where he gained his Football Blue and went on to become a Welsh International footballer. He trained for the ministry at Lichfield Theological College and was ordained in 1899 and licensed to Rushall, Lichfield. He came to Oyster-mouth with *"excellent credentials and with a reputation as a hard and steady worker. He will take charge at the new church."* wrote the vicar. He arrived on April 26th, 1903, and lived in Chapel Lane. He became curate-in-charge at St Peter's until 1907 when he left due to eye problems. He was presented with a purse of gold on his departure.

For awhile it seems the vicar experienced difficulty in filling the vacancy with a suitable curate for several changes are recorded in quick succession:

In 1907 the **Revd W. M. JENKINS** stayed only a few weeks until May when the **Revd D. L. WILLIAMS** came from Sutton in Surrey. However, he, also, only remained a short time and in June 1908 the curacy was filled by the **Revd G. M. WILLIAMS** of whom it is written: *"During the short time he was at St Peter's he had made himself liked and respected by most who attended the church. He left because he had accepted an offer of a living in Shropshire."*

From 1908 to 1913 the **Revd W. R. JONES, B.A.**, was the new assistant priest-in-charge of Newton district and he resided at Summerfield. With some relief the vicar writes: *"He promises to be the right man for the job. It makes the Vicar's holiday doubly restful when he can leave his large parish in such good hands."* However, in 1913 Revd R. Jones left St Peter's to go to Brecon to co-ordinate work among children in the diocese. On leaving he was presented with a silver pocket font with a baptismal shell from the Sunday School and a white embroidered stole and altar linen from the Bible class, and the choir gave him a photograph of the choir. He was temporarily replaced by the **Revd A. VAUGHAN WILLIAMS** until the **Revd W. J. WILLIAMS**, the eldest son of Canon W. Williams (Canon Missioner of the Diocese), served as curate between 1913 and 1915. He was a graduate of Oxford and had tutored at a grammar school before coming to Newton. He lived at Fairfield until the end of 1915 when he left to become an army chaplain.

During the 1914-1918 World War services were curtailed, but after the war the vicar was joined by two more curates who first helped at St Peter's before moving on to other churches within the parish.

They were the **Revd W. H. HARRIS, M.A. (Oxon.)**, (1919-1920) and the **Revd H. Victor WILLIAMS**, who was later appointed the first priest-in charge at Clyne Chapel in 1927. The next curate was the **Revd S. T. PHILLIPS** who stayed for three years (1920-1922) before going on to Christchurch in Swansea and then becoming the Vice Principal of St Michael's Theological College at Llandaff. Later he was Rector of Tallyllyn, in Breconshire, and Vicar of Roath and was also examining chaplain to the Bishop of Swansea and Brecon.

The Revd T. R. ROWLANDS, M.A., B.D., was the next appointed priest-in-charge at St Peter's, 1922-1926, and was described as *"a scholar and able preacher."* He left after four years to take up a living at Abercrave and later became Vicar of Holyhead, as well as Rural Dean (see photograph).

The Revd D. HILARY JONES, M.A., followed and served two years at St Peter's as priest-in-charge (1926-1927) before following his predecessor to become vicar of Abercrave where he was instituted by the Bishop of the Diocese on Saturday, August 6th, 1927. He was described as: *"Saintly"* and it was recorded: *"He writes very earnest and intense articles."*

The Revd D. J. DAVIES arrived in the September (1927-1928) from St Michael's Church in Aberystwyth where he had been assistant curate for four years. He had studied at Oxford and at Aberyswyth. He did not stay long at Newton as he was recorded as suffering from ill health and left after a nervous breakdown.

The Revd W. J. HICKIN, B.A., originally came for four weeks, in October (1928-1933), but stayed for another four years as priest-in-charge and then, when the new Parish of St Peter's, Newton, was formed he was appointed its first vicar.

1933 Formation of the new parish of St Peter's, Newton

The Revd Canon WALTER JOHN HICKIN, B.A. (1889-1961)
Vicar of St Peter's Church, 1933-1961

In February 1933 the parishioners were formally advised that the bishop had offered the new parish to Revd W. J. Hickin. They were pleased for he had been priest-in-charge of the church for nearly five years and his appointment was a popular choice. He moved, with his unmarried sisters, into a new vicarage at the top of St Peter's Road, on the left hand side, which had been generously given by Mrs Irene Caroline Richardson.

He was born in 1889. He studied at St David's College, Lampeter, and he qualified in 1912 with a

B.A. in Science. He went on to train at St Michael's College, Llandaff, and he was ordained deacon in 1913 and priest in 1914. His first curacy was at Mold, in the diocese of St Asaph. He was also curate in Brecon and then in Jeffreyston, Pembrokeshire, during World War I. He stayed until 1920 when he emigrated to Canada and became Rector of Rimby from 1921-1926. Later, after he had decided to return to Wales, he was granted permission to officiate in the diocese of Swansea and Brecon in 1927. He was then offered the position of curate in Oystermouth Parish and became priest-in-charge at St Peter's Church in 1928.

On February 4th, 1933, Revd Hickin was instituted, by the bishop, to the living in Newton parish, in the bishop's private chapel at Brecon as the bishop, due to illness, was unable to perform the ceremony in the church itself. A few days later, the vicar was inducted at St Peter's Church, on Thursday, 9th February, at a solemn ceremony performed by the Archdeacon of Gower. A number of clergy from the diocese attended and, afterwards, tea was provided by the ladies of the Mothers' Union in the Church Hall.

At Revd Hickin's first vestry meeting, he appointed Mr Gage to be his churchwarden and Mr E. T. Thomas to be the people's warden.

In his first letter to his parishioners, as their vicar, in the March 1933 church magazine, he writes in a reflective mood. In it he refers to times during the past five years when: *"clouds had appeared low and life a bit difficult,"* but admitting it was his fault. He goes on to express: *"his sincere gratitude to all the people of Newton for their great kindness and heartiest help."*

He is still affectionately remembered by some parishioners today. Memories of a child at the time: *"The vicar would come into the Girls Fellowship meeting once a month for a cup of tea . . . all the children loved Mr Hickin. He would attend every night when we put on a performance of entertainment. The vicar would accompany the choir and carol singers around the village every Christmas."*

One of his choirboys remembers: *"The vicar's long sermons were not interesting to us boys, so we used to talk and joke during the sermons and quite often the vicar would lean out of the pulpit, look towards us and give us a very unholy look."*

Another choirboy, now a vicar, describes W. J. Hickin as: *"Profoundly spiritual, very devout and quiet. He was a good man, of great integrity; never a populist; very modest – help always generously given. Not a good preacher but scrupulously honest. Not an innovator but good on the financial side. He was an accomplished pianist. There are marks in front of the choir stalls where Canon Hickin would beat time, with a silver topped rod, while conducting at choir practice."* His motto was *"Never push yourself – the Lord will take care."*

It must have been a difficult time for the vicar during the Second World War when several of the congregation and the organist were away on active service and various church organisations were temporarily disbanded. Mr

The Induction of Revd W. J. Hickin as the first vicar of the new Parish of St Peter's, Newton, 9th February, 1933.

Back row, left to right: Revd V. Williams, Mr E. T. Thomas (first Ch/W of St Peter's),
Capt. W. J. Ackland (Ch/W. Oystermouth), Revd E. Jenkins (Curate-Landore),
Revd D. Lyn Davies (Vicar-Killay), Revd D. S. P. Mackintosh (Vicar-Bishopston.
Front row, left to right: Mr H. M. Ward (Ch/W. Oystermouth), Revd W. S. Edmonds (Mansleton),
Revd Iltyd Jenkins (Curate-Oystermouth), Revd W. J. HICKIN (Centre),
Archdeacon H. S. Williams, Mr Hugh Bellingham (Solicitor), Revd Hilary Jones (Vicar-Abercrave).

George Johnston was his churchwarden and Mr S. Copleston was the people's warden. In 1944 the vicar was assisted by Revd D. Gerallt Thomas.

In 1954 Mr Hickin was installed as Canon of Brecon Cathedral and in 1959 he was appointed Canon Treasurer. At the same service the Vicar of Swansea, Canon J. J. A. Thomas, was installed as Archdeacon of Gower. He was the father of a future vicar of St Peter's, David Thomas, who writes: *"Throughout my time as vicar, the influence and teaching of Canon Hickin were still clearly in evidence. What a huge debt of gratitude Newton owes to its first incumbent who served 30 of the first 70 years of the parish."*

Revd Hickin reports in the church magazine on two events, in which members of St Peter's participated, which moved him to write at length. The first was in May 1953 when a remarkable parade took place in Swansea on the Good Friday. *"Over a thousand churchmen processed through the streets to the Brangwyn Hall to join a choir of two hundred strong. They were divided into ten companies each marching four abreast and in silence, followed by the bishop of the diocese, his chaplains, the rural dean and the Archdeacon of Gower. Before each company a wooden cross bearing an emblem of the Passion was carried. This solemn*

Act of Witness was concluded with a short service in the Hall and the Secretary General of the Churchmen's Society spoke. Over twelve hundred churchmen together paraded in Swansea streets which were lined with curious and understanding spectators as they made their sacred and silent Act of Witness to their Christian faith, in a very moving manner."

Secondly, in 1959 a big Evangelical Mission was launched in the diocese and special services held at St Peter's. The theme was Faith and Family aiming to fill the church, emphasising personal witness and for every Christian to be an active evangelist. This call has often been repeated throughout the ages.

During 1959 St Peter's lost its longest serving churchman, Mr Edward John Price. He had come to Newton sixty years earlier and he was appointed verger and sacristan in 1903 when the church was opened. He continued in that office until 1945 when illness compelled him to retire and he died peacefully on July 15th, 1959, at the age of 87 years. He was succeeded by Mr Bill Barrington, another very long serving and loyal verger.

It was with sadness the churchwardens had to announce the sudden death of their beloved vicar, Canon Hickin, on February 8th, 1961, exactly twenty-eight years after his Induction as Vicar of Newton. He was much loved and respected, serving the church and village faithfully for thirty-three years. He was described as: *"a man of great integrity, with strong and tireless administrative qualities; bearing the burden of an ever increasing parish without complaint; and fulfilling his good work right to the end."*

Apart from the several gifts (already referred to in chapter 6), given to St Peter's in memory of Canon Hickin, his ministry could also be seen as a lasting memorial for it is interesting to note that several members of his congregation later became ordained. These were: Timothy Ganz and Phillip Brenden Meager in 1962; Timothy Campbell Smith; and James Owen who was vicar of Little St Mary's, Cambridge, for many years and later became a Canon of Ely.

CURATES ASSISTING THE REVD CANON HICKIN

The Revd Hickin was assisted by only one curate and by a retired vicar:

The Revd W. BRIAN was a former Vicar of Whiteshill, near Stroud, and had retired early because of ill health and came to live in Newton. He was licensed in 1938 to help out, as required, at St Peter's.

The Revd GERALLT THOMAS was curate for only one year (**1944-1945**). **The Revd JOHN BOYLE** covered the vacancy after Canon Hickin's death, in 1961, for six months, until the arrival of the next vicar.

Canon T. KENNETH BRUNSDON (1908-2003)
Vicar of St Peter's Church, 1961-1976

Thomas Kenneth Brunsdon was born at Cwm-avon on 2nd September, 1908. For four years he attended the Merchant Taylors' School in London and worked in pharmacy for five years. In 1929 he gained a Welsh church scholarship and attended the University College Swansea until 1933 when he gained a B.A. Hons. in Philosophy.

He then went on to train for the ministry at St Michael's College, Llandaff, and was ordained as deacon in 1934 and priest in 1935. He went to Knighton as a curate from 1935 to 1940. While there, in 1936, he married Esther Jane Bowen Ph.D., lecturer in biology at the University College, Swansea. She later became a children's officer for Radnorshire C.C. and also served as a J.P. In 1940 he became Vicar of Llandegley, staying until 1947 when he went on to become Vicar of Builth. In 1961 he was invited to become Vicar of Newton. He had already been made a residentiary canon of Brecon Cathedral in 1958, and from 1961 to 1964 he was Canon Treasurer.

His Induction Service was held at St Peter's on Tuesday, June 20th, 1961, at 6 p.m. in the presence of the Bishop of Swansea and Brecon Dr J. J. A. Thomas. Afterwards, the visitors were invited to refreshments in the Church Hall. The following Friday evening, of June 23rd, more refreshments were served and adult members and friends of St Peter's Church were able to extend a warm welcome to their new vicar and his wife. In his own words he *"found it a tremendous change to move from a market town to a parish in an ever growing suburban area of Swansea."* However, he goes on to say how he *"welcomed coming to a loved and lovely church, its appointment and furnishing evidence of good Anglican ways and the result of good and instructed taste of generous past donors."*

Canon Brunsdon was very much a traditionalist but also proved to be an innovator. He was supported by his curate, Revd Norman Lea, and together they made some revolutionary changes for the time. They introduced the Family Eucharist at 9.30 a.m. each Sunday and adopted the use of a 'Nave Altar', a portable altar, to be erected at the foot of the chancel steps to be used for the service. They introduced an up beat hymn book, '100 Hymns for Today', to reflect the informal nature of the worship. Also, at this time, he formed a Youth Club with his curate who was under the guidance of Canon

Arthur Howells, the Diocesan Youth Chaplain. In fact, there were so many youngsters they ended up with two Youth Clubs!

Several parishioners have recalled their affectionate memories of him for he was a lasting friend to many: *"He was always a very caring friend, supportive in times of grief, ready to listen, comfort and give advice at times of trouble. He also had a great sense of humour in his rather quiet way."*

His curate, Revd Norman Lea, 1968-1970: *"If I had one thing to thank Newton for it would surely be my lasting relationship with my Vicar . . . who over the years has been my mentor, protector, advisor, guardian angel, but above all, a dear friend whose wise counsels I have always valued and who, in his own way, was an outstanding parish priest. This is also true for the people of Newton."*

During the vicar's incumbency, with the support of his churchwardens and P.C.C., several major alterations and building projects were undertaken which enhanced the church. As the vicar commented: *"The building programme had to be fitted in with the normal work of a Parish, the weekly round of worship, and work with the Sunday Schools, with Mothers' Union, Young Wives Fellowship, Girls' Friendly Society and the Choir. The generous and able help of many, according to their ability, met these challenges to the full."* This work included the cleaning of the woodwork in the church and treatment for woodworm before the new Hickin Memorial screen could be installed in 1961.

From 1963 to 1964 he became occupied with the building of the new vicarage. When it was completed it was blessed by the Bishop of Swansea and Brecon on May 29th, 1964. At that time a new carriageway around the church was created and the Lychgate was repaired. The church had a new heating system installed.

In 1967 the Church Hall underwent major restoration work on its foundations and general structure. In 1975 the hall was almost rebuilt and refurbished. Before the gift of a memorial window to Miss Kirkland could be fitted, on the west wall of the church, it was necessary to repair the stonework around the window.

In 1968 there were more improvements with new lighting and wall heating bars positioned on the columns. A house was purchased for the first curate and his wife in Melcorn Drive.

Repairs continued in 1971-1972 with the painting of the woodwork and troughing on the outside of the church and shortly after, the East window had to be repaired and guards placed around all the windows for protection. The organ also required new pistons and the choir stalls needed attention. Once again the choir were fitted with new robes.

1973 commemorated the 70th anniversary of the church with the printing of a booklet on the history of the church. New seats were replaced around the Garden of Remembrance and in 1974 heathers were planted around the grounds. It was also necessary to resurface the carriageway.

There was also much buying and selling of property, including the sale of the old vicarage in St Peter's Road and the sale of land adjacent to the new vicarage; the purchase and sale of the curate's house and the sale of School House, the funds being returned to the Diocese.

On his retirement Canon and Mrs Brunsdon were thanked by the churchwardens and the Parochial Church Council for: *"Giving of themselves untiringly. Thank God they came to Newton."*

Mrs Brunsdon was ill for a number of years during which her husband devotedly nursed

Canon and Mrs Brunsdon.

her. She died in 1989 and Canon Brunsdon gave to the church a silver Ciborium in her memory. He retired to Porthcawl.

It was remarkable that Canon Brunsdon's last visit to St Peter's Church was just a month before his death, when, although frail, he attended Sung Eucharist and the exhibition to commemorate the centenary of the church. He was accompanied by his former curate, Revd Norman Lea, a faithful friend throughout the years. It is also remarkable that at that service four out of the five vicars of Newton Parish were present and photographed together representing forty-two years of continuous service to the church. Canon Brunsdon died peacefully, a month later, at the age of 95 years, on December 22nd, 2003. His former curate, Revd Norman Lea, conducted the funeral service.

CURATE ASSISTING THE REVD CANON BRUNSDON

The vicar was assisted by only one curate, the **Revd NORMAN LEA, B.A.**, from 1968-1970. He trained at Mirfield and was ordained at Brecon Cathedral on December 21st, 1968. He had just married when he served his title at St Peter's, Newton, and he and his wife resided at Melcorn Drive, specially purchased for the couple at £4,050 from loans and gifts. He recalls some memories of that time. His first Christmas at St Peter's, within a week of his ordination, was an unforgettable experience as he was confronted by a huge congregation – some even sitting on the windowsills! The experience and guidance he gained from his vicar and supportive churchwardens were to remain with him throughout his ministry. Later, Norman Lea became Vicar of the parish of Cadoxton-juxta-Neath.

The Venerable HAROLD EDGAR WILLIAMS (1917-2004)
Vicar of St Peter's Church, 1976-1987

Harold Williams was born in 1917 and was brought up and educated in Llanelli. He trained at St David's College, Lampeter. Before continuing his theological studies he developed a taste for the sea by working his passage in a tramp steamer, carrying tinplate from Llanelli to Gravesend, and returning with other cargo. In 1939 he went to Kings College, London, to study for the A.K.C. course in Theology, and while he was there, during World War II, the college evacuated to Bristol. He was ordained as Deacon in 1942 in Chelmsford Cathedral by Bishop Henry Wilson and priested the following year.

His curacies were in contrasting parishes, St John's, Leytonstone, East London and St Mary's, Barnes. He then returned to Wales as curate of St Jude's, in Swansea, where he met and married Joan in 1951 and their first son was born.

From 1946-1948, Harold served in the Royal Navy as chaplain, firstly with the Home Fleet on H.M.S. *Dido* and later, in 1951, he returned to the Navy, until 1955, serving in Argyleshire, Dartmouth and joining the Mediterranean Fleet on board H.M.S. *Bermuda*.

During 1955-1956, he was appointed Bishop's Messenger and Warden of Ordinands by Bishop Glyn Simon who, at that time, was Bishop of Swansea and Brecon. He took up his first living in the Usk Valley, in the parishes of Llansantffraed and Llanhamlach where sons Phil and John were born.

In 1961 the family moved to Hay-on-Wye where Harold was Vicar of St Mary's. This was followed in 1967 by a move to Brynmawr. He was appointed Canon of Brecon Cathedral in 1972 and a residentiary secretary of the Provincial Board of Ordinands.

Thence, to his last appointment as Vicar of St Peter's at Newton from 1976 to 1987. By a happy coincidence, he was aware he bore the same name as the founder of the church and also occupied the same office of Archdeacon of Gower, to which he had been appointed in 1983, after being Chancellor of Brecon Cathedral.

1983 was also a significant year for St Peter's Parish Church as it celebrated its Golden Jubilee. Among the many special events to commemorate this occasion there was a B.B.C. 'Songs of Praise' and 'Any Questions' chaired by David Jacobs. A magnificent Flower Festival was organised by the Ladies of the Parish and ably supported by the Men's Society. The Cwmbach Male Voice Choir from Aberdare gave a concert during this festival. Also, on show was the Gold Cope which had been lovingly restored by Mrs May Lalor (Williams, H. E., 1990).

Harold Williams described his young curate, Revd John Cruse, as one who worked well with youngsters. He helped to form a thriving Sunday School where over one hundred children attended, as well as a Young Parents group. Sunday services were geared to parents and children. On one Sunday a month there was a Family Service (not communion). Children were also involved in Easter and Christmas scenes, offering gifts at Christmas and fresh eggs at Easter to be distributed to the sick and aged. For Mothering Sunday the children assisted in making a simnel cake, distributed to all at the service. For Harvest Festival children helped bake small loaves, and even Harold enjoyed having a few lessons. Mr Cyril Bowen was his organist and the choir mistress was Betty Thomas and during his time Mrs Wyn White was the first lady to be appointed sides-woman at St Peter's.

The Girls Friendly Society was led by Joan, his wife. There was also a Men's Society, a Mothers' Union, a Church Women's Fellowship and a Travel Society. The vicar and his wife enjoyed travelling to Rome, Athens and Paris with them. There was even an adventurous Walking Fellowship.

The Venerable Harold E. Williams retired on his 70th birthday, Easter 1987, but still restless for travel he took up part-time posts as chaplain in Matalascanus, South West Spain, Benidorm and Mallorca. When he and Joan eventually returned to their home in West Cross, Swansea, Harold wrote a fascinating recollection of his life called *The Parting Mist*. In chapter 12 he recalls what it was like when he first came to St Peter's: *"to settle in a young church, in an ancient hamlet, which still retained something of the country ethos, where the vicar was still the 'persona' who was welcomed in every home and community activity."* He observed that the 'old hamlet', with an increasing spread of new housing, was fast becoming a mix of village and new town. The congregation was made up of both young and old and all age groups were catered for. He described the worship as joyous (Williams, 2000).

He was succeeded by Revd David Thomas who writes: *"Archdeacon Harold and Mrs Williams were living nearby in retirement. I realised within a very few weeks of my arrival how determined he had been that St Peter's should*

Photograph courtesy of Joan Williams.

reach out into the wider, increasingly secularised local community and, above all, that children and young adults should find their way into the life, worship and witness of the church . . . His wife Joan shared his vision and commitment."

Harold was pleased to be fit enough to attend the service of Thanksgiving for the Centenary of St Peter's Church, but his health continued to deteriorate and he died on 12th October, 2004, at the age of 87 years. He had had a happy and fulfilling life in the Ministry, greatly encouraged and supported by Joan, and their kindness will long be remembered by many whose lives they touched.

CURATES ASSISTING THE VEN. HAROLD WILLIAMS

The Revd JOHN CRUSE also arrived, newly qualified, with his wife, to work with Harold Williams. He served his title at Salisbury after gaining his theological degree at Lampeter. He recalls the two years at St Peter's (1982-1984) as happy and fruitful ones. Certainly, it was a very active time in the church for his time covered the Parish Golden Jubilee in 1983. In addition to his normal duties he was involved with several church groups, having helped to form 'The Newton Circle' and he worked with young families in the 'Monday Group'.

There was music appreciation group, the Sunday School, the youth club, and the GFS to help look after. Throughout, he received wonderful encouragement and support from his vicar who, when appointed Archdeacon of Gower, was often away, thus entrusting to his young charge added responsibilities. Revd John Cruse writes of that time of *"the feeling of trust and encouragement. The whole atmosphere at St Peter's was one where faith was taken seriously but life enjoyed in good company."*

He aspired to carry this ethos with him throughout his ministry in various parishes, mostly in England and eventually to his present living as Vicar of St Mary's, Shalford, in Surrey. After leaving St Peter's he lived for awhile in the wilds of mid Wales before moving across the border, where he gained a teaching qualification and became involved in church educational work. His wife Jane is a lay-reader, having commenced her studies while at St Peter's. They have two teenaged sons.

In 1980 the Church in Wales had decided women could be ordained as Deacons, so during Archdeacon Harold William's last four years at St Peter's he had a lady deacon to assist him, the Revd Clarice Smith.

Revd CLARICE SMITH (1984-1988) and 1988-1995 (Honorary)

Clarice had worked for nearly thirty-three years in the civil service when she answered the call to serve God in the Ministry of the Church. So, in 1976, she took early retirement, and trained at St Michael's Theological College in Llandaff. The following year she was made a deaconess and her first appointment was as curate to the parish of Llaniwg, Pontardawe, until December 1980, including two months during a vacancy.

With the new ruling in the Church in Wales she was ordained deacon in September 1980 which meant she could now perform more duties including conducting marriage services. In the December of that year she became curate of the parish of Llwynderw, covering both the churches of Clyne and Holy Cross. During this time she also joined the team of chaplains at Singleton Hospital. Clarice remained at Clyne until August 1st, 1984, when she became the next curate at St Peter's where she worked with two vicars, Archdeacon Harold Williams and his successor Canon David Thomas, until her retirement in July 1988. She returned on a voluntary basis and she continued to assist and support the vicar, especially at times when he was without a curate and also during another vacancy. To quote David Thomas: *"I benefited greatly from this remarkable woman Deacon, from her example of prayerfulness and her deep love of the scriptures. I also learnt a great deal from her about the need for close attention to detail in pastoral matters."* She finally retired for the third time on her seventieth birthday in December 1995. Shortly afterwards, when the Governing Body of the Church in Wales legislated for the ordination of women to the priesthood, Bishop Dewi Bridges offered to ordain her but she declined. Thankfully, she has remained a faithful parishioner at St Peter's.

The Revd Canon DAVID THOMAS (1942-)
Vicar of St Peter's Church, 1987-1996

David Thomas was born on 22nd July, 1942, in Bangor, North Wales. He started his education in Swansea where his father, John James Absalom Thomas, was Vicar of St Mary's, and he continued his schooling at Christ College, Brecon. He went on to Oxford to study classics at Keble College, 1960-64, and theology at St Stephen's House. 1967 was a significant year for David when he married Rosemary Calton in the April and was ordained deacon in St Asaph Cathedral the following month.

For the next two and a half years he served as curate at Hawarden, in Deeside, with special responsibility for St Francis' Church, Sandycroft. He was ordained priest at St Asaph in June 1968. Earlier in that year Rosemary and David became parents when their daughter Felicity was born. Towards the end of his time in Hawarden, David was invited by Archbishop Glyn Simon to become a member of the Liturgical Commission of the Church in Wales. He continued to serve in this capacity until his retirement in 2008.

In 1969, he returned to academia – initially as tutor, then as chaplain, at St Michael's College, Llandaff. It was during their time at Llandaff that

Rosemary and David's son, John, was born. In July 1975, David returned to his *alma mater* in Oxford as Vice-Principal of St Stephen's House. However, the link with Wales was not broken for there were always students from the Church in Wales at St Stephen's House. In addition, David now became a member of the Church in Wales Doctrinal Commission, on which he served until it was dissolved in 1993. The family left Oxford at the end of 1979 for the parish of Chepstow, in the diocese of Monmouth, but their time there was short because David was asked to return to St Stephen's House as principal in summer 1982.

By the middle of 1987 David had been ordained for twenty years, of which he had spent only five in parish ministry. He and Rosemary were therefore delighted when the opportunity arose to return to parochial ministry in Wales following the retirement of Archdeacon Harold Williams from St Peter's, Newton. Recalling his memories of St Peter's, David Thomas writes: *"At St Peter's we learnt, as never before, about the deep and abiding joy of pastoral ministry . . . I found it to be a richly formative experience of Christian prayer as well. The daily offices, both morning and evening, and the regular celebration of the Holy Eucharist came alive for me in a completely new way. St Peter's is a really beautiful and very obviously holy place to pray in. I used to sit in the church on my own sometimes, just reflecting quietly on how the prayer of so many people in the twentieth century had somehow been 'soaked up' into the building itself."* This time was a very special experience for David and Rosemary.

He was grateful to 'inherit' Grahame Sutton as his warden and Steve Dunster as people's warden, as well as some impressively wise 'elder states-men' like Frank Jones, Werner Sivertsen and Viv Lethbridge. In the following years David Williams, Keith Davies and Anne Sutton were also wardens. Likewise, Miss Gwenneth Snow, secretary of the Parochial Church Council (P.C.C.) for many years, was indefatigably faithful throughout her long life. She assisted in the church in all sorts of ways and was associated in most aspects of its running. She looked after the Mothers' Union and ran a monthly prayer group at which she gave outstanding brief, devotional addresses.

The hard work of the wardens was complemented by that of Bill Howells, David Williams and Dennis Lenthall in the post of covenant secretary and Alan Grocutt as treasurer. All these people played a special part in guiding the parish through the financial straits caused by a threefold rise in the annual diocesan quota payments between 1987 and 1996. This swingeing increase made it necessary to hold a number of special fund-raising events: a revival of the annual church fête in 1988, and soon after began the week-long Petertide celebrations. The leading lights for these activities were Win White, and Finvola Davies who is still taking an active part in parish life.

Unfortunately, the financial climate of these years made it necessary to shelve work on the rapidly deteriorating Church Hall, although a fund for a replacement was opened. An organ restoration fund was also launched in 1989 and the £12,000 needed for urgent and essential work on the bellows was quickly raised.

David's ministry was both pastoral and ecumenical. Through the Mumbles Council of Churches he often shared pulpits with other denominations in the area. Relations with nearby Paraclete Chapel were cordial. He also inherited many active organisations. Rosemary, too, was busy, involved with M.U., C.W.F. and the Mission to Seamen Guild as well as working part-time.

The parish magazine required a large group of volunteers who contributed to the printing and circulation to 500-600 people in the parish and beyond. The editor was Leslie Griffin, whom David describes as: *"resourceful, indefatigable and patient beyond belief when, yet again, the vicar failed to meet the deadline!"*

Some changes were introduced to the services on Sundays, most notably the combination of the 9.30 a.m. and 11 a.m. services into a Parish Eucharist at 10 a.m. The monthly Family Service was retained, though it was re-timed to 11.15 a.m. Other services designed for young families included Christingle, the Animal Service and the child-friendly Easter Vigil Eucharist, which was always followed by fireworks and hot dogs!

In 1993, during a week-long parish mission in Holy Week, led by Dr George Noakes, large numbers attended the services, including several people from Paraclete Chapel. It was unfortunate that their minister, the Revd Arthur Harries, died very suddenly on the Palm Sunday.

Three vicar's of St Peter's (back row): Revd David Thomas, Ven. Harold Williams and Canon Brunsdon and three of the vicar's curates Revd Clarice Smith, on his left, and Revds. David Davies and David Swyer, front row.

On Sunday, 6th June, 1993, new choir robes were blessed in memory of Christopher, the son of Keith and Sue Davies. Two former vicars and three of his curates attended this service as seen in the photograph on page 96.

On Wednesday, 16th June, the vicar marked his Silver Jubilee as a priest by inviting Rt Revd and Rt Hon. Dr David Hope, Bishop of London (later Archbishop of York), to preach at a special Eucharist at St Peter's Church. There was another unusual occasion during Revd David Thomas' time, when there were three bishops in the church. It occurred during a Confirmation Service when Bishop of Swansea and Brecon, Bishop Dewi Bridges, was present. Also, in the congregation were two of his predecessors, both retired and residing in the parish. They were the vicar's father, Bishop J. J. A. Thomas (fifth Bishop of Swansea and Brecon 1958-1976), and his successor, Bishop Benjamin Vaughan, who was also Bishop of Honduras in 1967 and had retired to Newton in 1987 where he lived until his death in 2003.

In 1994, David Thomas served as High Sheriff's chaplain to a member of the St Peter's congregation, Mr Colin Rees. In the same year David was made a Residentiary Canon of Brecon Cathedral and, two years later, Rural Dean of Clyne.

It was announced early in November 1996 that David had been appointed Provincial Assistant Bishop of the Church in Wales. The parting, six weeks later, was not made any easier by the fact that everything had happened so quickly. The appointment was confirmed by the Sacred Synod of the Bishops

Left: The Revd David Thomas, High Sheriff's Chaplain to
Mr C. Rees, High Sheriff (2nd left), at his inauguration.

of the Church in Wales, at St Asaph Cathedral on 20th December, 1996, and David was ordained Bishop the following day. His new task brought with it a special responsibility to provide pastoral and sacramental care for those unable, in conscience, to accept the ordination of women as priests. The situation was difficult and confusing, and the need to hold church people together was paramount. Although the congregation were pleased for him they were sad to lose a friend all too soon. A parishioner recalls memories of the vicar: *"He was an outgoing man, ready to smile and a great family man, proud of his children's achievements. He was a good friend who would often drop in to visit and chat over a cup of tea."*

On 19th September, 2001, Provincial Assistant Bishop David Thomas returned to St Peter's to preach at a special service to commemorate the centenary of the laying of the foundation stone. Two years later he was again present for the special service to celebrate the centenary of the opening of the church. Also present were two of his predecessors and several former curates.

CURATES ASSISSTING THE REVD CANON THOMAS

During his ministry at St Peter's David Thomas was fortunate to be assisted by a succession of curates:

The Revd DAVID DAVIES arrived in 1990 straight from theological college in Llandaff with his wife, Donna, and their son Joshua and a second son was born while they were at Newton. It became necessary to find a larger home for the family as the curate's house in Croftfield Crescent was too small. A house in Summerland Lane was purchased.

Revd David Thomas, his vicar, writes: *"David did sterling work with young people in the parish and started a huge youth club. A very worthwhile by-product of this was the St Peter's Football Team.*

Sadly, neither of these ventures lasted long as they were short of people to help run them." David was much missed by the young people in the parish when he left in 1993 to take up a living in Powys. He subsequently became an army chaplain and served in Iraq.

His successor was the **Revd DAVID SWYER**. He came from a title in Killay in 1993 with his wife, Rebecca, who was a deacon at St Paul's, Sketty. David was a music graduate and set up an excellent little youth orchestra in the church, but, again, due to lack of qualified help, it did not survive after his departure, two years later in 1995. While at St Peter's, David, still a young man, had surgery for a total hip replacement.

The Revd **TUDOR GRIFFITHS** came to Newton with his wife Nelleke and their two sons, briefly, from January to May 1996. They had been working with CMS in Uganda and. prior to that, he had been vicar of a country parish near Crickhowell for five years. Revd David Thomas had already met him in the late 1970s when he was lecturing at Oxford and Tudor was a student at Wycliffe Hall. David writes: *"I, and, I think, also the congregation, gained enormously from Tudor's wonderful evangelical preaching. I also found it helpful to be able to share parish problems and challenges with him."* Tudor moved on to become Diocesan Missioner of Monmouth. Tragically, Nelleke was killed in a car accident a couple years after they left Newton.

The Revd **DOMINIC COSSLETT** arrived at St Peter's in 1996 from the College of the Resurrection, Mirfield. He had graduated from St David's University College, Lampeter, with a B.A. Hons. degree in Theology and then went on to gain a M.A. at the University of Leeds. He was ordained at Brecon Cathedral. Despite his youth and inexperience he immediately showed maturity beyond his years. David Thomas writes: *"He had considerable potential and I was looking forward to working with him as he found his feet in the pastoral, parochial ministry."*

Alas, his plan was frustrated, for, six months after Dominic was ordained as deacon, David left the parish to become a Bishop. Dominic handled a difficult situation and the vacancy with confidence that belied his youth.

The Revd CLIVE JONES (1940-)
Sixth Vicar of St Peter's Church, 1997-2006

Clive Morlais Peter Jones was born on November 20th, 1940, in Pembrokeshire. He was educated at the Narberth Grammar School and studied music at the University College of South Wales in Cardiff where he gained a B.A. Hons. and a Certificate of Education. Brought up as a Congregationalist, he became an Anglican at university and he eventually decided to study for the priesthood.

He left Wales, as a Powys Exhibitioner, to train at Chichester Theological College from 1964-1967 where he also gained his L.T.C.L. in music and a diploma in singing. He was tenor lay clerk in Chichester Cathedral Choir.

Clive was deaconed in 1966 at Llandaff Cathedral and priested the following year. He served his title at Llanfabon in Nelson, until he was invited back to Llandaff Cathedral as priest vicar from 1970-1975. While there he was appointed Music Director of Cardiff Palestrina Choir and continued to work with them during the ten years he was Rector of Gelligaer and at this time he held several other appointments. He married Diane in 1977 and they have one son, Richard, and are now proud grandparents. In 1985 they moved into the diocese of Oxford where Clive was Rector of Tilehurst, near Reading, for nine years. In 1994 there was a change of air and country when Clive's next appointment took them to the diocese of Europe and the chaplaincy of the Costa Blanca in Spain until 1997.

On September 4th, 1997, the Revd Clive Jones was inducted as the sixth vicar of St Peter's Church. It was an active time for both the vicar and the church during his eight and half years' incumbency. Father Clive contributed not only spiritually to the church but also used his personal skills, in business acumen and music, in a practical way and empowered many changes. In his first annual vestry report he stated: *"A new incumbent, wishing to make changes, should do so in the first six months. After ten years a parish needs a shake up or people become lethargic."*

Father Clive arrived like the proverbial new broom and within his first year there were noticeable alterations within the church, its grounds and the rectory which included repairs, restoration and disposal. To name a few: a side chapel was created in the south aisle; and the high altar brought forward; a new order of services was introduced; there was a new look for the weekly pew notes and the magazine and its cover; the nativity scene appeared within the altar at Christmas, enhanced by new crib figures given in memory of Miss G. Snow. In a similar style, there was also an Easter tableau. The processional Cross and sanctuary lamp were restored to their former glory and there was much re-gilding and touching up of faded brass on the altar furniture which became apparent. New book shelves appeared, worn chests were replaced by new cupboards.

There was much work done towards the maintenance of the church building both inside and out. The floors were sanded and sealed; the interior walls were cleaned; a new central heating boiler was installed making a noticeable improvement to the heating of the church; the vestries received a make-over and the squatter pigeons were removed from the bell tower which was then more usefully converted to a cleaning cupboard; even the vicar's washbasin was replaced!

Externally there were also a lot of improvements. The lychgate was refurbished and the surrounding stonework repaired. The grounds received a makeover, thus improving the visibility and appearance. Some trees were doctored, after a large one came down in a storm, in early 1998. The Remembrance Garden was enlarged. Nearby, climbing plants were grown up a new fence, and a new boundary fence was erected between the Church Hall grounds and the neighbouring property on the western side.

To comply with a quinquennial report the church roof and guttering received attention. All the external iron work of troughs, boxes and down pipes were cleaned up, replaced where necessary, and repainted. Several clerestory windows required re-leading, and, for protection, mesh guards were fitted to the stained glass windows on the east and north walls. The wooden framework of the bracket and gallows, housing the bell, also needed replacing. For awhile, the congregation patiently coped with the inconvenience of the church shrouded in scaffolding, and earth works, where drains were dug up to connect the storm water pipes to the main road.

The newly revised Disablement and Discrimination Act meant that a loop system had to be installed for the hard of hearing and large print service and hymn books made available. Car parking space for the disabled was allocated when the drive was partially re-surfaced. Hand rails were added and a permanent ramp was planned at the main entrance. A toilet for the disabled was included in the plans for the new hall. All these extra requirements had to be met in the budgeting as well as meeting the standards required for fire safety regulations. These were essential as the church is frequently used for public concerts and functions.

Soon after his arrival, the vicar also addressed the worrying financial state of the church with an ever increasing annual diocesan quota to meet. He firmly believed an improvement could only be made once the spiritual side of the church was on the right lines. He made helpful suggestions about budgets, use of money from bequests, and keeping a separate maintenance fund. In the following year a successful Christian Stewardship Renewal Campaign was launched. Also, fortuitously, at this time, the church received a very generous bequest, so easing the way to meet the hefty demands of the diocese quinquennial report in 2002. There were yet more changes, sadly, due to the deaths of the stewardship treasurer, Mr Denis Lenthall, and Mr Alan Grocutt, P.C.C. Treasurer. They were succeeded by Mr John Banbury and Mr David Allen respectively.

The vicar encouraged the congregation to re-examine the meaning of worship and the significance of the various services, particularly during the times of the Holy Festivals, as already established by former clergy. For example, the Ceremony of the Imposition of Ashes on Ash Wednesday, and time for reflection on the Stations of the Cross with the richness of the Liturgy during Holy Week. He introduced the washing of the feet on Maundy Thursday which brought a fresh and inspirational meaning to the service. Over a number of years, he introduced the congregation to the use of the *Church in Wales Alternative Order for the Holy Eucharist*.

The vicar also introduced a Healing Service, the Guild of St Raphael, once a month. For awhile, once a week, a Pram Service for mothers and children, below school age, was held, and a new Bible study group was set up. Later this was replaced by two home discussion groups once a month.

During Father Clive's incumbency he was assisted by one other curate and two non-stipendiary priests who are referred to at the end of this chapter.

The churchwardens, during Father Clive's incumbency, were:

Vicar's warden: Anne Sutton, Rita Pickard, and Philip Shaddick.
People's warden: Keith Davies, Mike Abbett, Steve Dunster, Judy Powell.

Sadly, within a short time of his arrival, the vicar received several unexpected blows. Anne Sutton was suddenly struck down with a stroke, Mike Abbett moved overseas, and, Steve Dunster died after a short illness.

Parochial Church Council (P.C.C.) meetings began with Eucharist and it was proposed to meet every six weeks. The maximum number of members was reduced to twenty. The long-standing secretary, Mrs Leslie Griffin, was succeeded by Mrs Joy Edwards and, on her retirement, she was followed by Mrs Cynthia Kelly-Jones. In order to make the meetings of the P.C.C. more meaningful and shorter, several new sub-committees were formed.

Fortunately for the church, Father Clive was well acquainted with the computer and technology. Gone were the old and laborious ways of printing and copying. The vestry soon became equipped with the latest technical equipment to help printed matter look more professional. The vicar also undertook to edit the monthly church magazine, making several changes.

His time at St Peter's coincided with some historic events both for the church and nationally, all of which required his skill as a planner and organiser. With the approach of the Millennium, followed by the centenary of the laying of the church's foundation stone in 2001, and, two years later, in 2003, both the 70th anniversary of Newton Parish and the centenary of the St Peter's Church, he set up the *Celebration 100 Committee.* This was chaired by Grahame Sutton (a

The Archbishop of Canterbury, with the Revd Clive Jones, on the occasion of his visit to St Peter's Church on Saturday, June 21st, 2003.

former churchwarden), for the purpose of *"identifying and putting into action imaginative projects and events appropriate for the forthcoming celebration of the Millennium and St Peter's Centenary."* Among the several schemes proposed by the committee was the replacement of the old chairs, many worm-eaten. Members of the parish and friends were invited to subscribe and donate a chair in remembrance of a relative or a significant event.

Throughout his time at St Peter's, Clive was greatly supported by Diane, his wife, and they formed a great team. They generously attended as many functions as they could together often helping in a practical way. Diane, also, had many hidden talents and it was soon discovered she was an excellent cook and hostess, and a very artistic flower arranger, as well as a fine soprano voice in the choir. She was branch leader of the Mothers' Union.

CURATES AND HONORARY PRIESTS ASSISTING THE REVD JONES

The Revd Dominic Cosslett stayed on for another twenty months to work with Father Clive until May 1999. He left to become Assistant Curate of St Mary's Priory Church in Abergavenny until 2002 when he was inducted parish Priest of St Mark's, Kingstanding, in Birmingham. He subsequently became a Roman Catholic. In December 2008, he was ordained as a Roman Catholic priest by Archbishop Vincent Nicholls of Birmingham.

When Dominic left St Peter's Father Clive doubted he would have another young curate to train as so few were now entering the ministry. However, in 1999 St Peter's was blessed to have yet one more curate, though briefly.

The Revd JONATHAN DAVIES, B.Th., was born and brought up in Carmarthen where his late father had been a parish priest. After he left school he served an apprenticeship as a mechanic and later became a sales executive for a Swansea Pneumatics Company. In 1991 he offered himself for the ordained ministry and he graduated from Bangor University, North Wales, in theology. He trained at St Michael's College, Llandaff, Cardiff, and was ordained in June 1996. Jonathan served the first three years of his ministry in the parish of Betws with Ammanford, in the diocese of St David's, before arriving at St Peter's in 1999.

Alas, his stay was only for six months as he encountered personal challenges and for a while returned to a secular job before his next appointment as priest-in-charge of St Luke's, Cwmbwrla, and also Tourism Advisor in the archdeaconry of Gower. He later went on to be Vicar of Manselton with Cwmbwrla and also chaplain to the Fire and Rescue service in Swansea.

It seems Father Clive's predictions were soon to be realised for Jonathan has not been replaced by another curate and the church has since made a bold decision to sell the curate's house in order to raise much needed funds for the building of the new hall.

However, St Peter's has been blessed to have the services of two non-stipendiary priests, and a lay reader, amongst its membership, who are:

1. The Revd JOHN L. WORKMAN who first came to St Peter's covering the vacancy following the elevation of Bishop David Thomas. He also covered the vacancy following the retirement of Revd Clive Jones and has continued, thankfully, as Honorary Assistant Priest at St Peter's. Throughout his long life he has always been involved in church life.

In the early thirties he was a choirboy at St Paul's Church, Sketty, and was educated at the local schools before entering business, becoming proprietor of a successful shoe retailers *'Penhales Footwear'*. At that time he was also an active member of St James' Church, Swansea, serving on the P.C.C., a sacristan and chorister. He continued his studies at home to become a licensed diocesan lay reader and after some years received two years theological training at St Deiniol, Hawarden. He was ordained to the priesthood in 1983 and was a Minor Canon at Brecon Cathedral for the next three years. From 1986-1995 he was Vicar of St Luke's, Cwmbwrla. At a time when many other men would be thinking of retirement, Revd Workman became hospital chaplain at Singleton Hospital, Swansea, serving from 1997-2002, and an honorary chaplain to the Guild of the Servants of the Sanctuary, and honorary chaplain to the Friends of the Young Disabled.

Father John has been married to Isa for sixty years and they recently generously shared their Diamond celebration with the congregation in a moving Thanksgiving service. He and his daughter sang with the choir and both his grandsons were servers. Throughout his parish work Mrs Workman has actively supported him. She has worked in the diocese as part of the Mothers' Union Executive. They have a son and a daughter and grand-children who are also active members of the church.

2. The Revd Dr JOHN THOMAS was a Swansea graduate in chemistry and later gained a Ph.D. at Leeds University. He went on to teach chemistry in Further and Higher Education and was Principal of the Worthing College of Technology. On his retirement he moved to the Cotswolds and was ordained priest in Gloucester. He served as a non-stipendiary curate in South Cerney until the death of his first wife.

He was later blessed to meet Ruth, a Doctor of Mathematics, whom he had known from student days. After they married they moved to Mumbles in 2000 and joined St Peter's congregation. This was an opportune time for the church as he was able to help out, when required, with preaching and teaching. This is what he feels led to do, and has given talks on science and faith as they relate to Christian belief. At all times he is greatly supported by Ruth and they have both been involved in hosting discussion groups.

The Revd CANON GEORGE E. BENNETT (1951-)
Vicar of St Peter's Church, 2006-

After a relatively short vacancy, St Peter's congregation were delighted to hear that their next parish priest would be their Area Dean. He was already a familiar figure to many in the parish for not only was he 'the next door neighbour' but also had skilfully orchestrated the previous intervening months so all had continued to run smoothly at St Peter's Church.

Both Father George and his wife, Rhona, originate from Swansea and had first met at their local church, St Nicholas on the Hill. From there he went to Aberystwyth University and gained a degree in history before moving to

Bristol to work for the Church Army, amongst homeless men, in the inner city. He then went onto study theology at St Stephen's House at Oxford where David Thomas, former Vicar of St Peter's, was the Vice-Principal. They were to meet again, much later, when Father George moved into the diocese of Brecon and Swansea. The Revd David Thomas had acted as his spiritual guide and confessor and he first became acquainted with St Peter's.

After Father George was ordained, his first curacy was at All Saints' Church, Clifton, Bristol, with its fine liturgical and musical tradition, which made a lasting impression on the young curate. From 1982-1993 he served as Vicar of St John, Newbury, Berkshire, where he worked with children and became involved with the building of two new church halls. He returned to Wales in 1993 when he was appointed Vicar of Llwynderw, with its two churches, Holy Cross at West Cross and Clyne Chapel at Blackpill, Swansea.

Father George Bennett and his wife Rhona.

He was greatly supported by his wife Rhona in meeting the challenges of helping two different church communities to work in partnership together. He also developed a team of pastoral visitors to attend a number of housebound worshippers. Thus, Father George arrived in his new role, suitably prepared from all the experience he had gained from these parishes. He was inducted at St Peter's Church on Friday, October 13th, 2006, the Feast Day of Edward the Confessor, one of his patron saints.

Father George's previous experience of being involved with the building of church halls was to be invaluable, for, immediately on his arrival he was thrust into the numerous decisions and meetings regarding the new village hall project with which the church was concerned.

Like his predecessor, on his arrival, Father George was required to steer the congregation into meeting the continuing heavy financial needs of the church. Together with the support of the treasurer and churchwardens a successful Stewardship Renewal was launched, the first since 1999. This helped to balance the books. The Stewardship Renewal also highlighted the need for not only financial giving but also the giving of time and talents.

The vicar was also anxious to meet the challenge of church growth and ways of attracting families and young people back into the church. He initiated a Parish Conference at Nicholston House, Gower, to enable the churchwardens and members of the P.C.C. to explore the theme of Growth within the church for the future. The day conference started with a thought provoking address from Archdeacon Robert Williams. Many helpful and positive ideas emerged and have since been worked on.

The vicar has been welcomed into Newton School where he has been able to lead the assembly once a month and has also resumed links with the uniform groups who now attend a number of parade services throughout the year. In the autumn of 2009 a meeting was arranged for the Revd Kay Warrington, Diocesan Children's Officer, to visit and discuss ways of attracting youngsters into the church by using the facilities of the New Hall when it is opened early in 2010. Volunteers were invited to initiate ideas.

Father George has built on the ministry, introduced by Father Clive, of lay Eucharistic assistants to take the Sacrament to the housebound. Also, during the summer of 2009, a training course was undertaken, by a small group from the congregation, to become Pastoral Lay Visitors, and they were Commissioned on 9th of August by the Archdeacon Robert Williams.

During his first year the vicar was appointed chaplain to the incoming Lord Mayor of Swansea, Councillor Susan Waller, who resides nearby, within the parish. St Peter's hosted the Civic Service in the autumn of 2007.

Throughout his time at St Peter's, Father George has been very ably assisted by the two honorary priests, the Revd John Workman and the Revd John Thomas as well as **Mr PHILIP SHADDICK** who was admitted and licensed as a Reader at the age of 69, at Brecon Cathedral on October 27th, 2007, by Bishop Anthony Pierce. He has been a worshipper at St Peter's Church for many years and in 2003 he received a call to preach and can claim to be the parish's first 'home-grown' lay reader. He is also currently vicar's warden and a member of the choir.

THE VERGERS

The office of verger is an ancient one. The title means 'staff bearer', derived from the Latin word *virga* meaning staff. St Peter's Church has only had three vergers. Memories of them have been recalled by Mr Bill Barrington, the last serving verger:

MR. EDWARD PRICE served from **1903-1944** and *"he was known as Ted to everyone. He was verger from when St Peter's was consecrated until late in the war years when he had a breakdown and was forced to retire. Ted was a gardener by occupation and was employed by Judge Morgan at his residence, Kiln Green, on Caswell Road. He was allowed any time off necessary to deal with weddings, funerals, etc. He also looked after the newly planted shrubs in the church grounds, cut the grass and swept the paths . . . he appeared to be always present in the Church where he opened and closed it, prepared everything for the services, looked after the lighting, tended the boiler for heating, rang the bell and dealt with members of the choir and congregation who fainted during the services."* A replacement would be a serious challenge but was found in:

Mr FRANK SMITH, *"an octogenarian and a retired manager of the Star Supply store who volunteered to fill the post until 'The boys come home' [from the war]. He filled the post valiantly from* **1945-1951** *whilst continuing to sing baritone in the choir."*

The 'boy coming home' turned out to be Mr Bill Barrington who had already a long association with the church and he continues with his story: *"I was born close to St Peter's Church just before it celebrated its 20th birthday. In those days it was customary for the first time a young mother went out, after her confinement, was to go to church for the baptism of the newly born . . . this was the beginning of my long association with Newton and its church. My mother was nursing me 'Welsh fashion' when she enrolled as a member of the Mothers' Union in the newly constructed Church Hall."* [Probably making Bill the longest attending member!]

He goes on to say that his parents then moved to Mumbles where his brother was born, but in late 1927 they returned to Newton and resided at East Lodge at Llwyn-y-Mor where his father was employed as caretaker to Mr Frank Gilbertson's property. It was there that Bill learnt his skills in central heating as his father had to attend to the boilers and radiators in the Big House. In 1928 Bill and his brother joined the church choir until in 1939 he left to join the armed forces and saw action in North Africa and the Normandy Landings in Europe. On his return the family had moved back to Mumbles where Bill became involved in a number of local groups and organisations including working as a Scout leader. It wasn't long before Canon Hickin invited Bill to become the next verger.

Mr BILL BARRINGTON became enrolled on Easter Sunday and served from **1951-1961.** Under the watchful eye of his vicar, Canon Hickin and his successor he soon learnt the valuable role which he has continued to serve tirelessly and with total commitment and much dignity in two other churches for more than fifty years. Unfortunately for St Peter's, at very short

notice, Bill, and his wife Veronica had to move to London where their very sick daughter had to receive treatment. Little did he envisage that a temporary move would extend to 22 years before he returned to his home town. During the time Bill was away he became verger at the Royal Military Chapel at Chelsea Barracks.

On returning to Mumbles he was invited to resume his duties as verger at All Saints Church where he continues to faithfully serve to this day and has become a well known and respected member of the community.

This remarkable achievement was recognised in 2003 when he was awarded an M.B.E. in the Queen's New Year's Honours List for his life service to the church, country and community.

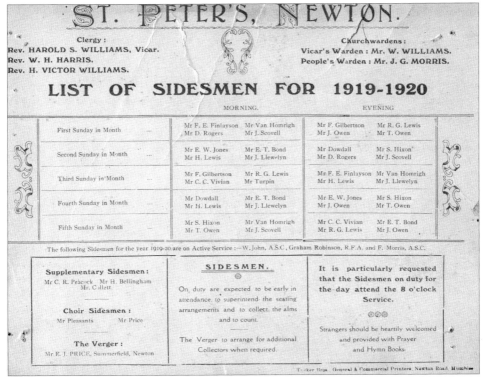

ST. PETER'S, NEWTON.

Clergy:
Rev. HAROLD S. WILLIAMS, Vicar.
Rev. W. H. HARRIS.
Rev. H. VICTOR WILLIAMS.

Churchwardens:
Vicar's Warden : Mr. W. WILLIAMS.
People's Warden : Mr. J. G. MORRIS.

LIST OF SIDESMEN FOR 1919-1920

	MORNING.		EVENING	
First Sunday in Month	Mr F. E. Finlayson	Mr Van Homrigh	Mr F. Gilbertson	Mr R. G. Lewis
	Mr D. Rogers	Mr J. Scovell	Mr J. Owen	Mr T. Owen
Second Sunday in Month	Mr E. W. Jones	Mr E. T. Bond	Mr Dowdall	Mr S. Hixon
	Mr H. Lewis	Mr J. Llewelyn	Mr D. Rogers	Mr J. Scovell
Third Sunday in Month	Mr F. Gilbertson	Mr R. G. Lewis	Mr F. E. Finlayson	Mr Van Homrigh
	Mr C. C. Vivian	Mr Turpin	Mr H. Lewis	Mr J. Llewelyn
Fourth Sunday in Month	Mr Dowdall	Mr E. T. Bond	Mr E. W. Jones	Mr S. Hixon
	Mr H. Lewis	Mr J. Llewelyn	Mr J. Owen	Mr T. Owen
Fifth Sunday in Month	Mr S. Hixon	Mr Van Homrigh	Mr C. C. Vivian	Mr E. T. Bond
	Mr T. Owen	Mr J. Scovell	Mr R. G. Lewis	Mr J. Owen

The following Sidesmen for the year 1919-20 are on Active Service :—W. John, A.S.C., Graham Robinson, R.F.A. and F. Morris, A.S.C.

Supplementary Sidesmen:
Mr C. R. Peacock   Mr H. Bellingham
Mr Collett.

Choir Sidesmen :
Mr Pleasants   Mr Price

The Verger :
Mr E. J. PRICE, Summerfield, Newton

SIDESMEN.

On duty are expected to be early in attendance, to superintend the seating arrangements and to collect the alms and to count.

The Verger to arrange for additional Collectors when required.

It is particularly requested that the Sidesmen on duty for the day attend the 8 o'clock Service.

Strangers should be heartily welcomed and provided with Prayer and Hymn Books.

Tucker Bros. General & Commercial Printers, Newton Road, Mumbles

Churchwardens at St Peter's Church Newton 1933–2008

THE REVD CANON W. J. HICKIN, 1933–1961

Vicar's Warden	People's Warden	P.C.C. Secretary	Organist	Verger
Mr F. Gage Died 3. 2. 1939	Mr E. T. Thomas 1933-1939	Mr S. Copleston	Mr W. Thomas From Oct. 1933 Mr W. G. Symons – 1939	Mr E. J. Price 1904-1944
Mr E. T. Thomas 1939-1952	Mr S. Copleston 1939-1944	Mr S. Copleston Died 9.10.1944	War Service	.do.
Mr G. Johnston 1942-1952	Mr E. Earrey 1945-1946	Mrs Copleston 1945-1954	Mr W. G. Symons 1945-1946 Mr W. Thomas 1947-1948	.do.
.do.	Mrs Copleston 1947-1952	Mrs Copleston 1945-1954	Mr W. Thomas 1947-1948	Mr Smith 1945-1953
Mr A. C. Gibbs 1953-1959	Mr G. A. Toomey 1953-1955	Miss Snow 1954-1985	.do.	W. Barrington 1953-1979
Mr A. C. Gibbs	Mr A. S. Kift 1955-1957	.do.	.do.	.do.
Mr G. A. Toomey 1959-1962	Mr F. B. Andrews 1958-1962	.do.	Mr Cyril Bowen 1958-1983	.do.

THE REVD CANON T. K. BRUNSDON, 1961–1976

Vicar's Warden	People's Warden	P.C.C. Secretary	Organist	Verger
Mr G. A. Toomey 1959-1962	Mr F. B. Andrews 1958-1962	Miss Snow – 1985	Mr Cyril Bowen – 1983	W. Barrington – 1979
Mr W. W. Sivertsen 1963-1979	Mr F. H. M. Jones 1963-1979	.do.	.do.	.do.

VENERABLE HAROLD EDGAR WILLIAMS, 1976–1987

Vicar's Warden	People's Warden	P.C.C. Secretary	Organist
Mr W. W Sivertsen – 1979 Mr V. M. Letherbridge 1980-1984	Mr F. H. M. Jones – 1984	Miss Snow – 1985	Mr C. Bowen – 1983 Miss J. Kelly 1983–
Mr G. D. Sutton 1985-1990	Mr S. G. Dunster 1985-1992	Mrs L. R. Griffin 1985-1998	.do.

THE REVD CANON DAVID THOMAS, 1987–1996

Vicar's Warden	People's Warden	P.C.C. Secretary	Organist
Mr G. Sutton – 1990 Mr D. Williams 1991-1994	Mr S. G. Dunster – 1992 Mr K. Davies 1992 – 1998	Mrs L. R. Griffin –1992	Miss J. Kelly now Mrs J. Thomas
Mrs A. Sutton 1994-1998	.do.	.do.	Mrs J. Thomas (née Kelly)

THE REVD CLIVE JONES, 1997–2006

Vicar's Warden	People's Warden	P.C.C. Secretary	Organist
Mrs A. Sutton – 1998	Mr M. Abbett – 1998	Mrs J. Edwards 1998-2006	Mrs J. Thomas assisted by husband H. Thomas
Mrs Rita Pickard 1999-2006	S. Dunster died April 2000	.do.	.do.
.do.	K. Davies 2000-2001	.do.	.do.
.do.	Mrs Judy Powell 2001-2009	.do.	.do.
Mr Philip Shaddick 2006–	.do.	Mrs C. Kelly Jones	.do.

CANON GEORGE BENNETT, 2006–

Vicar's Warden	People's Warden	P.C.C. Secretary	Organist
Mr Philip Shaddick 2006–	Mrs Judy Powell 2001-2009 Mr E. Partington 2009–	Mrs S. Bates	Mr & Mrs H. Thomas

9.

Music in the Church, the Organ and Choir

St Peter's has always had a choir. It may have been formed when the congregation met in the schoolroom, or founded just before the consecration, but it was in good voice for that event, assisted by the parish church choir and accompanied by an orchestra of local players. In all, sixty choristers assembled for the opening service conducted by Mr Donald Lott who was the first choirmaster at St Peter's. The Revd Montague Welby, a former Vicar of Oystermouth, hoped that the orchestra would continue to support the choir but Harold S. Williams was adamant that an organ was a necessity. However, for the first four years the singing was accompanied by a harmonium played by Gus Nettell, with Miss Stella Williams deputising, and ably assisted by Miss Violet Howells.

Newton Church Choir is first mentioned in the *Oystermouth Parish Magazine* in September 1902 when there is a report of them joining the annual parish choir outing. By the end of that year they were working with the Newton Choral and Orchestral Society to perform Gaul's cantata, *The Holy Week*, tickets priced 2/-.

In May 1907, Arthur Gilbertson, a Pontardawe industrialist, gave the church money for an organ which was built by Norman & Beard for £600. The Gilbertson family attended the afternoon service of the dedication of the organ at the end of September when the Archdeacon of Llandaff preached on the text *'Now bring me a minstrel, and it came to pass when the minstrel played, that the hand of the Lord came upon him'*. The service was followed by an organ recital given by Mr Arthur Hey, the organist of St Mary's, Swansea. Harvest Festival was celebrated in the evening.

Mr Barlow was appointed organist and Ernie Rosser was employed as organ blower until 1912 when he was replaced by Jack Groves, a burly docker, who lived in Slade Road. Jack remained at the post for the next twenty years but he was not available mid-week so, if there was a weekday wedding, two boys from Newton school were sent to deputise. One boy, C. A. Arnott, recalls: *"Going into a very narrow space behind the organ and pumping on a projecting shaft that took two of us to operate and we had to pump away to make a bobbin reach a marked height, then release it until it dropped to a lower mark before we pumped it up again."* The vicar wrote: *"Now nobody who has spent an hour behind the scenes, blowing St Peter's organ, knows what that means. Some few of who, in an emergency, have offered to take Mr Groves' place, on emerging from the hidden scene (in their case – scene of torture) behind the organ, have been heard to mutter, 'Never again'. It was really hard work."*

Mr Barlow had a good choir to work with, 15 lady and 12 boy sopranos, 3 boy altos, 4 tenors and 6 basses. He is reported as having been very strict with them, especially over punctuality. The choir worked hard and would often practice twice a week. They sang at both the 11 a.m. and 6.30 p.m. services on Sunday, and for festivals, such as harvest, they performed an anthem. It became a tradition at Christmas to sing carols after Evensong and also at the Glynn Vivian Home for the Blind in Mary Twill Lane. At Easter they sang a more major work, Stainer's *'Crucifixion'* and *'Gethsemane to Golgotha'* were repeated many times over the years.

However, it was not all hard work for the choir for there were regular summer outings, usually to Gower. Oxwich was a popular destination, the journey being taken in one of Mr Pressdee's brakes. Sometimes they went further afield, by train, to Llanwrtyd Wells. In the winter an annual church supper was laid on for them.

This was taken after the Dedication Service of the new organ, 1907.
Photograph by M. A. Clare (Courtesy of Carl Smith).

113

Oystermouth Parish clergy and St Peter's Choir, November 1912.
Men standing: Mr Pleasance, head gardener at Langland Court (far left);
Thomas J. Williams (3rd left); J. Barlow, organist (left, in front of Cross);
Ted Price, verger (holding Cross); 'Nobolo' Davies (4th right).
Middle Row: Revd H. S. Williams, Vicar (centre); 2 curates: Revd R. W. Jones
& ? Revd Latimer Davies; Beatrice Owen (2nd right).
Choirboys: brothers George Owen (1st left), Frank Owen (3rd left), Eric Owen (5th left).

By 1913 the original choir surplices were wearing out and Mrs Richardson, of Tawelfa, Langland Bay, provided a new set for both men and boys, which were worn for the first time at the Harvest Festival. By 1927 these, too, had seen better days and the Mothers' Union gave 3 guineas for replacements.

Mr Barlow was succeeded as organist in 1923 by David Price, a master at the church school in Dunns Lane, Mumbles. He used the old harmonium for choir practices in the chancel. In 1928 he moved to be organist at All Saints and the choir presented him with a silver rose bowl when he left. A new organist, Mr Thomas, was appointed at the end of 1928. He remained in the post until 1933.

Harold S. Williams, the vicar, was most enthusiastic about the benefits of electrification of the organ pump which took place in 1931. He aired his thoughts in the parish magazine in both June and December of that year: *"We, at St Peter's, are now in a position to blow the organ without help and those of us who were irritated by the weird groans and squeaks that used to come from the back regions, are extremely grateful to the more wealthy of the church people for their generous and prompt response."*

A Choir outing in the 1920s.
David Price, the organist, is wearing a cap.

In 1933, twenty-year-old W. G. Symons became the next organist. He was an enthusiastic and well liked man who arranged organ recitals and gave organ lessons, but in November 1939 he was called up to join the army. Mr Thomas returned to play at St Peter's for the duration of the war.

During the war the choir consisted mainly of 12 to 18 boys, plus a few men. There were no ladies among the singers. Choir practice was taken by Canon Hickin with Mr Thomas at the organ. The boys received between 2/- and 4/- quarterly according to seniority and a shilling for weddings, also an extra payment at Christmas. John Pickard remembers that the vicar would also give the boys a couple of apples each from the Harvest display.

Mr Symons returned as organist in January 1945 but left again two years later, when he took a job in Buckinghamshire. Mr Thomas was once more recalled and remained organist until his death in 1954.

In 1953, when the organ was nearly 50 years old it was given an overhaul. The pipe-work was cleaned, thumb pistons were added, the pedal board partly rebuilt and the leatherwork on the bellows was patched.

Cyril Bowen was appointed organist in 1954. He came from St John's, Hafod, where he had been organist and choirmaster for 25 years. The choir then consisted of about 10 boys and 4 or 5 men. In 1959 it became affiliated to the Royal School of Church Music and began to take part in festivals and workshops around Swansea and Brecon. Toward the end of the 1960s the number of choirboys dropped, so in 1969 girls were admitted. During this year a fund was set up to replace the choir robes.

Cyril Bowen, Organist and Choirmaster from 1955 to 1983.

A cheese and wine party by the Newtonians and a coffee evening by the choir helped to raise the money and the new cassocks and surplices were first worn on the 9th November.

Ladies did not join the choir again until Archdeacon Harold E. Williams became vicar. Gradually the number of singers increased and Mrs Betty Thomas, the choir mistress, extended the repertoire. On Good Friday, 1982, they sang choruses from the St Mathew Passion. When hymns were introduced at the 9.30 a.m. Sunday service an assistant organist was needed. Phillip Lethbridge played for four years and then Karen Bennett played until the two morning services were combined. When Cyril Bowen retired in 1983 he declared that the last twenty-four years at St Peter's had been the happiest of his life.

He was succeeded by Janie Kelly, who later married Huw, and became Mrs Janie Thomas. At first Mrs Betty Thomas continued to act as choir-mistress and after her death John Llewellyn became choirmaster, proving very popular with the young. The number of children in the choir increased considerably and in 1993 Mr and Mrs Keith Davies presented the much enlarged choir with new robes in memory of their son, Christopher.

During the time that the Revd David Thomas was vicar, the choir numbered over fifty. When they performed at Brecon Cathedral in 1995 one lady was heard to mutter: *"This isn't a choir – it's a blinking choral society!"*

The choir in 1995, wearing their new robes. Seated front row: Mr John Llewellyn, choirmaster; Revd David Thomas, Vicar; Mrs Janie Thomas, organist.

By 1989 the organ, again, urgently needed repairs to the bellows, the pedal boards and some of the pipes which had become silent. £10,000 was raised to cover the cost of the repairs and Hill, Norman and Beard were able to start work in January 1990. In October a re-dedication service was held. The preacher was Revd Timothy Ganz, Vicar of Tutbury, who had learned to play the organ on this instrument in the 1950s. Since 1990 the Swansea Organists Association has held several recitals on the organ with Janie, Huw and the choir participating.

When the Revd Clive Jones became vicar, Janie Thomas combined the roles of organist and choir-mistress. Her husband assisted at the organ.

The choir now sing at the 10 a.m. Sunday services and perform an anthem after Communion. They have built up a wide repertoire. Two young and talented choristers, Lydia White and Catrin Davies, both gained the Bishop's Award for young singers. In 2004, after a very long break, the choir again sang Stainer's 'Crucifixion'. There were a number of other memorable concerts and recitals, serious and light, held in the church. The vicar showed his skills as a fine tenor soloist, organist and conductor.

Janie and Huw Thomas, current organists at St Peter's.

In 1999, through a generous bequest from the late **Miss Maureen Blair**, the church was able to purchase a Boston Grand Piano. This has greatly enhanced the musical repertoire of the church. A piano stool was given in 2002 by **Cynthia Kelly Jones** in memory of her mother, Mary Kelly.

Another piano, an upright, was given in 2005 by **John Thomas Esq.** in memory of his wife, Betty, the former choir mistress. It is situated in the Choir Vestry where it is used for choir practice.

In the latter part of the year 2000 it became apparent that over £50,000 worth of work was needed to refurbish the organ. A successful organ appeal raised enough money for the work to start about a year later. The choir itself had organised many fund-raising events. *Nicholsons* of Malvern dismantled and restored the organ within three months. At this time the church was closed during the week days and the congregation became used to being accompanied by piano and digital electronic organ. A re-opening recital was given in February 2002 by Peter Irving, organist and choirmaster of Solihull Public School. He had spent part of his childhood in Newton and his father, David, helped enthusiastically with the fund-raising for the restoration of the organ. During June there were two recitals on the newly restored organ. Firstly, Peter Irving made a return visit and attracted a full church. Later in the month, the choir of St Mary's parish church performed, under the new directorship of Dr William Reynolds.

The choir attending the ordination of Dominic Cosslett by Rt Revd David Thomas at St Mary's Church, Abergavenny, July 1997.

10.

Outreach and Support for Overseas Missions

Mission has always been part of the church's ethos. Until 1933 St Peter's congregation joined with the other churches in the parish raising money to help local people and for missionary work overseas. Support was given to the Orphanage at Thistleboon, the House of Mercy at Eastmoor and the local fund to help the poor and needy. Missionary meetings were often held in the drawing room or garden of larger houses such as The Cliff, Cliff Edge, The Croft and Dolgoy. They started with a talk from a returning worker from Africa or Asia which was followed by tea and collection. One such meeting at The Cliff in 1908 was addressed by Hannah Riddell, once the proprietor of a Mumbles girls' school, who went to Japan and established a hospital for lepers. She received donations from the parish and Mrs Peel, of Sunnyside, acted as correspondent. The Society which featured most was the Universities Mission to Central Africa (U.M.C.A.) and support was also given to the Zenana Mission and the medical missions of the Society for the Propogation of the Gospel (S.P.G.).

In the early 1930s, Dr Elsie Davies, of Cliff Edge, was working at the S.P.G. St David's Hospital at Malacca, now Malaysia. In 1929 a Missionary Guild was formed at St Peter's and in 1931 the Guild raised £15 for one of Dr Davies' local girls to train as a nurse in Singapore. The following year the Sunday School collected 870 corks for use in the hospital dispensary.

During the Second World War mission work at home played a larger part. In 1942 the parish began collecting for the Waifs and Strays Society (later the Children's Society) following a talk given to the M.U. Miss Betty Evans organised a flag day which alone raised £25 and £33 was sent to the Society in 1943. This equalled the donation to the S.P.G. The third largest donation that year was sent to the Mission to Seamen. Also, a great quantity of warm, knitted garments, were made for the men at sea and presented to the Swansea Missioner. Many smaller donations were also given in 1943 to causes as varied as the orphanage at Eastmoor; Swansea Hospital; Diocesan Moral Welfare Association; Earl Haig Fund of the British Legion; the Additional Curates Society; The Society for the Promotion of Christian Knowledge (S.P.C.K.); Zenana Missions Society; U.M.C.A. and the Welsh Chaplaincy in Patagonia.

January 1948 saw a spurt of missionary zeal with monthly meetings in the hall chaired by Dr Elsie Davies. The first speaker was Miss Corbett, her former matron at Malacca. About a hundred people attended the next meeting with a showing of missionary films, while in March the speaker was from the Children's Society. For many years Mrs Betty Sivertsen (née Evans) organised the Children's Society house-to-house collections and the Sunflower Guild collecting boxes. Mrs Smith, of Nottage Road, took over from her in 1961 and Jill Price continued to empty the boxes for a while.

During the post war years Mrs Arthur Owen organised collections for the Mission to Seamen. After a break of some years, the Newton Mission to Seamen Ladies Guild was reformed. It was chaired by Mrs H. L. Gilbert with Mrs L. R. Griffin as secretary. They organised films, talks, coffee mornings, etc. and raised £4,000 in their first twelve years. The Mission has since been renamed Mission to Seafarers but the guild continues to flourish under the guidance of Mrs Joyce Haydn Jones, who has been chairman for many years. They hold two or three fund-raising events a year and are able to contribute about £1,000 to the Mission annually.

By 1967 donations to the now United Society for the Propagation of the Gospel (U.S.P.G.) were supporting individuals abroad. St Peter's supported a nurse at St Peter's Hospital, Madinare, Bechuanaland in Southern Africa; and through the 1980s paid for three boys at Sholua and girls at Canning, North India, to live at the U.S.P.G.'s hostel while they pursued their education. Support was also given to a series of students in Madagascar. In the later 1990s St Peter's started to support a child through World Vision. The first two children, Oscar and Carla, were from the Honduras. Tragically, Oscar died in an accident. When aid was no longer required in that country, support was given to Felix from Bolivia.

In May 1990 a mission came to St Peter's when the Clyne Deanery experienced a week of mission, led by Brother Ramon, an Anglican friar, to encourage our faith. The 1990s saw a new venture in support of the U.S.P.G. with provision of soup and cheese Lent lunches on the Fridays in Lent. This proved to be very popular and continued in support of other charities until the old hall was demolished. Since 1991 a black bucket has been put out, at the back of the church, at Christmas. Money was first collected for the Stepping Stones project at Killay for disabled children. It has since supported many other causes at home and abroad including, in 1994, the orphanage at Vlores in Albania where parishioners, Dennis and Deidre Lenthall's daughter was working. Clare Richardson, the daughter of another parishioner, Jean Haines, has also been supported in her work in setting up a Methodist Special School, for children with disabilities and special needs, in Gambia. She has kept the church in touch with her progress through regular newsletters.

11.

Social Activities

During the first half of the 20th century, when there was limited transport and no television or other distraction, people were more actively engaged in entertaining themselves. Within the church there were many societies which catered for different groups of people and provided an opportunity to socialise. The *Oystermouth Parish Magazine* records a series of events during 1902-3. These were performed by local people to mostly raise funds for the building of St Peter's Church, such as a Japanese Pastoral Play and other entertainment, performed in the grounds of the house of a parishioner, Miss Dillwyn Llewelyn, as seen in the notice below.

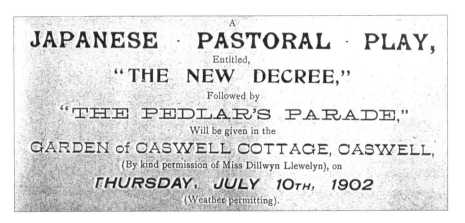

There seemed to be some form of entertainment each month. Serious concerts, lantern shows and light-hearted entertainments were popular. Fêtes, flower shows and grand bazaars all brought people together to enjoy themselves and raise money at the same time.

The Revd Harold S. Williams was determined to fund-raise for the new church *'without a bazaar'* but there were two such events organised in 1905 and again in 1907. These bazaars were held in the grounds of Oystermouth Castle over a number of days and opened by illustrious members of the Swansea gentry, such as the Duchess of Beaufort, The Dowager Lady Kensington, and the Hon. Elaine Jenkins.

Another big event in the early years was the annual St Peter's Social Gathering, with tea and stalls laid out in the Churchmen's Club, followed by a concert in the school room, across the road, which was given by children and talented local adults or an amateur group from Swansea. A more unusual entertainment, held in December 1912, was a recitation by Roger Beck of Dickens' *'Christmas Carol'* which was a sellout event.

In the early 1920s, whist drives became popular and were effective fund-raising events. The whist drive was followed by a dance to a band, such as *The Savana*, and it was not uncommon for 100 people to attend. From 1931 a whist drive was held in the Church Hall every Wednesday evening, throughout the winter months, in aid of hall funds. They were organised by Mrs Stirling Evans and Mrs Pressdee. Fred Foster was MC at first and later Mr Gilbey officiated. These drives continued up to 1939, when the meetings transferred to Thursday afternoons and the profits then paid for church expenses, as well as for knitting wool, to make items for servicemen at sea. Jumble sales appeared in the 1920s and concerts continued. In 1935 there was a series of organ recitals and over 100 people attended the first one.

Social activities at St Peter's were severely curtailed during the Second World War when the Church Hall and the Churchmen's Club were commandeered for war purposes. After the war, when the hall was returned to the church and had been renovated, a Social Committee was formed. Once more there were whist drives and social evenings. Games and dancing formed the programmes of the latter events and about seventy people regularly attended, even in 1947 when the *"present austerity conditions do not permit refreshments being served!"*

There have also been a few major productions of religious dramas. In December 1950 twelve young churchgoers performed a nativity play, *'The Madonna'*. They gave three performances, one for the children, and then two for adults. Fifteen years later, in 1965, Mrs Finvola Davies produced *'The Business of Good Government'*, and, at Easter 1967 a passion play *'Come Ye to Calvary'* was staged. Both plays involved large casts of actors, singers and designers drawn from the congregation.

To celebrate the Queen's silver jubilee in 1977, St Peter's held a concert by two pupils from Bishop Gore School, Debbie Rees, soprano, and Sian Jones, harp, both of whom went on to become international artists.

Arising from a music society formed in 1981, Clive John led a series of extramural musical appreciation classes for a couple of years which proved successful. Since then the Gower Festival has used the church, most years, for one of its concerts. More recently there have been many church organised concerts for visiting choirs, solo voice and instrumental music.

A discussion group was formed in 1983. It was known as the Monday Group which met fortnightly in various houses of members. The topics mostly covered 'Beliefs' and what it meant to be a Christian in the modern world. This lasted several years and something similar was revived in the new millennium, with two meetings once a month, one in the afternoons and another in the evenings.

Among the many events celebrated for the Golden Jubilee in 1983 was a most spectacular Flower Festival. It was organised by Mrs Win White, assisted by Mrs Joy Edwards, and was a great success, with about 1,500 visitors attending. It led to other festivals most notably in 1985 celebrating International Youth Year and again in 1995, during Petertide week, with musical presentations each evening. It inspired a number of ladies to form a flower arranging group, in readiness for celebrating the Millennium at Easter 2000. Toward the end of the 1980s, when the church was struggling financially, the summer fête and Christmas Fair were re-introduced, both proving to be good social occasions as well as financial ones. In 1984 the BBC programme *'Any Questions'* was broadcast from St Peter's. The team comprised of Michael Foot, Edward du Cann, Rosalind Gilmore and Paul Tyler, drawing a large audience. Around this time there were several other radio broadcasts recorded in the church which are described in chapter 16.

A Harvest Supper in the Church Hall was held annually for several years. The meal was followed by an entertainment and folk dancing. For a while it was discontinued until it was revived again in the mid 1990s. Later, for several winters, the choir organised an annual Barn Dance, until it was no longer possible to serve food in the deteriorating Church Hall.

During the Revd David Thomas' time the celebration of St Peter's patron saint developed into a week long Petertide festival at the end of June. It was intended to be a social occasion and Mrs Finvola Davies has undertaken to co-ordinate a variety of events ever since. These include concerts, strawberry teas, exhibitions and light entertainment such as excerpts from Gilbert and Sullivan or popular shows. This festival has continued to be one of the highlights of the year.

Other celebratory events followed to mark the Millennium, and in 2001, as part of the centenary celebrations for the laying of the church foundation stone. During 2003 the Centenary of the church was celebrated with a number of special services and social occasions (described more fully in Chapter 16).

The demolition of the Church Hall, at the end of 2007, curtailed many of the church and village social and fund-raising activities for a couple of years. During that time the church was used instead for some concerts and meetings while other hall users found temporary accommodation elsewhere.

12.

Organisations and Societies

1. The Band of Hope

The Band of Hope was begun in the Victorian era in order to instruct children in the ethics of temperance. It was extremely popular with the children, as a source of entertainment, for many of the meetings provided 'Magic Lantern' pictures.

Certificate of Merit awarded to Percy Luckham, September 1916.

Most churches and chapels held a Band of Hope meeting once a week. At St Peter's the meetings took place in the Mission Room in the old Newton School. Each summer the children took part in a Band of Hope Union procession, with other branches, led by the Church Lads' Brigade band. The All Saints, Norton, Wesleyan and Castleton Congregational branches all marched from the Parish Hall, Dunns Lane, to Newton where they were joined by St Peter's and Paraclete branches, and from there they marched to Southend and back to Dunns Lane. Some years there were over 500 children taking part.

In April 1908 the three Anglican Bands of Hope held a most successful meeting in the Parish Hall, Mumbles, for a number of competitions. The children were awarded medals for the following classes: *Girls*: Writing out Lord's Prayer; Letter describing Oystermouth; A worked bookmarker; Darning; Crochet work; Essay on Temperance; Performance of a Song, Recitation or Hymn. *Boys*: Writing out the Apostles' Creed; Letter describing a railway journey; Speech on Temperance; A drawing of the King; Model of a boat; Maps of England and Wales; A Letter answering an Advertisement; A Letter describing Christmas Day 1907.

The Newton Band of Hope children gave many concerts, usually in the schoolroom. The May 1906 *Parish Magazine* describes a concert which started with a cantata called 'Little Bo Peep' starring Adeline Owen and Gertrude Hixson, and a dance by May and Grace Hutchings. The other children, wearing wreaths of primroses, were a chorus of fairies. This was followed by a violin solo, a recitation and songs. The final item was 'Sleeping Beauty' performed by the children from Miss Dillwyn Llewelyn's Home for Orphans, at Caswell Cottage. Four years later they performed 'Bo Peep' again for a parish Sale of Work.

In 1906, the Newton children were hoping to have a piano, for concerts and other performances, but by 1908 they were still unsuccessful. They had to hire a piano, at a cost of £1.10s.2d per session, for their February entertainments, held over three days. They charged 2d per ticket and made 10s.6d, 12s.6d and 7s.2d respectively – a total of £1.10s.2d. Each year, the children had a summer treat. In September 1906 Graham Vivian gave the use of a field for the Parish Bands of Hope outing. The children from Newton and Oystermouth caught the Mumbles train from Oystermouth to join the Blackpill Band of Hope. Then the three groups processed up the drive of Clyne Castle and admired the gardens. They were given tea, followed by sports. The prizes were presented by Mrs Heneage Vivian, Miss Vivian and Graham Vivian. In August 1908, St Peter's Band of Hope had a picnic at Oxwich arranged by Mr and Mrs J. G. Morris and the Misses Aitken, F. Rayner and V. Taylor. They had lunch and tea on the green and were shown over Oxwich church by the rector and told of its interesting history. In November 1908 Mr Richardson, of Arnside, gave the children a most enjoyable evening with his gramophone. In 1910 they travelled in brakes to Porteynon beach for a picnic.

Thus, the Band of Hope continued with practical competitions, uplifting lantern lectures and many musical performances. Together with Sunday School they provided children with both a social life and also a sound religious education. As the years went on, a note of censure crept in for it was said: *"That which is lacking is the lively interest of parents in the movement."* By Autumn 1913 The Band of Hope had been replaced by the St Peter's Children's Guild.

2. *The Girls Friendly Society (The Edwardian Branch)*

The Girls Friendly Society was set up in the 1870s to befriend girls going to work away from home. Branches were started in many towns and the movement then spread to provide meetings for older and younger girls in many places. The Society was well established in Oystermouth parish by 1900. There were weekly branch meetings for candidates (girls) in Mumbles and Newton and an Associates branch, for young ladies, which covered the whole parish. They met for talks, festivals, conferences and outings. In January 1901 a course of cookery lessons organised by Miss Dillwyn Llewelyn of Caswell Cottage, was held in Newton schoolroom. The menu was an attractive one and included soups, pies, pastry and cakes, etc. The teacher, Miss McCelland, gave some excellent recipes for the dishes on the list. After paying the necessary expenses the proceeds of £2.9s.8d., were handed over for the New Church Fund. On Easter Monday, 1902, the Newton branch was lectured, by Revd A. Burrows, on 'Duty, the aim in life', after which they all enjoyed a tea. In a lighter mood it is reported in the *Parish Magazine* in 1906 that the Newton girls presented two plays to help pay off the debt on St Peter's building. The entertainment was arranged by Mrs Le Boulanger, the working associate for Newton. The first play was *'The New Degree'* in which Mildred and Beatrice Owen, Annie Lewis and the Hixson girls, Annie, Elsie and Gertrude took the characters. *"They all acted so well that it would be impossible to praise any one of them in particular. The second play called 'Aunt Jobson' was most amusing. The girls who acted also sold the tickets and handed over £3.9.0d,"* wrote the vicar. The following year, Mildred, Beatrice and Harriet Owen all received their 7 year membership cards. In 1909 the Newton branch was organised by the Misses Glascodine, Miller and Beor. It seems probable that the number of girls attending the meetings was dropping for the vicar exhorts parents to see that their girls attend at 6 o'clock in the schoolroom every Wednesday. This branch probably closed in the next year or two but the meetings of the Associates continued beyond the war years. 1912 saw the last Annual Diocesesan Festival at Llandrindod Wells, where Miss Dillwyn Llewelyn was elected President.

3. *The Children's Guild*

The Children's Guild was founded in 1913 under the supervision of Miss Freda Rayner, Miss V. Taylor and Messrs Morris and Graham. Meetings were on Tuesdays at 7 p.m. in the schoolroom. They soon had 50 children on the register and attendance averaged 40 a night. In 1922 the club moved into the new Church Hall at the earlier time of 6.30 p.m. These children also enjoyed performing. In 1922 they presented Bethlehem Tableaux just prior to Christmas and in 1931 and 1932 they produced two more shows: *'The Pied Piper of Hamelin'* and an operetta *'Happy Ever After'*. The Guild continued to flourish through the 1930s, with Ralph Symonds in charge, until 1940 when the hall was taken over by the military.

4. *Daisy League*

The motto or watch word was *'God Only'*. It was a more religious, organisation. The Daisy League, flourished for some years. It was started for St Peter's children during the 1st World War by Irene Caroline Richardson, widow of Ernald Richardson, but it spread to some other local parishes. She called the members *daisy-petals*, using the daisy to illustrate the text *'Abide with me and I in you'*.

Many children were enrolled at an after-noon service on Sunday, 14th May, 1917. This was possibly the first enrolment. Others followed. It is known that Kathleen Owen of New Hill Farm was enrolled in July 1923. The children attended a weekly meeting in the school building and their subscriptions paid for new brass vases and

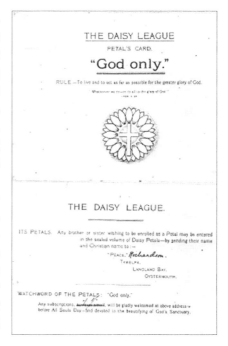

candlesticks for the altar, which were first used at Christmas 1921. After Mrs Richardson moved to Brecon in 1926 **The Daisy League** continued for a few more years. They took part in a Flower Service in July when the children brought flowers to church which they presented at the altar. These were later taken, by Miss Peel, to Swansea Hospital to cheer the patients.

5. *Young People's Guild*

At the time the new Church Hall was opened in 1922, a group called the Young People's Guild was started. It met at 8 p.m. on Tuesdays after the Children's Guild. In 1926 fifty members enjoyed an outing to Carmarthen. In 1927, under the leadership of Miss Rayner, they were enjoying lantern lectures, talks, games evenings, country and ballroom dancing, and acting. There was an elected committee with Maud Woollacott acting as Secretary and Doris Phillips as Treasurer. By 1937 this group had split into a **Girls Guild** which still met on Tuesdays, and a **Boys Guild** which met on Mondays, Wednesdays and Fridays. These groups ceased to function in 1940 when the hall was taken over by the army.

6. *Girls' Fellowship*

In 1946 a Girls' Fellowship was started and met on Tuesday nights under the leadership of Miss Penzer. Girls could join when they were seven years old and stayed on into their teens. Among other activities they did handiwork and embroidery and made items for their annual autumn sale of work. One of the girls would be chosen to present a bouquet to the lady who opened it, and felt greatly honoured. Valerie Owen remembers she was chosen one year and the lady gave her a box of lacy handkerchiefs. Another annual event was their variety show which filled the hall at each of its three performances. The girls acted sketches, sang songs and danced both ballet and tap, to Mrs Stirling Evans' piano accompaniment. Canon Hickin attended every performance, and would drop in on a meeting during the refreshment break.

The group flourished until Miss Penzer died at the end of 1956, when meetings ceased. Nearly two years later, in the autumn of 1958, a new Girls' Fellowship opened, which was led by Mrs Seaton and Miss Garlick, the latter being later replaced by Mrs Pressdee. These ladies retired in 1962, handing over the running of the club to Mrs J. Ll. Thomas and it finally closed in 1966.

Girls' Fellowship Variety Show.
Back row – *Josephine Richards, Janice John Angela Luckham, Valerie Owen,*
Ann Munday, Shirley Collier.
Middle row – *Ann Mossman, Margery Davies, Janice Barry, Barbara Goss, Doreen Bowen.*
Front row – *Esmee Owen, Mrs Stirling Evans, Miss Penzer, Mrs Elsie Jones, Jackie Ritchie.*
Kneeling – *Sylvia Davies.*

7. Cymry'r Groes

The official badge of Cymry'r Groes,
which means *Welshmen of the Cross.*
It is a Celtic cross with a
red dragon superimposed.

St Peter's Youth Fellowship began in November 1947 under the auspices of **Cymry'r Groes**, the official youth organisation of the Church in Wales. To be a member every young person had to be over fourteen years of age and they made a promise, among other obligations, to make Holy Communion the centre of their spiritual life. Mr Knight, Mrs Copplestone and Jean Young (Haines) were the leaders. Jean recalls her memories of that time: *"That winter (1947), every Thursday evening from 7 p.m. to 9.30 p.m., the Church Hall buzzed with enthusiastic girls and boys."* It was intended that a wide variety of cultural as well as social activities should be included in the programme. However, two 'old boys' Bernard Knight (later Professor) and John Wright (treasurer

Presentation of an engagement present to Jean Young (now Mrs Haines).
The group is standing on the site of the vicarage. Includes: Bernard Knight, John Wright,
Margaret Bowen, Joyce Griffin, Emily Jeffries, Mrs Copplestone, Maureen Rosser?, Jean Young,
Joy Griffiths, Sheila Lewis, JeanGriffin, Ken Jones.

from 1948 to 1950 until he went to university), both recollect the social side – playing snooker, table tennis, darts, chatting, etc., but memories of the cultural side of Cymry'r Groes are somewhat sparse! Practising carols came to mind and Sheila Lewis (Bond) remembered the vicar happily playing a selection of his opera records from time to time. Sir Bernard's poignant memory of rubbing French chalk into the floor of the hall, until his fingers ached, has remained with him to this day. This, of course, was for dancing practice, but as he said, *"I think I did more rubbing than dancing for I never learned a single step in my life."* The *Parish Magazine*, December 1949, reports Mr Delafield, of British Rail, giving a film display to a large crowd which also included the choirboys. A touch of culture perhaps! Visits were exchanged with other branches from Clyne, Oystermouth, St Gabriel's and Manselton. Summer evening meetings included tennis at Langland and walking to Pwlldu, but seldom getting further than Brandy Cove! The annual outing to Porthcawl was very popular. In 1951 a weekend school for leaders was held at Kilvrough Manor. Members over 17 years could apply at the cost of 10/6. A new hand book had been issued and all were urged to read it. Jean Young married in 1948 and the Knight family moved to Cardiff. The vicar and Mrs Copplestone continued to run meetings for another three years.

8. Youth Clubs

Since Cymry'r Groes other youth clubs have been set up but none has lasted more than a few years. One was opened early in 1962 and it had an average attendance of 40. There was table tennis and darts and a talk or activity. The following winter there were fewer members and by September 1964, the future of the club was uncertain. It closed soon afterwards. When the young curate, Revd Norman Lea, came in 1968 he reformed the Youth Club under the guidance of Canon Arthur Howells, the Diocesan Youth Chaplain. It proved popular and soon there were two clubs, one for the juniors on Wednesdays at 6.30 p.m. followed by the seniors at 7.45 p.m.

Unfortunately, the keen young curate moved on in March 1971, and in 1972 there was a plea for someone to help Mr David Meredith to run the club, which now seemed to consist only of the junior section. In 1974 it had disappeared altogether from the list of organisations. With the arrival of the next curate, Revd John Cruse, a club was started on Sunday evenings in the winter of 1982/3 for church members and their brothers and sisters. It was always short of helpers and closed with John's departure. Mr Michael Abbett ran a club in the winter of 1986/7 for 12 year olds upwards, but again it was short of helpers. The most recent youth club was run by Revd David Davies during his curacy. In early 1991 there were 130 on the register and a football team was organised but again no-one was available to take it over when he left.

9. The Girls Friendly Society (G.F.S.) – St Peter's, Newton branch

G.F.S. Banner made by Marjorie Ganz. Carried annually at the Rally Service.

A new Girls Friendly Society branch was set up when Archdeacon Harold and Mrs Joan Williams came to Newton. Mrs Williams had been leader of a branch in their previous parish at Brynmawr. She later became Welsh President while at St Peter's. With the help of Wendy Cope, Leslie Griffin, Carole Porter and Barbara Jenkins she started a junior and senior G.F.S. in 1978. It was great fun and made demands upon the leaders often supported by Mums (and Dads!) in order to maintain a varied and challenging programme within the ethos of the Christian faith.

The festivals of the church were not only a guide to teaching, but led to practical work. The girls helped with the decorating of the church at festivals, especially the children's corner, and made the loaf for harvest, having great fun using any spare dough for making 'church mice'. These mice were dotted among the flowers at the chancel steps and were not always appreciated by the choir girls, when a hungry church mouse appeared to taste their wares! The other culinary 'sortie' was making the simnel cake for Mothering Sunday, for distribution at the service on that day.

The annual Diocesan Rally was held in different parishes throughout the diocese and provided an opportunity for an outing. It was often the focus for presentation of 'Branch work', testing the skills, of both leaders and girls, in a variety of 'set' craft projects and written work. A wall hanging, of a collage depicting Welsh life over the years, was of such a high standard that it won the overall prize one year. It was hung in the church and appreciated by many. Later, it was taken to a World Conference by Welsh delegates. Another collage, with a Christmas theme, remained in the church.

Easter Frontal made as part of a Lent project.

Among other projects which the girls enjoyed making were an Easter frontal for the small altar; the knitting of 108 yards towards an attempt at the longest scarf in the world; knitting a blanket of squares for Oxfam; collecting food for the pets at the dogs' home in Singleton Park and a visit to the lifeboat as part of a project on the sea. They started the collection of used postage stamps for the Leprosy Mission which the church has continued to this day.

Some of the branch joined The Offa's Dyke walk from Chepstow in the South to the North Wales coast, undertaken by girls and leaders from branches throughout Wales. Each night they stayed in church halls, where blisters were dealt with and the girls fed. It was a challenge, but one of the rewards was the fellowship and friendships created. Another year some of the girls joined the G.F.S. summer holiday week at Winchester House on the Isle of Wight. St Peter's Church also played host one year to a Welsh holiday. The teenagers enjoyed weekends away. One member was happy to lodge in the G.F.S. hostel for students and working girls in Birmingham when she started a job in that city.

10. Newton Churchmen's Club

The club was officially opened on January 9th, 1906, by Mr Williams of The Cliff, the first president. The club was open from 7 p.m. to 10 p.m. six nights a week from September to April and membership cost 2s/6d for the season. An article in *Oystermouth Parish Magazine* welcomed the club as *"a real, practical and sensible contribution to temperance work. No man's religious views are a bar to membership."* The aim was to provide a meeting place for men, away from the

*Photograph taken at the celebration dinner held at the Osborne Hotel
after the Club won the Church Billiards League cup in 1951.*
People standing, left to right: *John Roberts of Slade Road; Northcliff Price, Southward Lane;
Richard & Dick Woolacott (Richard's father) of Thistleboon Farm; George Owen of Whitestone Lane;
Fred Wilcox, Nottage Rd; Mr Carr, a chorister at St Peter's; Arthur Beynon, Nottage Rd;
Dick Bowen; Jack Meyrick of Blackpill; Tom Stainton; ?; Theo Rowlands, hairdresser;
Sam Davies, Bryncerdin Rd; Ernest Billings, Mumbles; Bryn Critchet, Mumbles; ?;
Will Pearce, Southward Lane; Arthur Owen, St Peter's Rd.*
Front row, sitting, left to right: *Mr Lewis, Southward Lane; ?; Edwards, Mumbles;
Canon W. J. Hickin, Vicar; Bill Richards, Newton Rd; Ernie Richards; Ted Thomas of Newton Rd;
Mr Davies, Headmaster of Oystermouth School.*

pubs, in the winter months when they could not work in their gardens. It was envisaged that they would smoke their pipes, read newspapers, magazines or books and play draughts or chess.

The future direction of the club was indicated in October 1906 when a second hand billiards table was purchased for £40. Brick pillars had to be built under the floor to support the weight, and the gas light extended to illuminate the play. Later, in 1926, a 'ping pong' table was also acquired. Members competed to win the billiards cup presented by Mr Williams, and billiards and draughts matches were arranged against the Oystermouth Men's Club. Over the years the library was built up by gifts of books and periodicals. In the winter of 1933-34, a second billiard table was installed, the gift of Mr Mills of Lomey (later known as Langland Court). Snooker balls were purchased and the table tennis table sold.

As many of the members went away in 1939 to serve in World War II, and the building was requisitioned, the club closed until 1946. Expenses were higher so the membership fee was increased to 10/- a year, or 5/- for 18-20 year olds. Mr M. J. Llewellyn, who lived in the cottage next to the club, had been steward since it began but was not able to continue so John Roberts took his place.

In 1948 and 1951 the billiards team won the Church Billiards League cup. By the end of the 1950s the club faced a financial crisis and nearly closed, but with extra fund-raising it survived the predicament. For many years the club had raised money and a successful whist drive in the Church Hall helped with the funds.

The membership of the club appears to have peaked at around 50 and is now about 30. Reflecting a change in community needs, the club is now open twice a week in the afternoons and on alternate days in the evenings. Members are not required to reside within the parish but must be over 17 years old.

11. The Church Men's Society

In the early years St Peter's had its own branch of the Church of England Men's Society, but in October 1912 Mr H. Bellingham, the secretary, reported that this branch was to amalgamate with that of the parish church.

The Men's Discussion Group had its first meeting in October 1964 and, although it seems to have had a short existence, it may have been the inspiration for the setting up of the *Newtonians Men's Society*. This was launched in October 1967 when W. G. Sutton and S. J. Freeman organised a dinner for 34 church men at the Langland Court Hotel at which it was unanimously agreed that a society should be set up. The first meeting was on January 15th, 1968, at the Central Cafe, Mumbles. The meetings were social occasions, often a meal and a talk. Once a year they treated their wives to an evening out. By 1973 meetings began to be monthly with talks in the church hall, occasionally with a supper prepared. In 1980 the average attendance was 35, a figure that was maintained for several years. Over the next few winters the talks were linked to a theme, the first being Swansea, the next the Nationalised Industries and then Education. In 1986 the talks were about Mumbles. Trevor Parkes was elected chairman in 1983, replacing Alan Swain. Roy Jones and Bill Howells were treasurer and secretary. In 1989 the officers were Ray Cope, David Williams and Sid Freeman. At this time it became the custom to gather for a glass of wine before the meeting. Revd David Thomas remembered two excellent speakers from his time in the Parish. They were

Visit of the Archbishop of Wales to St Peter's Church Men's Society, February 1981.
Included in the photograph: Canon Harold E. Williams, Vicar; Cyril Bowen, Organist;
The Archbishop; Peter Davies; David Meredith; Peter Pickwick; Roy Jones; Frank Jones;
Werner Sivertsen; Bill Howells; Dick Slater; Eric Owen; Leslie Foster; Col. Vaughan Williams.

Gareth Wardell, MP, who gave a penetrating and a most amusing talk about life as an MP; and Dom Leo Bonsall, from St David's Priory in Swansea, who shared some fascinating insights derived from his experience as a Benedictine priest in Latin America. By September 1991 the membership had dropped away, so after an autumn visit to St Michael's Theological College, Llandaff, it was decided to close the society and the 1992 programme was cancelled.

12. *The Travel Society*

The Travel Society was formed in 1980 under the guidance of Werner Sivertsen and with W. H. Howells as secretary/treasurer. The first holiday that was organised was for five nights in Rome in February 1981, travelling from Luton Airport. Its success led to many other yearly trips attracting around 40 members and friends. In February 1982 they went to Athens and the following year it was to Paris in the springtime and then to Andalusia and to the Loire Valley in the succeeding years. By this time Mr Wyndham Jones had become secretary, Werner Sivertsen was chairman and Bill Howells continued as treasurer. In May 1990 a coach party at last enjoyed a tour to Bruges and to Ypres to visit the Menin Gate memorial, having had to cancel arrangements the previous year. In 1991 Maurice Edwards was elected chairman, Denis Lenthall became secretary and Viv Lethbridge was treasurer.

In early October of that year the first British holiday to York and Durham was arranged and, in May 1993, 36 people joined the coach trip to Scotland. In between these British trips the society returned to France again, this time to Brittany, staying at Dinard. At the end of 1993 Maurice Edwards resigned as chairman and although there were 75 members there was no-one willing to take his place. Eventually, Mrs Finvola Davies took over that office but a visit to Norwich had to be cancelled. A trip to Lake Garda and Venice in October 1995 did go ahead but this was the last holiday organised by the society. Unfortunately, the society was never revived but in 2000, the Millennium year, a group, accompanied the vicar, Rev. Clive Jones and his wife, travelled to Oberammergau, to witness the re-enactment of the Passion.

13. The Mothers' Union

The Mothers' Union branch at St Peter's has been in existence since the early days of the church. The meetings then were weekly, starting with a service, often followed by a sewing session, but sometimes by a talk. There were also records of outings which, judging from the description below, sounded quite adventurous: *"On August 12th members of the Newton Mothers' Union had their annual outing by Mrs Mainwaring's kind invitation. About 3 p.m. the somewhat unusual spectacle of the mothers in a motor car was seen by the villagers. Bracelet Bay was the destination and thither the motor car conveyed us at no mean pace. Arrived there, an excellent tea was served in one of the newest refreshment sheds. Afterwards a blow on the Mumbles pier and a stroll on the cliff served to pass the time pleasantly until our motor again appeared. The homeward journey was accomplished without mishap and with a final jerk and snort the motor discharged the mothers at the foot of Newton hill about 7 o'clock. They all agreed that a pleasant afternoon had been had and they were indebted to Mrs Mainwaring."*

Over the years an annual sale of work evolved out of the sewing afternoons. It raised £30 in 1927, a considerable sum, and continued to be very profitable. In the late 1930s the working parties also made garments for charitable causes. In 1939 they made baby clothes for moral welfare work, a parcel of clothing for the social service league and wool bed jackets for members of the MU's invalid prayer circle.

Talks were of a serious nature. The Mother Superior from Eastmoor and Deaconess Margaret Bailey of Landore spoke of their work and successive diocesan presidents and other MU officials gave addresses and many of the local clergy spoke to the meetings. From the beginning the annual outing was a highlight of the year. In 1908 the Mumbles and Newton groups went to Llanwrtyd Wells, probably travelling on the train from Blackpill and all thoroughly enjoyed themselves. Outings became more adventurous as transport improved. In 1930 they went by charabanc to Builth for lunch, then over the Sugar Loaf Mountain for tea at Llandrindod Wells and then to Brecon and another short stop before home. They always started out early and rarely returned before 10 p.m. In the following years they ventured to Devil's Bridge and Aberystwyth, Gloucester and Cheltenham, St David's, Fishguard and Cardigan. With the advent of the Second World War such trips ended. Unable to use the Church Hall for meetings the MU squeezed into the upstairs of the Schoolhouse in Nottage Road. They began knitting comforts for the Forces, dispatching large parcels to the Mission to Seamen. One parcel in 1940 consisted of: 19 prs. of seamen's grey socks, 11 prs. of seamen's navy socks, 16 prs. of ordinary navy socks, 16 prs. of socks of other colours, 2 sea-boot stockings, 16 helmets, 7 prs.of mittens, 7 prs. of wristbands and 1 pr. of gloves.

In 1940 the branch also decided they needed a banner. It was designed and made by the Sisters of the Church, also known as the Kilburn Sisters, for £19.18s.9d. It depicts mother and child on the inverted cross of St Peter. It was consecrated on 14th October, 1941. By the 1970s the banner was looking worn. After the death of MU member Mrs Marjorie Freeman, her husband, Sydney, made a gift of a new, handsome banner in her memory (on the left). It was made by Mrs Martin of Killay.

The first Tuesday of the month meeting was a devotional meeting for the Mothers' Union and the other Tuesdays were more informal. From 1946 the later meetings were known as the ***Ladies Guild***. All church women were invited for more hands meant more goods being made for the annual bazaar, the church's main fund-raising event, organised by the Guild. This started well, but support dwindled and the group closed about 1953. An attempt was made in 1949 to increase the membership of the Mothers' Union by starting a ***Young Wives*** group which met on Thursday afternoons, finishing in time to collect the children from school. The group organised speakers and many events such as whist and beetle drives, coffee mornings, jumble sales and a children's bazaar and Christmas Fair, but it did not result in younger women joining the older MU, so in 1959 Canon Hickin called a meeting to disband the Young Wives and start another more independent organisation, ***The Church Women's Fellowship***.

Memories by Mrs Betty Sivertsen, daughter of Mrs Stirling Evans, who was an active member of the Mothers' Union in the late 1930s: *"My mother was Secretary of the of the Mothers' Union in the days they met every week. After the opening service they would knit, sew and embroider for the church's annual Bazaar in November. Whilst doing this they would read a chapter from the latest book. Also there were speakers, as today. Bill Barrington lived in the Lodge at Llwynymor, and his mother too was an active member of St Peter's Mothers' Union. On the afternoons of Mothers' Union, Bill and I would race from school before they finished and if we kept very quiet we would be rewarded with a piece of delicious home made cake. They all had cake with their tea – usually made by Mrs Bossom, the Vicar's housekeeper."*

Mrs Sterling Evans membership card.

As Canon Hickin was a bachelor he had no wife to lead the Mothers' Union, so the group had produced Enrolling Members from within the branch. Mrs Evan Thomas was the Enrolling Member before the war and handed the post to Mrs Russell in 1941. She resigned in 1953 and Mrs Henry Thompson led the branch until the arrival of Canon and Mrs Brunsdon. Mrs Brunsdon became the first vicar's wife to be Enrolling Member followed by a succession of other vicar's wives: Joan Williams, Rosemary Thomas and Diane Jones. One of the faithful members, Miss Gwenneth Snow, also served for a short period. The present leader is Mrs Louise Hughes. Rosemary Thomas (the vicar's wife, 1987-1996), wrote of her time as leader: *"In addition to the monthly meetings, we always held a few social events each year. The main one was the Shrove Tuesday Coffee Morning. This was always a marvellous occasion with the hall full of chatter and activity as our members served on the various stalls and made and served coffee. (The proceeds of the morning always went to help the work of MU at home and overseas.) We had the occasional outing as well, and each year an Epiphany Tea Party in the vicarage. The fact that we had a good social life doesn't mean that we forgot the MU's essential purposes of prayer, worship and service. We used to have a carefully drawn up annual programme of subjects for our meetings. No less important in this respect, of course, were the annual MU festivals, the deanery retreat and quiet days, our corporate Holy Communion on Lady Day and, of course, the MU Wave of Prayer. By the time David and I left, there were 45 members in the branch."*

Since then the branch has continued to flourish and carry on with a similar programme. In 1998 the members once again plied their knitting needles, knitting 120 vests and other baby clothes for Rwandan babies. In 2002 two members, Veronica Barrington (wife of Bill, former verger) and Betty Sivertsen celebrated 50 years of membership.

Mother's Union outing in 1926.
Some of those present: At the back: *Mrs Geo Rogers, Mrs Snow, Miss Bosworth (High Pool Farm)*
Mrs Meyrick, Mrs Owen (Newton Farm), Mrs Childs, Mrs W. Barrington,
Rev. Hilary Jones (in Trilby), curate-in-charge.
Front row: *Miss Gladys Talbot, Mrs Talbot, Mrs Gibey, Mrs Stirling Evans (with fur wrap) and child,*
Mrs Geo Thomas (her mother), Mrs Davies (M.U. President), Mrs Hilary Jones in front of husband
(holding wrap) and Mesdames Walters, Rosser, Scovell and Bowen.

14. *Thursday afternoon Whist Club*

The weekly Thursday afternoon whist drives in the Church Hall were started by Mrs Stirling Evans in the autumn of 1939 to raise money to buy wool for the Mothers' Union working party which knitted garments for the Mission to Seamen to distribute to mariners during the war. Her daughter, Betty, remembers the wool was kept in their front room, and being of an oily nature, did not have a very good aroma! With the end of the war the ladies continued to meet and the money that was raised was given to missions that St Peter's supported, such as the Korean Mission, The Universities Mission to Central Africa (UMCA) and the Society for the Propagation of the Gospel (SPG). By the mid 1950s the profits were being used to help St Peter's to pay its 'quota' to the Church in Wales, as this commitment rose steadily year by year. Luckily, the Thursday Club's donations also rose steadily. By 1981, when Mrs Stirling Evans retired, the club had donated over £4,000 to the church. Mrs Elaine Misson took over the running of the club. Over the years the number of players dwindled to about 4 or 5 tables and the club moved into the smaller hall in the 1990s.

Three or four times a year the members met at the Langland Court Hotel for lunch followed by some hands of cards. Every year there was a summer outing, and at Christmas a dinner, prepared by the members, was held in the hall, but in 1975 outside caterers were used for the first time. The Thursday Club closed in 2002 when Mrs Misson retired due to ill health.

15. The Church Women's Fellowship (C.W.F.)

Banner made by Marjorie Ganz.

The Church Women's fellowship was started in October 1959. Its opening followed the demise of the Young Wives Group, and many of those ladies formed the nucleus of the new society. The first chairman was Mrs Sheila Byrde. Miss Christine Sutton was secretary and Mrs Sylvia Marshall was treasurer. The pattern of weekly Thursday evening meetings with a speaker, continued through the years until recently, when meetings became fortnightly. Breaks are at Christmas, Easter, and the summer holidays.

Over the years a wide range of interesting talks have been heard covering topical issues, travel and more light hearted subjects. There have also been many informative demonstrations of some specific skill. In earlier years there were local evening visits to places such as the Coal Utilisation Centre, the Swansea BBC studios and the Mission to Seamen's centre in the docks. There are certain events which continued yearly like the combined CWF/MU party in January and the teas the Fellowship provided for Sunday School parties. They also arranged a tea and an outing for the church children in the summer. Twice yearly jumble sales were held to raise extra funds which were mostly donated to the church. Other forms of fund-raising have included coffee evenings with an entertainment. In the 1970s Cockett Gilbert and Sullivan Singers were the performers. Nowadays the funds are raised from subscriptions, and recently donations have been made to the new Hall Fund which was originally started by several members of the CWF.

In the early years, as the church's Lent services or study evenings were on Thursdays, their meeting night, and, as the congregation was largely made up of CWF members, the CWF programme was in abeyance until after Easter. Later the Lent services moved to Wednesdays and the CWF followed its own Lenten programme. It also became a tradition, until very recently, for the CWF to make the Palm crosses for Palm Sunday. Now they are purchased, ready made. In December there is a Christmas dinner, and the year finishes with an evening of carols. There were regular summer outings to places like Tenby, Oxford, or Badmington House, where the group were shown round by the Duchess of Beaufort. In 1986 Gareth Wardell MP gave the fellowship a tour of the House of Commons. Recently the trip has been replaced by a summer meal.

In 1984 the CWF celebrated its Silver Jubilee with a party for 77 people. Mrs Marjorie Ganz gave the fellowship a photograph album to record events

Summer Supper, 8th August, 2002, organised by Eileen Ash; catering by Jean Whetton.
(Photograph supplied by Eileen Ash).

and the Fellowship gave the vicar a silver ciborium (used to hold the communion bread) to mark the occasion. Over the years the CWF has maintained an average membership of about 50, with many of the original members still attending, so the average age is somewhat more mature. Many of the members contribute to other aspects of the church life.

16. Altar Guild

This title refers to the ladies who arrange the flowers in the church, week by week. The first organiser is believed to have been Mrs Bellingham who retired at the end of 1942 after twenty-four years of service. Miss Hilda Davies of The Cliff replaced her. Later Canon Brunsdon drew up the list each year and allotted each helper a date. Ever since his retirement Mrs Joy Edwards has taken on the responsibility of organising the rota and over the years she has been involved with the flower arranging, having originally taken classes with Mrs Irene David in her home in Groves Avenue. Now there is an excellent team of flower arrangers who also contribute to the beautiful arrangements at festivals in the church and at other special events.

17. 5th Mumbles (St Peter's) Scouts and Cubs

St Peter's connection with the Scout movement began in the mid 1930s when Canon Hickin was on the committee of the Mumbles Boy Scouts Association.

He arranged for the District Scouts and Guides to hold annual church parades. In April 1942 the 5th Mumbles Wolf Cub Pack was started by Miss Monica Hinds (Cubmistress) and Miss Betty Evans at Canon Hickin's request. Due to wartime conditions, Newton boys were unable to join any of the Mumbles packs. They met on Mondays in the schoolhouse in Nottage Road, the only available space at that time. It was very cramped in the small rooms in winter although, once the weather improved, the play-yard could be used. Badge work was done in winter and outdoor activities in summer, in Caswell Valley, on the beaches and in Brandy Cove. The pack started with 30 boys and green and gold were the scarf colours. After Miss Hinds left in 1943, Mrs Sivertsen (née Evans), began her long service as Cub Mistress. Her first assistant was Jean Griffin, who was followed by Esme Owen and Bonnie Melville. Esme and Bonnie were both married in 1959 and Mrs Bunty Guest became the assistant. Clare Haines, Ann Cundy and Judith Canning all helped for a time and were followed by Anne Matthews who stayed with the pack for many years. The Church Hall was back in use in 1947 and so was the field behind the hall (now the site of the vicarage). The farmer took the cows out of the field on pack nights, and many frazzled beans and blackened sausages were consumed out there. Every year the cubs took part in Bob-a-Job Week and usually raised about £14. In 1960 they won the Mumbles Division Sports Shield. Around Christmas time they had a party and in 1963 were treated to a visit to the pantomime. Anne Matthews and Barbara Cule Davies ran the pack after Betty Sivertsen retired in the early 1970s. In 1971, Betty was awarded the Scout Medal of Merit. In 1998, Dr and Mrs Davies were presented with a joint High Sheriff's award for their long involvement with the Group, and in 2005 Mrs Davies had completed more than 45 years of service and she was awarded the bar to the Silver Acorn.

The 5th Mumbles Scout Troop started in 1945 under Mr Len Evans, leader of the 1st Mumbles, until their own leader Norman Long qualified as Scoutmaster and was assisted by Mr Marcus Long. They, too, met in the schoolhouse, at 7.45 p.m., after the cubs. Later, the cubs stayed with Monday meetings but the scouts moved to Fridays. Norman was called up for National Service and in 1948 another scoutmaster, Michael Robinson, ran the troop. It seems this troop was rather short lived for by 1950 the scouts had disbanded, however, the cubs continued to prosper. In 1968 the scout troop was reformed, under the leadership of Mr G. Golden, and the following year they won the Sims cup in the camp competition. Mr Geoff Evans followed him as leader in 1970 and since then there have been many more. Mr Bruce Bowbanks has taken a leading part and interest in the Troop since 1977 and later became Assistant District Commissioner, and his wife was the first lady Troop Scouter amongst the Mumbles Troops. In 1970 fund-raising began for a

5th MUMBLES CUBS WITH THE DISTRICT SPORTS SHIELD, 1960.
Includes: Roger Blyth, Philip Jordan, Andrew Brown, Roger Walmsley,
Robert and Charles Radcliffe, Nicholas Gethin, Gerald Gabb, David and Philip Guest,
Richard Budge, Paul Sivertsen, Howard Davies, Andrew Rolfe, and scout David Phillips.

headquarters in Newton for the scout movement. Numerous bazaars, coffee mornings and evenings were held and another fundraising event was a concert in church on 27th October, 1974, by the Gower Orchestra. A site was acquired at Picket Mead when the Group were able to lease some land from Welsh Water. A Scout Hut was erected and officially opened on 12th June, 1975, by Betty Sivertsen, who was then Assistant County Commissioner for the Cub Scouts.

The cubs and scouts no longer meet in the Church Hall but the link with the church is not broken as St Peter's is the sponsor of the 5th Mumbles Scouts Group. Church parades have resumed at St Peter's with the current Vicar. 2004 was a significant year for the Group, for, in May they held a 60th Reunion Party, which was attended by Scouters and Group Executive committee members from all periods of the Group's existence. In the same year Kevin Williams, the present Group Scout Leader, was awarded a Medal of Merit, and Dr Elwyn Davies was the distinguished recipient of the Silver Wolf, the highest award in scouting, for giving over 45 years of service. Also, in 2006 there was another cause for celebration when Robert Hixson was the Group's first recipient of the Queen's Scout Award.

(Information kindly supplied by the late Dr Elwyn Davies, writer of *The History of the 5th Mumbles Scout Group*).

Cubs on the Church Hall gate, c.1953.
Includes – Alan* and Charles Clewett, David Hagger, Stewart Andrews, Philip Guest.
(N.B. * Alan, went on to become County Commissioner for West Glamorgan
and Deputy Chief Commissioner for Wales.)

5th Mumbles (St Peter's) Cubs.
Back row: *?Jeffreys, John Pickard, Keith Richards, John Bowen.*
Middle row: *?, Betty Sivertsen (née Evans), Jean Llynfi Davies (née Griffin); Donald McKay.*
Front row: *Billy ?, John and Selwyn Hixson.*

18. 1st Mumbles Guides and Brownies

The 1st Mumbles Guides and Brownies first met in the stable loft at Glan-y-Coed, Newton Road, in 1928, and were there for many years. Later they transferred to the Scout Hut in Merton Lane when it was opened in 1975 and they attended St Peter's for Church Parade. They continue to meet once a week, the Brownies on a Tuesday and the Rainbows and Guides on a Wednesday, under the leadership of Mrs Hixson, with a few assistants to help. They look forward to their annual pack holiday at Parkmill and have also enjoyed special overseas holidays to Switzerland three times since 2000.

The 1st Langland Brownies was originally started by Elizabeth Hunt and met at the stable loft at Fensala, Higher Lane. They moved to St Peter's Hall at the beginning of 1986 when Mrs Sue Butler returned to the area from overseas. Her children were Brownies and Sue took over the leadership until 2005. She still continues links with the pack. Sue was succeeded by Sheila MacLaren as leader for the next three years. Alexandra Lang is now the current Brown Owl. It is pleasing to see the uniformed groups back in the church, at regular parades during family services and they are looking forward to returning to the new hall for their meetings when it is completed. The young ones undertake to decorate the children's corner at the major church festivals. They also take part in helping with the serving of the strawberry teas during the Petertide festival, as part of their hostess badge.

In 1988 the Church Hall was equipped with a fridge, cooker and other necessities for Brownie pack holidays. Many holidays were enjoyed there in the following years by other packs, such as Blackpill.

1988 in St Peter's Church Hall.
1st Langland Brownies presenting a new 'Baby Jesus' to the
Unitarian Church, Swansea, to replace the one stolen from the crib.

Guides and Brownies outside St Peter's after Church Parade.
Presentation of Queen's Guide to Elizabeth Hunt, 1962, 1st Mumbles.
Back row: *Penny Hunt; Frances Dale; Maureen O'Sullivan; Helen McGairl; Lynda Steadham; Mrs Kwantes (Commissioner); Carol Whiston; Elizabeth Hunt; Susan McNamara; Susan Tucker; Ann Meyrick.*
Middle row: *Catriona Macdonald; Joanna Wattis; Jane?; Jill King; Tessa Davies; Joanne Parfitt; Christine Williams; Cheryl ?.*
Front row: *Julia Davies; Eleanor Dale; Christine Ash; Yvonne King; Lynne ?; Lindsey Davies; Sally Haines.*

1st Mumbles Brownies, 1957.

13.

The Evolution of the Parish Magazine

In February 1899 the *Oystermouth Parish Magazine* made its debut and in the first edition the vicar, Harold S. Williams, as editor, wrote of his objectives in an introduction:

1. to chronicle church events;
2. to be a means of communication between clergy and people;
3. to keep the church and its people in touch;
4. to record local news considered of interest to readers.

The magazine was to contain a little publication *The Dawn of Day*, published by S.P.C.K. [Society for Promoting Christian Knowledge] and pages of local matter, two with advertisements, to help pay its way. It would cost 1d. a month and the vicar urged those who could, to pay an annual subscription, in advance, of one shilling.

The early magazines had a wine coloured cover and on the front there was a contemporary photograph of the Parish Church, as well as names of the clergy and times the church was open daily for prayer and meditation. It was printed by The Cambrian Printing Works, of High Street, Swansea. During the years of 1900-1902, while the vicar was busily involved in his scheme for church extension at Newton, he took the opportunity to circulate his appeal for the New Church Fund, and to keep the parishioners informed of progress. In 1903 the cover was simple and uncluttered, with few words.

The following extract is of a letter from the magazine, written in 1904, by the vicar, which makes amusing reading: *"My Dear Readers, Here I am again at the beginning of the New Year 1904 . . . Well, I am a big boy now, I am five years old, going on six, going strong, too . . . They say I have a splendid circulation – 800 a month. They say, too, I am considerably popular in Oystermouth, and it must be true, for I am welcomed in nearly every house in the parish. The rich like me, and so do the poor, and I like them, and so there it is in a nutshell . . . my friends continue to give me a place by your fireside and I will try and make myself pleasant and agreeable. Like most people in this world, I have to rely upon my own efforts to live; I have no public means . . . I have no relatives; I was born an orphan. The family of*

Oystermouth Parish Magazines were unknown until I came. They are all over the place now. I have to thank many kind friends for my present position: First, I must thank the gentleman that writes me [i.e. Revd Harold S. Williams]. *He does get very cross with me sometimes – throws me into the wastepaper basket, and says it's the best place for me; but in the end he turns me out somehow. Secondly, there's the gentleman that prints me. He does it very nicely but he does use very impolite language, because he has to call in his whole staff, and a few newspaper boys, to help decipher the Editor's writing, which he says is awful. Thirdly, my good friends the advertisers . . ."*

Ten years after the first publication, the circulation had risen to 850 and the cover shows a different view of the church which changed again in 1920. The cover was white and it depicted two photographs of both All Saints' Church, with its new extension, and the new church at Newton looking rather bleak on a treeless plot. It was now printed by Tucker Bros. of Mumbles and contained a new pull-out publication entitled *The Sign*, and was priced at 2d. By the end of the 1920s the circulation was up to 900 a month. In all of the magazines there were a large number of advertisements which make interesting reading as they are a reflection on the produce and services of the time.

After the formation of the new parish of Newton, in 1933, the magazine was called *THE CHURCH MAGAZINE for the parishes of Oystermouth and Newton*, otherwise the cover remained the same. In the February edition there was a full report announcing the new parish of Newton, defining its boundaries, as well as an account of the induction of the first vicar, Revd W. J. Hickin. The December 1938 magazine recorded the retirement of the vicar, now archdeacon, Harold Williams and his final letter as editor.

In the early 1940s St Peter's Church at last had its own magazine entitled *The Parish Magazine Newton* on a white cover which showed a new view of St Peter's Church standing in a more mature setting. From then on, for the next three decades, the style changed little, and became very perfunctory, with just the vicar's letter and church notices included in the insertion.

In the 1950s the names of the clergy, officers and services were also printed on the front cover and the cost was 3d a copy. The vestry notes of 1963 reported the concern of the P.C.C. of a £10 deficit of magazine funds, and suggested a change of insert to *The Welsh Churchman* in the hope of increasing the circulation. Later the insert changed again to the *Church News Magazine*.

Shortly after Archdeacon Harold E. Williams arrived in 1976 he conceived a new format for the magazine. He too was keen to harness some of the local talent he had noticed in Newton, as well as create a sense of community and fellowship in the village as a whole. It occurred to him that one method of achieving this would be by St Peter's producing and printing its own magazine. His intention was similar to that of his namesake, the first editor. The vicar called a meeting at the end of the summer 1977 for members of parish organisations and other interested parties. Mrs Jean Haines was appointed editor and the first issue was produced in time for Midnight Mass on Christmas Eve of that year and was distributed free, after the service.

Thus, another form of the *NEWTON PARISH MAGAZINE* was conceived. Jean Haines cut all the stencils and Joan Williams, the vicar's wife, drew by hand the cover design. It was a copy of a wood carving from the Philippines, the motive used for the 1972 GFS World Council. The magazine was run off in the vicarage, on a Gestetner machine by the vicar and his wife. By the time the next edition was prepared three long carriage typewriters had been acquired and a new Gestetner machine donated. For a long while Miss Gwenneth Snow supervised a hard-working band of volunteers and a production team of 'gatherers, folders and staplers' was formed and the magazines were then bundled for distribution by yet more volunteers.

ST. PETER'S CHURCH
NEWTON

Cover designed by Valerie Ganz, 1978-1998.

Mrs Leslie Griffin was the next editor for nearly twenty years and during that time the white cover had a coloured ink drawing of the north aspect of the church, designed by the prestigious local artist, Valerie Ganz. Then, other artists, who were also parishioners, namely Grahame Sutton and Philip Shaddick, contributed their designs based on some feature of the church. Over the years typewriters came and went and with the advancement of technology so printing methods improved. Later the magazine was printed at Eastmoor, until its closure at the end of the C20th. During that time the dedicated team of volunteers complained that their fellowship time was dwindling away with less to do!

When the Revd Clive Jones arrived he undertook the editorship himself, for fortunately he was computer literate, and he introduced a variety of computer designed covers, each on a different colour paper and depicting a topical theme for the month. The vicar's vestry soon became crowded out with 'high tech machines' which produced a very professional result under the eagle eye of Mr Les Evans and Mr Huw Jones, the next editor. There is still a large input from faithful helpers who help with the monthly compilation and delivery to 370 homes in the parish and beyond, so continuing to keep people in touch. All those involved look forward to the day when all the equipment can be moved into an office in the new hall.

No. 1.　　　　**FEBRUARY.**　　　　1899.

OYSTERMOUTH

✝

PARISH MAGAZINE.

"Lord, I have loved the habitation of Thy house, and the place where Thy Honour dwelleth."

THE PARISH CHURCH.

Clergy :

Rev. HAROLD S. WILLIAMS, L.Th , Vicar. "Beachmont."
Rev. T. OWEN PHILLIPS, L.Th , 4, Walters Terrace.

The Church is open daily from 8.30 a.m. to 5.30 p.m., for Prayer and Meditation.	The Clergy ask to be informed of any persons who desire, or need, to be visited.

" O, how amiable are Thy dwellings, Thou Lord of Hosts."
" My soul hath a desire and longing to enter into the Courts of the Lord."

PRICE, ONE PENNY.

Print of first magazine.

14.

The Church Properties

1. *The Church Hall*

Vicar Harold S. Williams could see the need for a Church Hall in 1910 but, possibly due to the 1914-1918 war, plans were delayed for another ten years. However, in 1920 the vicar procured a strip of land, L-shaped around the church, in order that a hall and, in time, a vicarage could be built. The Church Hall was officially opened on Thursday, 29th December, 1921. The occasion was described in the *Oystermouth Parish Magazine* (February 1922): *"The opening of St Peter's Church Hall by Mrs Richardson proved a most enjoyable function. The vicar presided over a large gathering and all enjoyed the excellent refreshments served by the ladies. After the dedicatory prayer an interesting programme of speech and song followed. The musical items were contributed by Mrs Marten, Mrs Hughes-Rice, Mrs Pearce, Mr Barlow and Mr Ben John. The following day the children enjoyed their treat of a tea-party, followed by a cinema entertainment kindly given by Mr Henderson."*

Photograph of the Church Hall by Mr Les Evans.

By 1927, the hall was already needing additional building works and improvements which led to a £45 deficit in the hall fund. A whist drive and concert were arranged to wipe out the debt, but the fund always had a struggle to break even throughout the 1920s. There were more alterations and redecoration needed to be done in 1931 which were paid for by weekly evening whist drives through the winter, run by Mrs Stirling Evans and Mrs Pressdee. The single lean-to room, behind the stage, was divided into two rooms, which was more convenient when used as a dressing room for plays and concerts. The hall was repainted inside and out and provided with new curtains for the stage and the windows. New electric lighting to replace the gas lighting was also installed.

The hall was well used by church organisations for men, women and children and by other village societies such as the Women's Institute and the Newton Horticultural Society and was available for fund-raising, whist drives, social evenings and dances. It was therefore a blow to the parish to be denied its use when it was requisitioned by the army in 1940, becoming the mess for the Sussex Regiment and later the American troops. Many church organisations closed then, but the Sunday School continued to meet in Newton School and the Mothers' Union met upstairs in the schoolhouse.

When the hall was finally returned to the parish it was in a dreadful state. In September 1946, Canon Hickin wrote in the magazine that: *the hall is still not available for use due to difficulties in getting licences for the work and after that, materials and labour. It seems to be getting more and more difficult to make a start. The Nissen huts have been removed from the field but the foundations and general debris still remains.*

The following January the vicar records that the hall was still almost completely derelict, and it was not until November 1947 that it was fit to be used, although it was still without heating. Clubs were started again and the social life of the village revived. The next few years saw refurbishment taking place. A local resident recalls attending a party for Newton schoolchildren in the hall to commemorate the Coronation in 1953 for which a hundred new cups and saucers were given. In 1956 fifty new chairs were bought, Mrs Christie paid for interior redecoration and new window curtains were made, and the Mothers' Union provided new stage curtains.

A survey of the hall in 1965, by architect Colonel Portsmouth, was followed by work on the roof, which was given a bituminous coating. Also, the west wall was almost completely replaced and renewed; there were improvements in the kitchen and toilets, erection of a porch entrance, and construction of a minor hall, in place of the old lean-to. Electric fittings were overhauled and the whole building was decorated. The cost was over £4,000 resulting in an overdraft of £2,500 at the bank. When the work was finished in September

1967, Canon Brunsdon organised an 'At Home' for parishioners. He thanked all the organisations who regularly used the hall. These were the Sunday School, Mothers' Union, Church Women's Fellowship, Whist Club, Scouts and Cubs, Women's Institute, Horticultural Society, Keep Fit Group, two badminton clubs, and a ballet class.

When the scouts moved from the hall to their new hut in Murton Lane in 1975, the main hall was again repaired and redecorated. A suspended ceiling and new windows were put in, the walls were panelled and strip lighting and individual heaters were installed, under the guidance of Mr Vergette. The W.I. then gave a piano for use in the hall and the C.W.F. paid for new orange plastic chairs. The success of the hall work led to the kitchen being panelled in 1979. This was done by church members Tim Hill and Ted Cope. More chairs and new tables were purchased in 1981 from donations given by the C.W.F. and the Women's Institute.

Originally the hall grounds had a gate at the entrance, but by the 1970s only a gate post remained. In 1987, when the Sunday School was bursting at the seams, guard rails were erected to prevent children dashing on to the road. Through the 1980s many more organisations were using the hall besides the ones already mentioned. These included: Mens' Society; Girls' Friendly Society; Travel Society; Toc H; Toddler Club; 1st Langland Brownies; and the Choir.

In 1991 another survey was carried out on the hall by Gilbert Mellors, a retired architect and member of the P.C.C., who reported that the hall was fast approaching the end of its life. He drew up some plans for a new hall and a building fund was started. Unfortunately, large increases in the parish Quota meant that the rebuilding was postponed.

In 1998 the need for a new hall again came to the fore and architect Clive Jenkins designed a new building which would cost about £350,000. Some parishioners did not like the idea of access directly from the hall to the west end of the church and others were worried about the proximity to the Garden of Remembrance. In the end this plan was rejected. However, a valiant group of church members persevered with the aim to get a new hall for Newton, especially after a survey confirmed this was the wish of the parishioners and wider community. A structural engineer revealed it would be more cost effective to build a new hall and that the kitchen was no longer of sufficient hygienic standard to be used. A sub-committee of the Parochial Church Council was set up in 2002 known as the Hall Management Committee. This was chaired by Mr Bert Harris and faithfully supported by Les Evans, and the late John Ash (Treasurer) and the late John Budge. Over the last eight years others from the church and outside have joined the committee and have persistently worked away to get funding, new plans drawn up and accepted,

HALL MANAGEMENT COMMITTEE, 2009.
Les Evans; Colin Rees; Will Watson; Tony Porter; Bert Harris (Chairman);
Revd Canon George Bennett (Vicar); (Absent: Norman Hixson); Jo Breckles (Treasurer);
Celia Jones (Fund-raising). Inset: *the late John Budge (left) and the late John Ash (right).*

and deal with all the negotiations between the planning department and the builders.

Progress was slow as investigations into ownership of the land on which the hall stood took two years to resolve. It was decided that although owned by the church the building would serve the whole community so should be known as Newton Village Hall. This would also assist with community fund-raising and grants. An energetic fund-raising committee was set up in 2004, led by Celia Jones. That year they raised an impressive £7,603 and they continue to work away, tirelessly. There have been many varied and successful events including a 'Bookshop' in the minor hall and a monthly community cinema, as well as concerts and a variety of imaginative sales which have raised over £36,000. This has helped towards the ever increasing costs and keeping the project fresh in the community's minds.

The hall site falls within a conservation area, which caused the new build-ing to be subject to strict planning regulations and presented many challenges. There were also further delays before the old building could be safely demolished. First, the hall had to be inspected for owls and bats and work on nearby trees was scrutinised as they were protected by a preservation order. At last, in November 2007, it seemed that the builders could proceed. The old hall was closed just before Christmas but its demolition was delayed due to the discovery of a live gas pipe and the asbestos in the roof had to be carefully removed. Later, there were still more frustrations lying ahead which included a long search to find the correct slate for the roof and stone for parts of the exterior wall of the new hall, in order to comply with the Planning department's specific requirements. All this, and more, inevitably increased the cost of construction and fund-raising functions were more difficult to organise without a suitable premises.

The Lottery eventually awarded a small grant which, although not sufficient to cover any of the cost of the building, did however help towards valuable funding for furnishing and some landscaping. There have also been many generous local donations including the fitting of the new kitchen by T. W. Thomas, to which the Newton W.I. has also generously contributed. It was with much optimism that in May 2008 the numerous members of the hard-working committees, and their supporters, witnessed Councillor Susan Waller, in her last month as Lord Mayor, cut the first sod and the project received a blessing from the Reverend Canon George Bennett.

Swansea Lord Mayor, Sue Waller, cuts the first turf.

Sadly, by the end of that year it was realised there was still a considerable deficit in funds and the contract with the first builder, *Jehu*, was terminated while there was a strong drive to raise the required amount of £46,000. This was done in a number of forms which included a £5 challenge which produced a fantastic community reaction and over £10,000 profit. An invitation was issued to the wider community to offer interest free loans producing again encouraging results. It was a great relief when a new building firm, *Ecobuild Wales Ltd*, picked up the gauntlet and at last a steady progress of work was to be seen from June of 2009. Completion was scheduled by Christmas but yet more frustrations were encountered. This time they were caused by the weather. The autumn had more than a fair share of rain and then it was followed by a very cold winter of ice and snow causing further delays. It is realised the Hall will have a budget deficit for some years to come so fund-raising will have to continue to repay the shortfall. However, the reward for the persistence and vision of the hard working committee will be the knowledge that the Newton Village Hall will be a focus to the whole community in bringing everyone together in friendship and sharing for many more years as was the vision for the first hall which stood for eighty eight years.

NEWTON VILLAGE HALL – OPENED APRIL 2010.   (Les Evans)

2. The Vicarage

Although the Vicar of Oystermouth, Ven. Harold Stepney Williams, had procured land in 1920 in order that, besides a hall, a vicarage could one day be built for St Peter's, it was to be another forty years before that vision was realised. Until the 1930s the church was served by one of the vicar's curates.

The first Vicarage in St Peter's Road.

It was not until 1932, when the prospect of St Peter's being a separate parish arose, that the need for a vicarage in Newton became more pressing. Mrs Richardson, a generous benefactor, gave to the church a house on the top corner of St Peter's Road which would be used as a vicarage until 1963.

When the Bishop, Dr J. J. A. Thomas, visited for the institution and induction of Canon Brunsdon in June 1961, he spoke of the urgent need for a new vicarage. Plans were made during 1962. A plot of land, in Mary Twill Lane, beside the proposed new vicarage, and the house in St Peter's Road, were sold that year to help finance the building work. Luckily, the parish was able to call on the expertise of parishioners to arrange estate and legal matters and direct labour was used to minimise expense, although at one time work was held up by a shortage of plasterers.

Canon and Mrs Brunsdon moved in at the beginning of 1964 and on May 29th the Bishop attended the blessing of the new vicarage. After Evensong, in the church, the congregation processed to the new house where they witnessed the blessing and then they filed through the ground floor before returning to the hall for refreshments.

[The Bishop never anticipated that one day his son, Revd David Thomas, would occupy the house and that later he too would reside there.]

By the 1990s the parish was finding it harder to meet all its financial commitments and an arrangement was made with the Representative Body of the Church in Wales, for the Diocesan Parsonage Board to take responsibility for repair and maintenance of the vicarage while the house remained the property of the parish.

The vicarage in Mary Twill Lane.

3. A House for the Curate

A number of houses within the parish have been provided by the church for use by curates during their time at St Peter's. The first curate was Revd Norman Lea, who came in 1968. In order to purchase a house for him and his wife, 30 parishioners loaned £100 each and **18 Melcorn Drive** was bought. When he moved in 1971 the house was sold as there was no prospect of another curate at that time.

It was 1982 before another curate was appointed. Revd John Cruse and his wife Janice came to live in **72 Croftfield Crescent** which was purchased by borrowing £15,000 from the Representative Body of the Church in Wales. Clarice Smith later lived there and was followed by another curate, David Davies and his family until the birth of their second son, when a larger house became a necessity, so a move was made to **29 Summerland Lane** in 1992. When David moved to his own parish in Breconshire the parish was without a curate for a while. The next occupants at this address were Revd Tudor Griffiths and his wife and family who needed accommodation on their return from Uganda. Curates Dominic Coslett and Jonathan Davies followed in turn, living there.

After Jonathan left St Peter's, the P.C.C. was told that it was unlikely he would be replaced due to shortage of curates. So, after a period of lettings, a decision was made to sell the house in 2004 and the money was placed in the much needed Hall Fund. All aspects of the sale were managed by the Hall Management Committee.

18 Melcorn Drive.

72 Croftfield Crescent.

29 Summerland Lane.

4. Newton Churchmen's Club

The club stands opposite the church, on the corner of Nottage Road and Caswell Road. It was opened in January 1906. The premises had been built after money was raised from a number of fund-raising activities, including a 'Rustic Fête' held in the field, in which the club, and the houses alongside, now stand. Activities at the fête included 'Guess the weight of the sheep' and a tug-of-war between Newton and Mumbles which was won by Newton.

Churchmen's Club. Photograph by Mr Les Evans.

The club is a wooden building with a corrugated iron roof and originally it was lit by gas and heated by a coal stove. Electricity did not arrive until 1926. During its early years many church events were held in the building until the new Church Hall was built. September 1939 saw many of the members off to war and in 1940 the club was closed altogether due to the building being requisitioned by the National Fire Service. It was the end of 1945 before it was released. The club finally reopened in the autumn of 1946. In 1985 the possibility arose of acquiring the freehold of the club site which was then held by the Electricity Board. In 1987, the ensuing covenant saw the church buying the site for £500 and the Churchmen's Club now leases the building from the church for a peppercorn rent. Since then a new roof of plastic coated sheeting has been fitted, with the help of a grant from the Community Council, as well as other repairs and renovations.

Members of the Churchmen's Club enjoying a snooker social in 2004.

15.

The Church Grounds

For the first two years after the church was completed the grounds were left unattended and were an 'eyesore' according to Harold Williams but in the winter of 1905/06 the area was cleared and levelled. To meet the require-ments of the original indenture (signed 10 July, 1901) for *"construction of a proper boundary wall, at least 3-6 feet high"* a dry stone wall was erected on the northern and eastern sides. This was set back from the original field boundaries, to allow for the widening of the road and construction of a footpath, necessitated by the considerable amount of traffic using the road to Caswell Bay during the summer months. Iron railings were erected on the southern and western sides of the grounds and there were two iron gates. A gravelled carriage drive was laid around the church and a gas lamp was installed by the main entrance. The remaining garden was planted with shrubs and trees. These included a traditional yew tree, and a number of coniferous trees which have grown to a great size over the century. During that time several have had to be felled or trimmed, for the sake of safety, on the advice of an arborist, who regularly inspects them.

In the summer of 1906 Mr Arthur Gilbertson gave money for the erection of a lychgate (see Chapter 6). A breach was made in the wall where it turned the corner in Caswell Road and the handsome, roofed gate was built during November and December of that year. Much later, in the 1960s, there was a proposal to move it but fortunately this never took place, although over the years it has required several repairs after damage and deterioration.

On winter nights the church grounds were very dark, until, in 1927, Mr Turpin gave a gift of another gas lamp outside the church to help the congregation find their way from the porch to the steps of the lychgate with greater ease. Later, when electricity was installed, the lighting was further improved. More recently, security lights have been added and to mark the Millennium, a generous donation from the Mumbles Community Council enabled the siting of flood lights around the grounds. Unfortunately, these have been subject to vandalism.

In 1931 the entrance to the hall was gravelled and the grounds improved as part of a full refurbishment scheme. A privet hedge was planted to mark the boundaries with the Church Hall grounds and along the roadside of both the hall and the church. Later, in the 1970s, Mr Harris, of Blackpill Nurseries, planted the remaining borders with shrubs and trees. In 1971 a footpath entry was replaced by a driveway which led around the church. In 1974 it was widened, asphalted and generally improved to give better access for funeral and wedding cars as well as for the congregation. Further widening took place on the south side of the church in 2005 to make disabled parking spaces and modifications were made, to improve access to the north entrance, by the construction of a ramp. In July 1968 a teak bench, the gift of Mrs Hunt and family, was placed in the grounds in memory of William Jenkins. There is also a more recent seat given in memory of **Stephen Dunster** who had served as a churchwarden and died in 2000. Another memorial gift was given in 1973, marking the 70th anniversary of the church, when 150 heathers were planted in memory of Miss Mary Francis. Other improvements have been the laying of a flagstone path leading from the church to the hall grounds in 1989 instigated by Keith Vaughton. In the early 1990s, Rosemary Thomas, the vicar's wife, suggested that the Mothers' Union plant daffodil bulbs in the church grounds. They continued to do this for the next three autumns, producing handsome results. To celebrate the Millennium, a flagpole was erected beside the entrance into Mary Twill Lane and it flies the flag of the Diocese of Swansea and Brecon.

The Remembrance Garden

In June 1957 preparations were made for a plot of ground to be prepared for the disposal of ashes after cremation. This was to be located at the west end of the church grounds and the site was to be marked by a simple cross of granite stone. On Friday, September 20th, 1957, the bishop and diocesan registrar held a short service to consecrate the plot. Later, a Cross was sited on the ground and a link chain fence was placed around the perimeter. Mr Barrington and his son Bill, the verger, first helped to make the Garden.

Burials prior to 1980 were in individual plots which are clearly marked on a plan. Subsequently, cremated remains have been poured into specially constructed underground vaults which are sealed when full. Originally there were three but over the years it has been necessary to increase the number and enlarge the area several times. Likewise the fencing posts have been replaced. The ashes of Bill Barrington's mother, Rhoda, were one of the earliest to be placed in The Garden after those of William Morris, of Glynn Vivian Home for the Blind, who was the first and those of John Edwards, Charles Smith, and George H. Jones on 20th February, 1958. Memorial vases are discreetly placed along the west wall of the church. There are no other listed monuments or gravestones in the churchyard.

16.

Special Events Throughout the Life of St Peter's Church

First Recorded Services

A License was granted, on August 17th, 1867, to the Vicar of Oystermouth, the Revd Montague Welby, to perform divine services in the Newton school-room. A report in the *Mumbles Chronicle* (October 20th, 1888) records the annual thanksgiving service for the gathering of the Harvest which was held in Newton School: *"The room was prettily decorated by the loving hands of the ladies of the parish. The decorations were described as being chaste and profuse and included flowers, miniature sheaves of wheat interspersed by grapes, fruits and ferns. Mr John Gwynn presented an excellent mow and rick which reflected his skill as maker. It is an act of love and charity he performs every year and the rick and mow are exhibited in all the churches in the parish at Harvest festival A most practical sermon was preached by the Revd Secretan Jones."*

The wedding of **David John Rees to Margaret Ellen Eynon** was recorded as having been performed also in the schoolroom on the December 14th, 1902. The official opening of St Peter's Church was followed the next day by the first **BAPTISM** on November 20th, 1903, of sisters **Dorothy Emma Celia Hixson** and **Edith Norah Euphemia Hixson** on January 8th, 1905. The **first twins** to be baptised in St Peter's were **Eric and George Owen** and overleaf is their certificate and photograph.

In 1907 there is an interesting story recorded (Thomas, 1978) about a baptism of a gipsy baby at St Peter's Church: *"The first child was baptised at St Peter's Church, Newton, when two ladies of the congregation were god-mothers. Under kind encouragement, the mother overcame her nervous reluctance, and accompanied by friends, she soon became at home in her unusual environment."* The vicar was also later involved in a second baptism of a gipsy baby, this time on Blackpill Common.

On **26th December, 1903**, the first **WEDDING Ceremony** was recorded at St Peter's of **John James Bragg to Georgina Irene Blanch Morris**: *"The marriage took place at the new church of St Peter, Newton, on Saturday (Boxing*

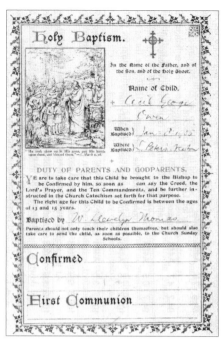

First twins to be baptised in St Peter's were Eric and George Owen.

Day) morning of Miss Irene Morris, second daughter of Mr & Mrs John Morris, Fairfield Villa, Langland, to Mr John Bragg, Castleton. An unusual amount of interest was manifested in the auspicious event primarily on account of the fact that this was the first marriage celebrated in the new church, and secondly because the contracting parties are well known in the locality. There was a goodly number of relatives and friends and other interested persons in the church, when at 11 o'clock the ceremony was performed by the Revd Harold S. Williams, Vicar of Oystermouth, assisted by the Revd W. Ll. Thomas (curate). The bride who was prettily attired was given away by her brother Mr John G. Morris and the bridesmaids were the Miss Edith Morris and Miss Bragg. Mr Albert Lloyd acted as best man. In pursuance of an ancient and interesting custom, the vicar, in the vestry later on, presented the smiling couple with a beautiful **Bagster Bible***, *bearing the following inscription: 'Presented to John James Bragg and Irene Georgina Blanche Morris, on the occasion of the celebration of the first marriage at St Peter, December 26th, 1903'. The wedding breakfast was partaken of at the residence of the bride's mother. The presents were numerous."* (*Mumbles Press*, 1st January, 1904).

---

* **BAGSTER BIBLE** – A comprehensive version of the Bible, sold by a very religious bookseller, Samuel Bagster of The Strand, London, from 1830s, often arranged in parallel columns, exhibiting 6 important translations or a polyglot version and contained thousands of references, maps and a number of valuable study aids. Many of the Bibles were luxuriously bound in tooled morocco, with gold edge and lettering, brass corners and clasp.

John Bragg continued to be an active member of St Peter's Church. He died on October 16th, 1918, age 40 years. and his wife on October 3rd, 1953, age 73 years. They are buried in Oystermouth Cemetery along with their son Ronnie, who also died young at 30 years old in 1935, and his wife.

On **March 31st, 1904**, the first **CONFIRMATION** was administered by Lord Bishop of St David's who requested that the service be held at St Peter's as he had not yet seen inside. He expressed great admiration for the building.

On June 29th, 1904, the first **PATRONAL FESTIVAL** was celebrated on St Peter's Day. Preacher: Revd C. Hayward Phillips of St Mary's, Pembroke.

Three very significant happenings in the life of the Church in Wales then occurred, the first having been delayed due to the First World War, namely: **March 31st, 1920**, the **Disestablishment of the Church in Wales** from this date The Church in Wales, comprising the four ancient dioceses of St Asaph, Bangor, St David's and Llandaff was created as a new province and separated from that of Canterbury, under the provisions of the Welsh Church Act 1914. In its early years, the young province founded two new dioceses, by proportioning two old ones, in the large, densely populated areas in the south; the diocese of Monmouth was carved out of Llandaff in 1921 and the diocese Swansea and Brecon out of St David's two years later.

On **June 24th, 1923**, the See (seat) of Swansea and Brecon came into existence and the Priory Church of St John, Brecon was chosen as its Cathedral. For administrative purposes its territory was apportioned between two archdeaconries: Brecon and Gower. The first Archdeacon of Gower to be appointed was Harold Stepney Williams.

February 1933: a Parochial division was formed out of its western part of Oystermouth Parish, which permitted the creation of the new parish of St Peter's, Newton. On February 4th, 1933, the Revd Hickin was instituted, by the Bishop, to the living in Newton Parish, as its first vicar (Phillips, E. I. E., 1973).

Jubilee Celebrations in the church

A special service was held at St Peter's on **November 19th, 1953**, to mark the **Church's Golden Jubilee**. It was attended by Ven. Harold S. Williams and a small group of people who were present at the original consecration service, fifty years earlier. The Vicar of Swansea, Canon J. J. A. Thomas, officiated.

A **60th Anniversary Service** was held on November 19th, 1963, conducted by the Bishop. Invitations were sent to all clergy in the Rural Deanery and to others outside the parish. Refreshments were served after the service, supervised by Mrs Brunsdon. The proceeds from the collection were devoted to church expenses.

The **70th Anniversary of the Consecration of St Peter's** was marked in **1973** by a number of events held throughout the year. Several preachers who had been connected with the church were invited to preach at various services. It was also the year of the **Golden Jubilee of the Diocese of Swansea and Brecon**. Mr E. I. Phillips, historian, compiled notes and anecdotes of the Parish of Oystermouth, including Newton, during the first half century of its life within the new diocese.

The **Queen's Silver Jubilee** in **1977** was celebrated by a service on June 5th. Also, later in June, during the Patronal Festival, there was a very successful Floral and Music Festival with concerts and receitals. Swansea Little Theatre put on a production of *'Under Milkwood'* and the Mothers' Union held a garden party.

The **Parish Golden Jubilee** in **1983** was celebrated throughout the year following the theme of thanksgiving and rededication. Three big services were arranged, the first in February to mark the anniversary, to which the bishop was invited to preach. The second was on St Peter's Day, in June, and another of thanksgiving at the end of the year. During the year a number of clergy were invited to preach who had associations with the parish. There was a pilgrimage to Caldey Island and special Lenten lectures given. Three services were broadcast and a recording of hymn-singing for *'Sunday Half Hour'* was on Radio 4. St Peter's people joined with others for the televising of *Songs of Praise* from Oystermouth Church. *Any Questions* was originally planned to be broadcast in the church during Jubilee Year but was deferred to January 1984. An illustrated talk on Newton 1933 was held at an open meeting of the Men's Society and an exhibition of memorabilia held in the Church Hall. A spectacular Floral Festival was held, during the Patronal Festival week. A souvenir booklet of a brief history of the parish was compiled and written by Miss G. P. Snow and Mrs Leslie Griffin.

Church Centennial Celebrations

Within the first three years, at the start of a new twenty-first century (2000-2003) three significant dates in the history of St Peter's were celebrated in the church. First there were many celebrations planned to mark the **Millennium**. A logo was devised, and the vicar wrote a new prayer for the Centenary of St Peter's Church. Throughout the year Mr Leslie Evans recorded all aspects of the parish life at Newton on video and a shortened version was made available for sale. The year was also marked by a successful Flower Festival based on the theme *Celebration 2000 – looking at the Christian influence on the Arts.* It was supported by the recently formed Newton Flower Group and open to the public. The local children of Newton Junior School were each presented with a Biblical book to mark the turn of a new century. During the week of the Petertide Festival, in June, the theme was *'Time'* and an exhibition was staged honouring the church's Patron Saint entitled: *"In the footsteps of St Peter, from Jerusalem to Rome and to St Peter's in Newton".* A special souvenir programme was printed to mark the occasion. There was also a walk organised to St Peter's Well and chapel, nearby, in Bishops Wood, referred to in chapter 1, 2000 was, appropriately, also the year of the Oberammergau Festival, in Austria, and a group from the church, joined by the vicar and his wife, attended.

2001: the **centenary of the Laying of the Foundation Stone** was remembered in September by a special Choral Evensong when Bishop David Thomas returned to preach. Also present was his wife, Rosemary, and another former vicar, Chancellor Harold E. Williams and his wife, as well as several other clergy including the Archdeacon of Gower, the Ven. Robert Williams. On the following Monday an Edwardian Soirée was organised with many folk present wearing appropriate costume of 100 years ago. There was also a small exhibition and a booklet was produced which briefly covered the church's history since the foundation stone was laid.

2003 was a milestone in the life of the parish when the **Centenary of St Peter's Church** was celebrated. The year also marked several other important dates in the history of the church. Firstly, to mark the **70th anniversary of the Institution of the Parish of Newton** a special Choral Evensong was held on February 9th and the Archdeacon of Gower, the Ven. Robert Williams, was invited to preach and the choir sang two anthems. Several neighbouring clergy from the deanery attended and tea was served after, so people had a chance to view a small exhibition.

Another highlight was the visit of the **Archbishop of Canterbury, Dr Rowan Williams**, who presided over a special Sung Eucharist service on June 21st, 2003. On the actual day of the consecration, **November 19th**, a **Centenary Sung Eucharist** was held and the guest preacher was the Revd Canon Roger Royle, a media celebrity. It was remarkable that three former vicars of the parish were also able to attend: Canon Brunsdon (it was sadly to be his last public outing for he died shortly after), the Ven. Harold Williams and the Rt Revd David Thomas.

During the actual week of the centenary, in November, an exhibition of memorabilia, photographs and records depicting the hundred year history of the church was held in the hall. This was followed by a Christmas Fayre.

*Clergy from the deanery attending Choral Evensong, marking the 70th anniversary
of the Institution of the Parish of Newton.
The Vicar, Revd Clive Jones in the foreground with the Archdeacon, Ven. Robert Williams.*

*St Peter's Centenary Service.
Canon Roger Royle, preacher; Archdeacon Harold Williams; Revd Clive Jones (Vicar);
Canon Kenneth Brunsdon; Bishop David Thomas.*

17.

The Sunday School

1. *Religious Education in Newton*

In the late 1600s and early 1700s few people thought it necessary to provide schooling for the lower classes, who would rarely move far from their native parish, or from the occupations of their forefathers; so a type of school was established during this period by religious organisations whose motive was the salvation of the souls of the poor, by introducing them to the Bible. In 1699 the Society for the Promotion of Christian Knowledge (S.P.C.K.) was founded. This society provided Bibles to help disseminate biblical and Christian values.

In 1731 the Revd Griffith Jones, Rector of Llanddowror, requested the S.P.C.K. to supply him with small Welsh Bibles to use in a school which he would set up in his parish. His request was granted, and his school successful. He then sent out itinerant teachers (usually poorly paid Anglican clergymen) to other parts of Wales to follow his example. The schools they set up usually lasted about 3 months, then the teacher moved on, but they did frequently re-visit. They were called *"Circulating Schools."* The first, and greatest number of these schools, were taught in Welsh, until it was realised that the few English-speaking areas were left out. This was remedied and thus Newton, in the Parish of Oystermouth, benefited from these visits and the pupils, of course, could be children or adults. The records report the numbers taught to read in Newton, viz: in 1743-44 there were 89 pupils, in 1744-45 there were 66 pupils, and in 1745-46 there were 55 pupils. People felt that the intensity of three months with the *Circulating Schools* interfered with the weekday labour of the children and adults, thus lowering their already poor standard of living. The end of the *Circulating Schools* in 1777 left a gap, but, in Wales, in 1785, a Calvinistic Methodist Minister, the Revd Thomas Charles of Bala, attempted unsuccessfully to revive them.

2. *The first Sunday Schools in Oystermouth Parish*

The Revd Thomas Charles of Bala discovered that regular weekly Sunday Schools were preferred, rather than the occasional *Circulating Schools*. As a result churches and chapels began to set up Sunday Schools for adults and children, in order to teach them to read the Bible.

The first Sunday School in Gower was set up by All Saints' Church in Oystermouth in 1805. Later, the Independents, or Congregationalists, established a Sunday School in Newton in 1818, when Paraclete Chapel was built, and in 1825 a Wesleyan Sunday School was set up in Oystermouth.

The Church Sunday School at Oystermouth had 74 pupils, twenty-one of whom walked more than a mile to get there. The meetings lasted for three and a half hours! The two dissenting Sunday Schools (Wesleyan and Congregational) had 116 pupils between them, 31 of whom were over 15 years of age. At that time the population of the parish of Oystermouth, covering Southend, Oystermouth, Newton, Norton and Blackpill was 1,482. In the 1841 census, an appreciative pupil, aged 25, described himself as: *"Farm labourer on weekdays, scholar on Sundays."*

Thoughts on Sunday School by Archdeacon H. S. Williams

"The Diocesan Authorities are making an effort throughout the whole Diocese to arouse greater interest in the Sunday Schools, and to improve our Sunday School methods. The Rural Dean has been asked to organise the effort in this Deanery of East Gower. A Meeting of the Teachers of the Swansea Churches was held on January 16th, when the Central Hall of the Oxford Street National Schools was crowded out. It was decided. 1. to appoint a committee composed of two representatives from each school. 2. to have an annual Children's Festival. 3. to have an annual Teachers' Service. 4. to have an annual Social gathering of the Swansea teachers and 5. to have Conferences to discuss Sunday School problems. The committee appointed are now meeting and will take immediate steps to bring these resolutions into effect."

Archdeacon Harold S. Williams also wrote later in the magazine: *"The Sunday School has got into a rut. It must be lifted out of it. The average Church-goer takes but little interest in the Sunday School. Many regard it as a pious fad of a few good people. Whereas it is the most important organization in the parish, everyone should be interested in it. What's the position today as to the religious education of the child?"*

Where is the child to get religious education? The only place is the Sunday School. If the Concordat becomes an accomplished fact, it is hoped that satisfactory instruction will be given to all children. But that day is not yet. There are many difficulties to face. Even if the Concordat does become a fact, the Sunday School will be very necessary to give our children instruction in Church Faith. From whatever point you look at it the Sunday School is a supremely important institution." (Oystermouth Parish Magazine, February 1922).

Ed: This article is just as pertinent today, nearly a hundred years later!

3. *Sunday School activities in Newton in the C20th*

The following records are extracts from the *Oystermouth Parish Magazines* and later the *Newton Parish Magazines.* They give an insight to the varied activities of the children throughout the century:

August 1908: Miss Dillwyn Llewellyn of The Cottage, Caswell, very kindly invited St Peter's Church children to a party at Caswell on Saturday afternoon. An address was given by one of the members of the Universities Mission to Central Africa.

August 1912: The 1st Flower Festival took place at St Peter's, as there were now too many children to get comfortably into All Saints. The children brought bunches of flowers, which were later taken to Swansea Hospital.

February 1913: Sunday School presented a silver pocket font with baptismal shell to Revd R. W. Jones, the curate, who was leaving.

April 1927: Sunday School performed a short missionary play, *"A Girl's Life in India,"* on 5th April. The Langland Orchestra played. In July the Sunday School children brought eggs, fruit and flowers to be sent to Swansea Hospital.

April 1932: Sunday School held a jumble sale to raise money for Sunday School funds. In **July** the children collected 870 corks to use in the dispensary of the Malacca Mission, at St David's Hospital.

October 1942: Sunday School children were given envelopes for the Waifs and Strays War Emergency Fund. They raised £4-4s.

October 1943: Hospital Sunday: The Children collected £1-7s-6d in place of the pre-war collection of eggs.

December 1949: Sunday School joined in the prayer book pageant at Stewart Hall, Sketty. St Peter's had the last scene, "Burial of the Dead".

December 1955: Sunday School children supported the "St Peter's Newton bed" at St Francis Hospital, Manahapur, India, run by the S.P.G.

March 1980: Sunday School children brought fresh eggs to the Family service on Easter Day. The eggs were distributed to those ill in the parish. During Mothering Sunday a Noah's Ark play was performed. In **September** for the first time, Children's pages were introduced in the *Newton Parish Magazine* – Joanna Parcell was editor and Catherine Cope, assistant.

December 1981: Bronwen Evans, Sue Evans, Catherine Rees, Zoe Bragg and Fenella Butler collected £3.72 at a Halloween party for the Children's Society.

August 1983 – Flower Festival. The children worked very hard at a delightful floral display, with a little help from the flower arranging ladies. Jan Dunster helped the tinys display the mustard and cress they had successfully grown.

June 1984: St Peter's took the "Last Supper" scene in a play performed by the Clyne Deanery Sunday Schools at All Saints'. At Christmas the children took part in the musical *"Hello Jesus"* by Leslie and Penny Ryan, with other Sunday Schools in the area.

August 1985: Diocesan Sports Weekend at Morfa. 24 children entered track and field events. Results were: Rachel Davies – 1st in 100 metres (7-9 yr olds) and 1st in long jump. Eve Daniels – 2nd in long jump (7-9 yr olds); Vanessa Butler – 1st in long jump (10-11 year olds); Michael Langford – 2nd in 100 metres (over 11) and 2nd in javelin.

February 1987: The 3-6 year olds had their party in the afternoon. The over six-year-olds and choir children met in the evening for games, disco music and chips. In December sixty Sunday School children went to The Grand Theatre to see *'Joseph and his Amazing Technicolour Dreamcoat'*. They were accompanied by parents, leaders and Revd Clarice Smith and the vicar, Revd David Thomas. On **20th December**, at a performance of the Nativity Play, the children collected £100 for the Ethiopian Famine Appeal and a further £326 was collected at the service.

May 1988: There was an outing to Brecon to "Meet the (new) Bishop" (Bishop Dewi Bridges). In the morning there was practice for orchestra followed by a picnic lunch with the service at 3 p.m. In **June** there were 132 Sunday School children, 10 leaders and 3 younger assistants. Revd Clarice Smith was commended for her work with them, encouraging teachers and children, and for her great assistance with workshops. At the Christingle Service the children brought Smartie tubes filled with pennies for the Children's Society. They raised £81.

1989: From the beginning of the year the time of Sunday School was changed from 11 a.m. to 9.30 a.m. so that the children could be in the church during the preparation for Eucharist. On the 2nd Sunday in the month there was a Family Service at 11 a.m. In **October** an outing to Dan-yr-Ogof Caves and Dinosaur Park and then to Craig-y-nos gardens was arranged.

1990: Sunday School children were congratulated for the orderly and reverent way they conducted themselves at the Eucharist at 9.30 a.m. Later in the day the infants brought teddies and dolls for a party and the juniors had a Tramps supper. In **July** the children from St Peter's joined a children's Mission Afternoon at St Hilary's, led by Brother Ramon. The annual outing was to Oakwood Park. 75 children, parents and grandparents went by double-decker bus.

1992: Children performed *"Hello Jesus"* again before Christmas.

1993: Mrs Ruth McNamara wrote a Nativity Play which the children performed. £100 was given to the Barrackpur Hostels project.

1994: July Children made a banner and performed a **tableau** about **Noah**.

1995: Smartie tubes at Christingle Service produced £85. £100 given for children's hostels at Canning and Shdua (India).

1996: Children now joined church members in church for the last part of the 10 a.m. service.

July 2000: The children attended a Diocesan children's Fun Day.

4. *Parties, trips and treats*

The children of Newton used the schoolroom of old Newton School for their Sunday School. In the early days the Sunday and Day schools of the whole parish combined for summer outings and Christmas festivities. In August 1903 all the children joined together for their annual treat in a field in Thistleboon. The older children, clergy, teachers and superintendents walked in procession through the village, then through Bracelet, led by the Mumbles Brass Band. The younger children were conveyed in brakes. 600 children sat down to tea, as well as a large number of parents.

After tea there were sports: running, skipping, 3 legged races and walking, a new craze! Before dispersing at 8.30 p.m. the children were given buns and sweets. The field was loaned by Mr T. W. James and his wife provided the sweets. The brakes were loaned by Mr Griffin and Messrs Baldwin and Ward. The offertories at July and August services defrayed the cost of food and prizes.

This was very much the pattern of Sunday School summer treats for many years to come. Similarly, at Christmas time there was an annual Christmas tea with prizes. Newton Sunday School held it locally in the schoolroom. In January 1906, at the tea party, good attendance prizes were given to Mabel Higgs, Jenny Roderick and Minnie Stephens. Class prizes were given to Adelaine Leonard and Ida Owen, Joan Francis, Stanley Hixson and Fred Bond. Entertainment consisted of a waxworks show, a Zimophone Band (instruments of combs and paper) and songs by Messrs Harold Williams and Llewellyn Jones, Miss F. Rayner and Miss S. Williams.

In May 1908 the vicar, Revd Harold S. Williams, made a request in the May magazine that: *"the congregation contribute £40 for the summer treat for 700 Sunday School members and 100 junior choir members. He did not feel it was too much to ask . . ."* In the June magazine he: *"regretted that only £35 had been collected, therefore he wished those, who had not been in church on May 31st for the collection, to send what they might have given, if they had been present."*

Over the years, and with the increase in road transport, outings and entertainment became more sophisticated, starting with Mr Bond's gramophone performance in 1908 followed by lantern slides, fancy dress competitions and outings to Port Eynon by bus. Port Eynon was the preferred destination for many years and in July 1940 the Sunday School children travelled in the yellow Swan buses, but it was to be their last summer outing for some years to come due to the outbreak of war.

When the war was over, treats were resumed. The Sunday School children, in 1948 were taken to the cinema. In 1956 the Young Wives took them to the circus, and in 1980 they went to Margam Park to enjoy rowing on the lake, the pets' corner and the adventure playground. In 1981 the children enjoyed an outing at Craig-y-nos Country Fair. 1983 saw them visiting Afon Argoed Country Park and in 1986 they travelled by double-decker bus to the Pembrey Country Park.

5. Memories of Sunday School and Outings

By Jean Haines: *"I probably started Sunday School in 1937 and continued for many years. I have few abiding memories of the school. At first school was held in Newton Infants School and there were at least two classes. Miss Rees was my teacher. As a spur to attendance we were given an album with spaces for each Sunday in the church year. When we attended we were given a stamp to stick in the appropriate space in the album. My strongest memory is of a Sunday School treat, an evening outing to Port Eynon probably in 1938. We had 2 Swan coaches and I was very disappointed to have to travel in the little Bedford coach and not in the large luxury coach in which the older children travelled. At Port Eynon there was a small fun fair and I can remember sitting on the floor of a swingboat between Miss Rees and another adult who were operating the boat. We also did a lot of chasing and sliding in the sand dunes. Later, during the war, I can remember having classes in the church under a Mrs Rosser, who I believe lived in Gloucester Place, Mumbles."*

By Valerie Peters (née Owen, in the late 1950s): *"When the war was over the Sunday School moved back to the Church Hall. Miss Snow was in charge and all of us who were learning the piano had to take our turn in playing the hymns. This I hated. One year all the Sunday Schools in Swansea had to take part in a pageant. St Peter's had the final Easter scene – I was Mary and I can still remember moving to the tomb entrance and seeing the stone rolled away. The scenery was marvellous. It was very moving. Shirley Collier, Margaret Davies, Angela Luckham, John Hixson, Ken Pickard and Richard Bowen were also in it. The Sunday School Christmas parties were always great fun. We always had chocolate spread sandwiches which were a real treat after wartime. Our Sunday School outings usually went to Horton* *and Port Eynon. When I was 16 Miss Snow asked me to teach in the infant Sunday School. I had always intended going into teaching so it was good practice".*

Our Sunday School outing, Saturday, 14th July, 1984, by Helen Clarke and Cathryn Dunster: *"I met my friend, Helen, at the Post Office. We got some sweets ready for the journey. We were going to Pembrey Country Park. We met our friends outside the vicarage at 10.30 a.m. The double-decker bus came and we rushed to the top, and downstairs the parents were in luxury! . . . We spent some time at the Adventure Playground. We had our lunch there and played cricket and then went for a long walk through the forest. Helen, Lucy and I were the only ones with a map, so we lead the way. The walk took us past the bird hide and onto the beach. It was very windy. Helen and I, and a few others went into the sea for a swim. We discovered later that two grandparents also braved the wind and long walk to the sea for a swim – it was really warm. We saw pieces of jelly-fish and told people to look out for them. Someone thought we said there were GIANT jelly-fish and ran to her mother screaming! . . . We had a picnic tea near the bus, prepared by some of the Mums . . . We got back to the church at 6.15 p.m. – tired, but happy."*

   The Sunday School Outing 1986. Writer unknown: *"I am writing this with my head still ringing! The Sunday School trip, which started after the family service on September 14th was a great success. Sixty-eight of us, aged from one to seventy-four went to Pembrey Country Park on a double-decker bus, taking lunch and tea. Mrs Meyrick led the swimming party and some children enjoyed donkey rides and the dads played football until exhausted . . . Later, the vicar and Clarice arrived and it was beautifully sunny.*

   We then moved in extended line to the adventure playground and the miniature railway. Dads and Mums and Grannies collapsed and the children worked off their last bits of energy until teatime.

   The bus ride home was the opposite of 'sensory deprivation' – I didn't know that children could make so much sustained noise! We were all safely home as the bell was sounding for the evening service. Thank you Jan, for organising the trip.

   Thank you, Mr Williams [the vicar], and Clarice, for having a word with the boss about the weather!

6. Sunday School Teachers in St Peter's

Sunday School teachers and helpers have always in demand and below are records of some who have helped over the years:

In **1912** the Sunday School Superintendent was Mr J. G. Morris and in **1913** the Sunday School teachers were: Misses H. W. Beor, Peel, V. Taylor, F. Rayner,

D. Trick and Mr J. G. Morris but by December **1913** it was "All change" for the teachers. Miss Naylor replaced Miss Beor, Miss Rayner led the boys' class and Miss Enid Evans was to oversee the music. Graham Robinson looked after books and boxes, and provided everything for the teachers so that they did not need to leave the children. Freda Rayner was now Superintendent and Miss V. Taylor was in charge of the mission boxes.

In **1954** the Swansea Sunday School Teachers Association attended Evensong at St Peter's and was entertained with light refreshments in the Church Hall afterwards.

In **1956** Josephine Richards, one of the teachers, was given an electric kettle by the Sunday School, on the occasion of her marriage to Jim Pressdee and in **1959** the Sunday School presented Miss Esme Owen, a teacher for many years, with an alarm clock to mark her forthcoming wedding.

In **1961** there was another exodus from the Sunday School, although the ever faithful Miss Snow was still in charge of the seniors. Miss Bossom retired, and was presented with a prayer book and hymn book as a memento of many years of faithful service. Misses Margaret Meyrick, Sandra Timothy and S. Bland were in charge of the juniors until Margaret Meyrick left to train as a nurse, and Penelope and Elizabeth Hunt took her place.

1979: Teachers were: Mrs N. Taylor, Mr G. Whattley, Mr J. Pickard, Mr R. Clarke, Mrs Haigh Elizabeth and Joanna Parcell, Katrina Penn and Caroline Thomas and thanks were recorded for their help over the years. However, in **1981** there is a cry for help – 3 young teachers were leaving to go to university. Mrs Taylor was still in charge of Sunday School.

In **1983** Jan Dunster led the Sunday School with Keith Davies, Meri Quinn, Valerie Cope and Andrea Penny, but in September Meri Quinn returned to Australia, Valerie Cope returned to College and Andrea Penny was not able to travel from Gowerton. By **1987** there was an enormous and flourishing Sunday School with an impressive team of leaders, including Jan Dunster, Pauline Vaughton, Grace Thomas, Jo Coulson and in **1989** Graham King joined. In **1991** Jan Dunster retired as leader after 8 years of service and Pauline Vaughton, another very experienced member of the team, took over.

A Letter from the vicar, David Thomas, expresses his great appreciation for Jan's leadership and co-ordination of Sunday School activities: "*She has done an enormous amount of sheer hard work in this capacity – Superintending the Sunday School week in week out, holding regular teachers' meetings, recruiting teachers and other helpers, organising all kinds of events from Nativity plays to parties and theatre trips . . . Running a Sunday School is a most important ministry within the Christian fellowship. It is largely thanks to Jan, with her deep commitment and infectious enthusiasm that our Sunday School has prospered and flourished so dramatically. When taking a confirmation class . . . which consisted entirely of Sunday School children, I was extremely impressed by how conversant they already were with the Bible and the basics of the Christian faith."*

He ends his letter with a quotation: *"Train up a child in the way he should go, and when he is old, he will not depart from it."* (Proverbs 22:6).

1992: It was felt that the Family Service should be tied more closely to what Sunday School was doing. The curate, David Davies, helped out some weeks.

1993: Ruth McNamara led the Sunday School and wrote the Nativity Play.

1994: Vivienne and Victoria Knill, Judy Partington and Ingrid Bowen continued to keep the Sunday School going. Mrs Vivienne Knill gave up in 1996 and Sue Evans and Jane Thomas took over.

In **1999** there was an appeal for someone to come to the rescue of the Sunday School and in the September the Sunday School was re-launched under the direction of Jane Thomas and Eirlys Oliver.

SOME SUNDAY SCHOOL OUTINGS FROM THE PAST . . .

18.

Day School Education in Newton

1. Day School Education in Newton in the 1800s

The widespread establishment of Day Schools took place in the early 1800s. Two societies substantially supported them: the National Society, which worked on behalf of the Established Church and the British Society, which was a non-sectarian organisation. In 1833 the Government gave grant aid to both these societies, and in 1839 a Committee of the Council of Education appointed Inspectors to ensure Government Aid was spent wisely.

The area of Gower, which included Newton, was given little aid, as the managers of the Gower Schools could not afford to provide either the schoolrooms or certified teachers required by Government standards. So the establishment and maintenance of the Gower Schools depended almost entirely on local benefactors, regular subscribers, and the trickle of weekly school pence from parents.

2. The Private Adventure School, 1819-1850

In 1846 a Commission of Inquiry into the State of Education in Wales was set up by the government. The results of the enquiry were bound in blue and sent for Government perusal. As they were less than complimentary to the mainly Welsh-speaking schools, they became known in Wales as *The Treacherous Blue Books.*

The Commission noted in its report, that there was, in Newton in 1847, "*A private Adventure School*" which had been supervised by an ex-naval purser since 1807. It had been established to educate the sons of wealthy farmers. The master was described as "hale and sharp". He had taught almost all the parish, and had then, with him, the grandsons of former pupils. He was recorded in the 1841 census as: "James Bennet, aged 70, schoolmaster in Newton."

However, it has now been discovered from the deeds, shown by Dr Stuart Cousens, that James Bennet took possession of "Pickett Mead Field and Close"

Pickett Mead House, Newton.

from John Kift in 1819 and established his school in Pickett Mead House, overlooking Pickett Mead. It remained there until 1850. (Sources: National Library of Wales. Dr Stuart Cousens.) [N.B.: Pickett as spelt in the deeds.]

3. Newton National School

The old Newton School in the early 1900s stood at the top end of Nottage Road, next to the old Nottage Farmhouse and the farm buildings. It was stone built and whitewashed with lime-wash every spring.

The original Newton School.

Newton National School was opened as a designated Church School under the auspices of the National Society in 1860. It was supervised by Church Managers, which made them responsible for the education, and the upkeep of the school building.

Mrs Henry Crawshay, wife of the Merthyr ironmaster, who had a summer house nearby at Langland Bay, was recorded as having held a garden fête in the grounds of their house in July 1862, in aid of funds for a new school room in Newton. She was also a benefactor of the school. The log book records numerous visits by her between 1867 and 1882.

In 1865 Newton School came under Government Inspection. All Government grants awarded to the school depended on the outcome of the inspections. The grant was often reduced as a result of the inadequate teaching by monitors and unqualified teachers.

The first inspection took place in 1867 when there were 52 children at the school. The report ended thus: *"As this test has not been satisfied by the examination of your school . . . My Lords have ordered one tenth to be deducted. Grant reduced."* Signed: *Secretan Jones*, vicar.

In 1869 the next H.M. Inspector's Report stated: *"A slight improvement in attendance and attainment of the scholars . . . My Lords will look for improvement another year."*

In 1878 things went from bad to worse. The registers were not marked, and 400 meetings were not registered, therefore . . . *"My Lords report that they are unable to make any grant for the past school year."* Thus the Managers came to depend on the charity and help of the local gentry, and the 'school pence' of 2d per week paid by each pupil.

In the school Log Book we are told of visiting ladies and gentlemen who helped with various lessons, including reading, sewing, knitting and scripture. Amongst them were the Misses Harriet, Emma and Annie Strick, Mrs Welby (the vicar's wife), Mrs Crawshay, Mrs Mainwaring, Miss Havergal and Miss Young. Others donated gifts of slates, jars of ink, pencils, copy books, wool, knitting needles and calico. Samuel Gillespie Prout Esq. presented the Mistress with a Sovereign to purchase a map of Palestine, and Scripture Books for the use of the children.

The school-pence from the parents were a regular source of income for the school. Defaulters must have been unusual, for only one is mentioned in the School Log Book. Willie Mock was sent home twice for his school fees – the second time he brought 2d instead of 8d. The School Board Officer called at his house as Willie Mock had been absent from school four times in the last week. His mother said he had not been kept home, and that she had given him all his school fees – naughty Willie Mock!

It can be seen that, for the first years of its existence, Newton National School was always in need of financial assistance.

4. Staffing

The Mistresses and Headmistresses of the
Old Newton School, 1865 to 1968

1865-1866:   Mary Howells, Mistress
1867-1871:   Mary E. Thomas, Mistress
1872-1878:   Lucie Wiseman, Mistress
1878-1891:   Sophia Mitchell, Mistress
1891-1924:   Ellen Howard, Mistress
1925-1928:   Wini L. Phillips, Headmistress
1928-1957:   Lilian M. Rees, Headmistress
1958-1968:   Gwladys Ferris, Headmistress

Women teachers in charge of a school were known as Mistress until the term 'Headmistress' was first used at the end of the 19th century by Frances Mary Buss, who ran a school in N. London for 44 years and died in 1894.

From 1860 to 1891 Newton School was staffed by unqualified Mistresses, which resulted in the loss of government grants. In order to improve the grant situation the managers decided in 1891 to appoint Miss Ellen Howard as Certified Mistress of Newton National School. She had completed her training at Carmarthen Training College for teachers.

When Miss Ellen Howard took up her post at Newton School, the Monitorial system of teaching was in existence, having been introduced into the National schools in the early 19th century by Dr Andrew Bell. The Mistress taught selected bright senior pupils, then they, in turn, taught classes of younger children. The School Log Book mentions several young monitors:

On April 25th, 1892: *"Edith Bailey commenced duties as a monitors."* In 1894 Edith signed her Indentures to begin training as a Pupil Teacher.

May 21st, 1895, records: *"Lilian Hixson, the monitor for the Infants class, having left school was temporarily replaced by Elizabeth Owen."*

February 24th, 1896: *"Georgina Dartnell began her duties as paid Monitor. She will have charge of the Infant class with occasional help from one of the 6th Standard girls."*

The Monitorial system evolved into the Apprentice System of Pupil Teachers, whereby promising young people signed indentures to study while teaching. They took examinations to qualify as certificated teachers. In September 1906 Edith Hartnett was appointed as a Pupil Teacher for 3 years at a salary of £7 for the 1st year, £8.10s for the 2nd year and £10 for the 3rd year. She could attend the classes for Pupil Teachers at Gowerton County School, provided that there was accommodation and that she paid her own railway fares.

There were many difficulties with salaries. In 1905 two assistants sent in their resignation, as the L.E.A. refused to pay them the whole of their salary, and the Managers were not able to make up the balance. Later in 1905 the County Council refused to pay any salaries for the month of August. However, a cheque for August salaries was received on September 22nd.

In the same year Miss Howard writes; *"Miss Symons intends sending in her resignation at the end of this month. She has been very dissatisfied for a long time, having passed the King's Scholarship nearly 2 years ago and is still earning only £30 per annum."*

5. Diocesan Examinations

In addition to Government Inspections, which examined the academic progress of the children, the standard of teaching and the condition of the buildings, there were regular and frequent Diocesan Inspections, which tested the children's religious education, their knowledge of the catechism and the Bible. In 1866 Mr Harriman Fisher visited the school and examined the children in reading, writing, spelling, arithmetic, scripture and catechism. There were monthly examinations and in 1891 the Annual Inspection took place in December. In July 1906 the Diocesan Inspector gave the following report on religious knowledge: *"The infants answered quietly and reverently. In standards II and III the work was thoroughly known. Standards IV, V, VI are a very interesting group."*

June 1912 Newton School Religious Inspection was supervised by Revd D. W. Thomas the Diocesan Inspector, who wrote in his report: *"Very good work is done in this school and the tone and discipline are excellent."*

March 1930 report of the Diocesan Inspectors on religious instruction states: *"The work was well done, and deserves very high praise. The oral work was*

This is Percy Luckham's Certificate which shows that Newton Church School was in the Diocese of St David at this time.

very pleasant to carry out, scholars being eager and alert to answer their questions. The written work was also very gratifying to read. The tone and discipline were excellent. The school deserves high praise also, for the work rendered in the infant department."

In October 1933 Newton Church of England School was transferred to the Council, and came under the control of the Local Education Authority so there were no more Diocesan inspections. Nevertheless, Religious Instruction in the school would still be given by the local vicar or curate.

6. A Village School

In the late 1800s and early 1900s, irregular attendance was sometimes a problem at Newton School. Farming was an important part of the life of the community, and all were expected to take part in the seasonal labours and even the children did their share. During the summer season donkeys were required to transport visitors from Oystermouth to Newton, Langland and Caswell. The older boys were in charge of the donkeys, so missed school.

Children were needed for the wheat harvest, the corn harvest, to set potatoes, to gather in the potatoes, and to help with haymaking. Seaweed was needed as a fertiliser for fields and gardens. Girls and boys took time off from school to gather and transport it from the beaches. Many of the older boys delivered milk in the morning, before school. They were often late or absent when the weather was wet, having found it necessary to go home to change their clothes. Parents took their sons from school to visit the Cattle fairs and ploughing matches. The children were taken from school by the teachers to the rickyards to see the threshing machine at work, or to see the new young lambs in the fields which surrounded the school.

They were often taken on rambles to look for specimens for their lessons – to show them which plants were poisonous, or to gather wild flowers for drying and pressing, finding as many as thirty different varieties. In springtime the children gathered primroses to decorate graves for Palm Sunday, and so earned a few coppers for themselves.

Although time was taken off from school for the regular farming tasks, the children worked hard at school work. In 1900 they learnt 'The Trial Scene' from the 'Merchant of Venice' and the 'Battle of Blenheim'. A parcel of toys was received from Sunlight Soap, as prizes, won for a writing competition for children under ten years old. Several of the older scholars in 1904 left to go to Higher Grade and Intermediate schools, whilst others left at the ages of 12, 13, or 14 to start work. Before a child could leave they had to be examined for a certificate of Proficiency (seen on page 182).

The threshing machine at the Nottage Farm, next to the School.

Newton Church School 1901.

In 1901 Ernest Rosser, who was almost 13, brought a note asking permission to leave school that day, as he had the chance of a situation as Messenger Boy at the Newton Post Office.

NOTE: He must have returned to school for this photograph (bottom, page 184), as he is the boy, with hat and pouch, standing next to the curate on the right.

In 1909, May Tarant, from Miss Dillwyn Llewelyn's Orphan Home, at Caswell, wished to leave to take up a place as kitchen maid, under her mother, who was a cook in a gentleman's house in Devonshire. Cecil Hughes, in 1910, needed a certificate of Proficiency, as his father wished to take him into his office as a typist. In 1917 Charles Talbot, who was nearly 14 years of age, applied for exemption having obtained a situation in the Post Office. At the same time Jack Dixon, aged 12 and in Standard V, applied for exemption in order to work at the local bakery. In 1923 Thomas Howell passed the Entrance Examination for Glanmor School. The children of the Village School were always happily occupied – never idle.

7. Interesting Snippets from the Newton School Log Book

The School Log Book gives us an insight into the joys and sorrows of contemporary life as they affected the school There were many more epidemics necessitating closure of the school in the earlier years, than in later times. In 1870 and 1875 fever was prevalent in Newton, and in 1870 there was also an outbreak of smallpox in the village. A high incidence of measles was noted in 1908. Influenza epidemics caused closure of the school for many weeks in 1918, 1919, 1922 and 1933. In January 1917 a goodly number of children were absent with broken chilblains on their feet. The opening of school was deferred for two weeks in September 1938 owing to an outbreak of Infantile Paralysis (Poliomyelitis) during the holidays.

Two great Lifeboat disasters are recorded, one in February 1903, and one in April 1947, when the entire crew of the Mumbles Lifeboat was lost. On each sad occasion the school was closed so that the children could line the route of the walking funerals to Oystermouth Cemetery. Many local families in Newton and Mumbles were affected by the deaths of these brave men.

From the 1890s water was pumped up from the fresh water stream at Caswell Bay. This supplied water to the school. But in 1910 the Water Works were damaged by storms, so there was no water on the school premises, for flushing the lavatories, or washing. The Mistress sent two boys through the village to 'Whetstone' pump to fetch water to dilute the disinfectant being used.

The school pupils in 1903.
Note the immaculate turnout of these village boys and their Mistress.

In September 1901 the school was given a holiday for the laying of the Foundation Stone for the New Church at Newton, and in November 1903 for the opening and Consecration of the newly built St Peter's Church.

The visit of Bostock Wantswell's Menagerie to Mumbles in May 1905, gave the children great excitement, and a half holiday.

On June 27th, 1906, there was an earthquake! Miss Howard reported it in the Log Book, thus: *"We were all rather startled by the earthquake. The partition shook and rattled violently. The goldfish bowl gave a lurch and the pictures swayed. The children took it very calmly. Not a child moved and in a very short time all settled down to work, as if nothing had happened."*

The Mistress was allowed to close the school for a half holiday in September 1907, so that she might hear the great Madame Patti singing.

During the First World War Miss Howard recorded the war efforts of the school. Wool was donated to be knitted into socks, helmets, body belts and scarves for the soldiers. The senior girls gave one hour extra time for this, every afternoon. Concerts in aid of Red Cross Funds were given, in 1915 and 1916. In 1917 Miss Howard wrote: *"The children gave a concert to the wounded soldiers, some of whom were old pupils of Newton School, and others were fathers of present scholars."* Later that year the children took part in a concert on the Mumbles Pier.

In 1919 the children were given an extra week's holiday to celebrate 'Peace' at the end of the war. In the same year Miss Howard wrote: *"A small school – several children having gone to a tea given for 'soldiers' orphans.'"*

Senior class with Miss Howard, c.1913/1916.
Gwyn Bowen, David Ripley, Edgar Long, Tommy Howell, Phyllis Rogers, Florrie Owen,
Cyril Luckham, Gwen Dixon, Violet Ripley, Ella Luckham, Lena Beynon, Kathleen Barry,
Alice Symons, Dolly Rosser, Averil Vaughan, Gladys Talbot, Billy Williams.

Newton School pupils, circa 1920.
Here we have Miss Lilian Hixson and Miss Ellen Howard with the following pupils:
Doris Roberts, William Jeffery, Tommy Powell, Graham Howell, Alfie Powell, Annie Ripley,
Eileen and Chrissie Rosser (twins), John Davies, Charlie Arnott,
Muriel Evans, Jimmy Mathias and Nellie Rosser.

1924.
John Smith, brother of Diney Smith is sitting Left of photo (he was killed at El Alamein).
Also included are Billy and Lewis Skilbeck, who lived in Nottage Farmhouse, adjoining the
school playground. Other pupils are thought to be: Flossie Rosser, Charlie Long, Milton Moore,
Lily Jones, Gordon Walters, Stella Jones, Dolly Butcher and Edith Hixson The teacher, Miss Davies,
had to resign from her post when she married to become Mrs Bell, as was the rule in those days.

In 1924 there was great excitement when the Prime Minister, Mr Ramsay Macdonald and his wife paid a visit to the Glynn Vivian Home of Rest for the Blind. Miss Howard took the children to Mary Twill Lane to see them arrive.

After their Coronation, in 1937, King George VI and Queen Elizabeth visited Swansea. The children travelled by Mumbles Train and bus to Trewyddfa Common, Plasmarl, to view the procession.

From 1939 to 1945 school was greatly disrupted by wartime air raids and restrictions, but normal school activities continued.

8. Newton School in the 20th Century

In 1904 the School became a **Church of England School**, under the authority of the Glamorgan County Council but still controlled by church managers. The vicar, Revd Harold Williams, as chairman of the school management committee, made an urgent appeal for funds to meet the expenditure of £320 required to meet the LEA's demand for improvements and certain alterations, as required by the new Education Act of 1902. If these requirements were not met within a certain time there was a real threat that the school would have to be closed.

The Borough Extension Scheme came into force on November 9th, 1918. The school then passed from the Glamorgan Authority to Swansea Education Authority.

In 1921 the school was divided thus:

(1) Infants department   (2) Standards I and II   (3) Standards III and IV.

(4) Standards V, VI, and VII.   The school leaving age was 14.

A reorganisation took place in March 1925. Newton Church of England School, with an age range of 5 to 14 years became an infant/junior school. Standards V, VI and VII – all the senior pupils – were transferred to Oystermouth Council School, a larger school, for all ages.

In October 1933, Newton Church of England School was transferred from the control of Church Managers to the Council. It was now to be known as **Newton Council School**. However, Religious Instruction was still in the hands of the local vicar.

From the beginning of the 20th century under the guidance of qualified Mistresses and Headmistresses the children made good progress, as shown by the Inspectors annual reports:

1904: As usual the report began: *"The room is far too crowded for efficient teaching,"* but went on to say: *"The lessons, however, are intelligently given, and, if the conditions were more comfortable, it is certain that the Mistresses would make this a very good school. The general tone is decidedly pleasing . . ."*

1921: *"English is generally a strong subject. The older pupils are eager readers which is reflected in free and fluent composition . . . the children evidently like to think for themselves. The tone and discipline left a highly favourable impression."*

1932: *"This is a happy little school, in which the staff has won the confidence of the pupils, so that they respond readily and make satisfactory progress . . . Individual records of progress are well kept . . . The work is carefully graded, the teaching conscientious and the pupils are anxious to give of their best . . . In general the school is a pleasant place to visit, and its condition reflects credit upon the Head Teacher and her two assistants."* [This was the last year in which Newton was a Church of England School.]

1937: *"The classroom is a delightful place, where modern ideas of Infant training are efficiently put into practice, with children who respond eagerly and naturally . . . Sound work is done in elementary subjects. Original composition showed a good range of ideas and of expression. Written work is neat and accurate . . . It was gratifying to note the importance attached by the Head teacher to the inclusion of good speech habits . . . The atmosphere of the school is very pleasant."*

From the beginning of the century the school building was gradually improved and modernised. A new cloakroom was added in addition to the porch in 1904. Then the schoolroom was extended by 9 or 10 feet, and a glass folding partition was erected, so as to form a separate room. At the same time the playground was improved, so that the children could have 'Physical Exercise Lessons'. More renovations were carried out in 1935. The school was re-roofed; large windows of a modern type replaced the old ones; the old lavatories were demolished and modern replacements were built – still outside. A portion of the yard was covered with asphalt and part of the boundary wall was rebuilt. The rooms of the School House, in which the Headmistress had previously resided, were converted for the use of the school. Finally, electric light was installed throughout the building, replacing the old gas lighting. These major alterations brought the school up-to-date.

In 1909 **School Medical Inspections** and visits from the School Nurse began. The school was connected to the main drainage system in 1910. In 1934 milk was supplied daily to the school in ⅓ pint bottles at a cost of ½d per bottle. In 1938 one of the rooms in the School House was equipped as a Staff and Medical Inspection room, and another as a craft room.

World War 2 disrupted school life from 1939 to 1945. School times were constantly changed. Air raids by day and night disturbed the children. Holidays were staggered. Gas masks were always carried to and from school. In 1941 an air raid shelter was erected in the school yard. After the war the school moved back to normal routine.

In 1947 wireless sets were installed in both classrooms. In September of that year another reorganisation took place. J3 children were to be transferred to Mumbles Junior School. However, there was a lack of accommodation at Mumbles Junior School, so J3 remained at Newton School for another year.

9. Changing Times

After the end of World War II there was a great building boom. The old village of Newton was expanding into a suburb. As a result Old Newton School was bursting at the seams. The Local Authority felt that the solution was to send children from Newton to the Grange School at West Cross, and Mumbles School in the Dunns, both of which had spare places. A public meeting was called at St Peter's Church Hall, in order that parents should be told of the plans by the Local Education Officers, and also meet the Heads of the two appointed schools. The meeting did not go the way the Local Authority had expected. Parents felt that as no transport would be provided, the distances were too great for young children, and the roads too dangerous. Apart from which, land had long been set aside in Newton, for a new school. They protested vehemently that they wished their children to remain in Newton. Canon Brunsdon offered the use of St Peter's Church Hall as temporary classrooms for the excess children. This offer was accepted, and later demountable classrooms were set up in the school playground. The new replacement school at Slade Road was occupied in 1968. The old School was sold to be converted into a hotel and restaurant. Without the determination of those 1960s parents, there would have been no school in Newton.

Class Photos

1948.

1955.
Photograph includes: Mrs Davies, Ruth John, Mary Evans, Janette Scott, Susan Cousins, James Webborn Gerald Gabb, Iain Fairley, Menna John, Susan O'Nions, Suzanne Rolfe, Elaine Walters, Christine Francis Brian Owens, Robert Radcliffe, Robert Harris, Jimmy Thomas, Robert Fairley, Roger Blyth Michael Pickard, Philip Jordan, David Hutchinson, Timothy Douglas Jones, Howard Davies.

Class 1957.
Photograph includes: Richard Budge, Geoffrey Thompson, David Haines, Andrew Mathieson
David Frame, Robbie Evans, Bruce Rolfe, Alexandra Bloxham, Anne Davies.

St David's Day, 1959.
Canon Hickin at the entrance to the old school, with Mrs Ferris.
The children in Welsh costume are: Nia Morris, Elaine Morris, Jane Lewis, Lynne Lewis.
Phillip Jordan holds the flag.

Newton School Staff, 1960s.
Back row: *Mrs Pickering, Mrs Jones and Mrs Price (the dinner ladies).*
Attendance Officer: Mr Ron Price.
Front row: *Teaching staff: Miss Thomas, Mrs Ferris, Mrs Davies, Mrs James.*

1968.
The children playing on last day at the old school.

19.

A Brief Account of Life in Newton
in the Early 20th Century

Occupations in Newton in 1901

Farming
(Information contributed by Mervyn Owen and Valerie Peters, née Owen)

According to the 1901 census the occupations of Newton inhabitants were many and varied but were predominately farming, fishing, quarrying and stonemasons. The village was predominately a farming area at the turn of the century. There were 11 Farmers employing 9 Farm Labourers, and 8 Market-gardeners. Many of the farm holdings had fields scattered about the village. They were not compact as seen further north of the parish in the Ordnance Survey Map of 1899. Plot 422 was to be the site for the new church, to be named St Peter's Church (see also Tithe map page 16).

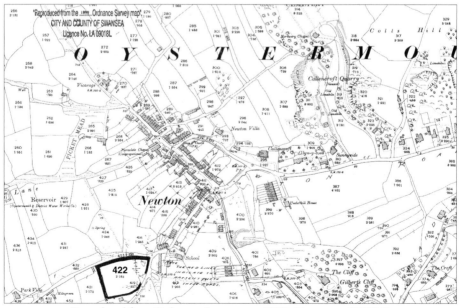

Reproduced from Ordnance Survey map 1899. (Courtesy of WGAS).

Newton Village in the early 1900s.
(Photograph by A. E. Way).

Nottage Farmhouse stood at the sharp bend opposite St Peter's Church. It was not easily seen until about 1900, when the present road, from Southward Lane to St Peter's Church, was made. Before that, the old road to Caswell Bay from Oystermouth passed through Newton Village via Nottage Road.

Nottage Farmhouse in the early 1900s.
(Photograph supplied by Mrs Annie Noakes).

Farm buildings of Nottage Farm.
They were demolished to build Nottage Mews.

The farmhouse was built in about 1630, and was a good example of a type built for moderately prosperous farmers, and even for the lesser gentry, in the late 16th and early 17th century. The Grove family owned the farm, which was tenanted by various farmers: 1843–Richard Parry, 1861–Samuel Cook, 1871–Phillip Gwynn and 1910–John Woollacott, whose son William occupied the farmhouse. The Grove family remained the landowners until the farmhouse was eventually demolished. Their Estate owned the land on which St Peter's Church was built (see also page 30).

Sketch of cutting the chaff at Newton Farm.

New Hill Farmhouse was built in 1776 by Samuel Gammon, who was a surveyor. It sits just above Paraclete Chapel in Newton Road and was built as a replacement for the small cottage adjoining it, in which John Owen, his wife and family lived.

When John Owen died, Samuel Gammon married his widow, and subsequently enlarged and modernised the Owen farm. He was an extremely well educated man. During the 19th century the Owens held many posts of authority, being Guardians of the Poor, as well as acting as Jurors at the Court Leet. The farmhouse was occupied by the Owen family until the end of the twentieth century, when Mervyn Owen the last of the main line died. At the beginning of this century the restoration of the farmhouse, the original cottage, and the barns took place, thus keeping a part of old Newton intact.

New Hill Farmhouse.

Farm Buildings of New Hill Farm.

The old farm buildings – cow shed, stable, cart shed, etc. are older than the house. Apparently they were originally small cottages with half lofts, which had ladder access. They were called tallots. Farm hands hired at the Hiring Fairs slept in the lofts. New Hill Farmhouse still exists at **163 Newton Road**.

Nottage Cottage is where twins, George and Eric Owen, were born in 1904. It is situated in Nottage Road, next to the Old Newton School. Their father, 'Thomas', farmed there, and the cow-stalls were built behind the house. The cottage has now been modernised.

Whitestone Farm

The farm house was built in Whitestone Lane with outbuildings of cow-stalls and stables, etc. for Thomas Owen, on land he owned. He and his family moved there in 1908.

In 1982 George Owen, his son and owner, described farming in Newton as it had been eighty years before: *"Newton was a locality of small farms, seven in all, with less than 50 acres each, where they kept a few cows and one or two had sheep. The milk from the cows was delivered to the houses in the area in cans, measured out to customers at their doorstep into jugs twice daily.*

"In those days the ploughing was done with two horses pulling a one-furrow plough, with the man walking at the handles of the plough. Then came the hay harvest. The hay was cut with the mower, left to dry for a day, after which it was turned by hand with wooden rakes and then raked into rows with the horse rake. When it was harvested, it was pitched into the cart by hand picks.

Until the reaper and binder arrived on the farming scene about this time, the corn was cut by hand with the scythe and we followed the scythe cutters, binding the swathes into sheaves and putting them to stand in stooks, six sheaves to a stook. After a few days drying they were pitched with pitchforks into a cart which had a wooden frame fixed on it called a Treble and when the load was well up, it was taken to the yard.

"About October a big Steam engine pulling a threshing machine arrived on the scene and went around each farm and threshed the corn. This was the time when all the local farmers joined together and helped each other – a very busy time indeed.

"Next the potato harvest came. This was done with a plough-like implement which split the row open and the potatoes were raked out of the earth with a tool called a Gaff, then the boys picked them up. The root crop was next on the calendar. Mangolds were grown

A sketch of the new threshing machine.

197

George Owen and son, Ivor, delivering milk.

for the cattle in the winter, so these were brought in and stored in big long heaps and covered with earth to keep the frost out.

"These, then, were the main items of the farmers' year. In the winter, of course they were kept busy hedge cutting and keeping the fences tidy."

A sketch of John Owen's Farm

John Owen's farmhouse can still be seen today and is now **135 Newton Road**. It belonged to John and Maggie Owen. He was the brother of Thomas Owen and uncle of George Owen of Whitestone Farm.

He was always known locally as Bowler John because he invariably wore a bowler hat, be it for hay-making, milking or bringing in the cows. Every local farmer lent a hand at haymaking. Later, the barn was burnt down.

Bidder's Farm. This was a small farm at the lower end of the village, seen on the right of the photograph. The farmhouse has long since been demolished.

Bosworth's Farm.

Bosworth's Farmhouse was at Highpool. Highmead and De Mowbray Housing estates are built on their fields. To the left of the photograph the site of the old barn can be seen. It has since had a modern barn conversion. Miss Bosworth used a yoke to carry the pails of milk.

Quarrymen and Stonemasons

The limestone of Gower was also evident between Caswell and Newton and it provided a livelihood to several of the local quarrymen. The names of Kiln Green and Kiln Cottage suggest that there may have been a limekiln in the vicinity just as there was at nearby Norton. The limestone quarry at Colts'

Hill employed 16 Quarrymen and Stone Masons. It was one of the quarries from which Mumbles Marble was extracted and manufactured at West Cross in earlier years. Several local men, living in or near Nottage Road were employed as stonemasons working on the building of the new church, nearby. Fred Bessant (seen opposite) was one of the Newton stonemasons who built St Peter's Church. He was the grandfather of Clifford Bessant and Margaret O'Brien who still live in Newton.

Other occupations (1901 Census)

Amongst the wealthier people in Newton were 14 people who had their own means. In addition there were: 1 East India Merchant, 1 Coffee Merchant, 1 Timber Merchant, 1 Iron Merchant, 1 Colliery Proprietor, 1 Land Agent, 1 Hardware Manufacturer and 1 Stocks and Shares Broker, an Inland Revenue Officer, 1 Bank Manager, 1 Solicitor, 1 Solicitor's Clerk, 1 Book Keeper, 1 Clerk, 1 Railway Clerk and 1 Miller's Clerk, all of whom possibly worked in Swansea.

The large houses scattered around the village also required staff. The gentry probably employed most of the 23 General Domestics, 13 Cooks, 11 House-maids, 1 Ladies Maid, 1 Governess, 1 Manservant and 8 Groom/ Gardeners.

The Village had 1 Music Teacher, 2 Dressmakers, a School Attendance Officer and 1 Police Constable to keep order. Three people kept boarding houses and 2 kept hotels. They were the probable employers of 1 Barman, 1 Waiter, 1 Waitress, 2 Chamber Maids, 1 Stillroom Maid and 1 Victualler.

The Matron and Under Matron, of Miss Dillwyn Llewelyn's Home for Orphans, at Caswell Cottage, lived in Newton, as did 4 Nurses, 1 Monthly Nurse, 1 Sick Nurse and 2 Laundresses.

Provisions were supplied by 1 Coal Merchant, 4 Bakers, 2 Butchers, 1 Chemist, 1 Grocer, 1 Boot-maker, 1 Shop Assistant, 1 Fishmonger, 1 Watchmaker, 1 Mattress Maker, 1 Wheelwright and 1 Seaweed Seller.

In 1913/14 there was a small farm behind the inn, The Rock and Fountain. Next to it was a baker's shop with a stone oven. [The baker's shop possibly belonged to the Howell family, which, in the 1800s exerted great influence in the village of Newton, and continued to bake bread until the mid 1900s.]

The sea gave employment to 1 Ship Owner, 1 Ship's Rigger, 3 Merchant Sailors and 1 Fisherman.

Some of the 22 General Labourers were probably employed by the 2 Builders. There was also 1 Road Labourer.

Newton must have appealed to retired people. Living there were 1 Retired Ship's Master, 1 Retired Chemist, 1 Retired School Mistress, 1 Retired Draper and 1 Retired Ship Broker.

The fact that the 1901 census records only one person in Newton as *"living on the Parish"* [today's Social Security] illustrates that Newton was a prosperous area, with hardworking inhabitants.

At this time the Swansea and Mumbles Railway Co. ran steam trains to Oystermouth and the L & NW steam trains had a station at Blackpill, nearby, so improving communications to Swansea and further afield.

Donkey transport

(Notes from Betty Sivertsen's memoirs in early C20th, *Walks around the Newton of my childhood*)

In the late 1800s and early 1900s the accepted mode of transport for visitors to and from Newton was the donkey and local people walked (shank's pony!): *"The donkeys were kept in a field, by the Castle, in Mumbles. They would be taken down to the station when the Mumbles Train came in. When they had taken their passengers up the hill to Newton they were rested, until required again, and fed in the ground behind the middle cottage of the village. They were led through an archway which was used as a back entrance for the adjacent cottages."*

This was often the job for the older school boys who were usually in charge of the donkeys, as may be seen in the School Log Book in the early C20th: On April 19th – *"The donkey season commenced."* On July 24th – *"A very nice day. All elder children required for the donkeys."* On September 7th – *"The donkey season: trade very brisk"* and on November 3rd – *"Donkey season over."*

Donkey carts outside Oystermouth Castle, c.1910.
(Photograph by Williams and Curmuck, Newport, Mons.).

201

The Inns of Newton Village

(Sources: Brian Davies and Diana Smith)

Older residents of Newton can remember hops growing wild in the hedgerows. Farmers and cottagers all cultivated hops and brewed their own beer. The old inns also brewed their own. There have been four inns in Newton.

The first inn was the old **Ship Inn**, probably dating from the 1700s. It occupied the site on which we find Newton Garage today, and was probably a smallholding as well as an Inn. It carried on business until 1860.

Next, was the **Rock and Fountain**, opposite the Ship Inn. It was probably established about 1750. The landlord was described as a *"Brewer, Farmer, Undertaker and Wheelwright"* – a Jack of all trades.

In about 1836 John Woollacott became victualler. In 1863 it was handed on to his son Richard, who ran it until 1911. He left it to his son Thomas. After the death of Thomas, his wife Louisa became the licensee until after the 2nd World War, when she sold it to Gerry Munday. The Rock and Fountain had been in the Woollacott family for 111 years.

In the early 1920s there was a fire at the "Rock". The fire cart from Mumbles could not get up the hill so all the available men from the village formed a chain, passing buckets of water from the pump outside the Post Office and so extinguished the fire.

The **Ship and Castle** came next in the 1840s. It was built across the road from the old Ship Inn. The Swansea Old Brewery Company owned it until 1912, when it was transferred to Hancocks, who had their beer delivered by horse drawn dray up the steep hill of New Well Lane. Going down the hill was even more hazardous for the horses, so the dray was held back by huge metal bars.

The Ship and Castle later became the Newton Inn.

202

In 1927 the Ship and Castle became the **Newton Inn**, in order not to be associated with the Ship and Castle at Southend, in Mumbles, which had been prosecuted for allowing the premises to be used as a brothel. The first victualler, in the 1840s, was John Davies. John Gammon became licensee later. In the 1920s the Heckler family were licensees. Iorrie Evans took over and ran the inn for about 30 years. The Rock and Fountain and the Newton Inn are both an important part of the village today.

Little is known about the fourth inn, which was the **Caswell Inn**, in a good position to serve travellers, visitors and villagers.

This is the house which John Smith extended front-wards in the late 1800s. The Caswell Inn was situated at the rear of this house in Nottage Road opposite Roger Woollacott's shop.

Health in the Village

During the nineteenth century there had been two serious outbreaks of cholera in Swansea and districts, which included Oystermouth and Newton, caused by primitive sanitary arrangements and overcrowding. At the time of the last outbreak a medical report stated that: *"In 1849 Newton village was found defective in a remarkable degree . . . in the Nottage area there were several stagnant pools . . ."*

A non-existent drainage scheme and lack of efficient water supply continued to be a problem almost up to the end of the century. Sewage matter permeated sections of the ground adjacent or near buildings and a number of wells were contaminated as a result. At one time it was not unusual to see notices in Newton with warning messages that "the water from the wells was not fit for drinking or cooking purposes". The Public Health Act of 1875 led to the formation of the Oystermouth Urban Sanitary Authority. It was run by a board of twelve who set about addressing these matters.

The estimated population had increased by leaps and bounds since 1896 and rose even further during the summer months. This meant greater numbers of inhabited dwellings. Regular public health reports were issued.

In 1901 the Medical Officer of Health for Oystermouth Urban District (which included the village of Newton), was Dr Arthur Lloyd Jones. In his report the doctor stated that the population of Oystermouth was 4,460 (including 33 based on board vessels) made up of 2,540 females and 1,920 males. The area of the district was 2,615 acres, with 1.7 inhabitants per acre. There was an average of 104 births and 61 deaths per annum. The infant mortality was small compared to other areas in Glamorgan and there was a low general death rate as a result of the health and longevity in the district. Dr Lloyd Jones remarked that there was a wonderful exemption from infectious diseases. Only 30 were notified during the year – 3 of sporadic scarlet fever, 4 of diphtheria and the remaining 6 were of whooping cough and erysipelas.

The total number of deaths during the year was 77 (41 males and 36 females). Causes of death were: 10 senile decay over 65 years, 8 heart disease, 4 paralysis, 15 natural old age, 19 consumption, 5 respiratory, and 18 infancy. However he recorded that there was an increase, so he felt it was necessary for notification of diseases and consequently supervision of adequate housing, drainage, feeding, clothing, and disinfection.

An efficient **Water Supply** had an important bearing on the sanitary state of the area. When an epidemic of sickness and diarrhoea at Newton was reported it was ascribed to the drinking water and the effluvia emanating from Newton's open sewer. He observed that in the district there were 28 dairies, cowsheds and milk shops.

Sewage Disposal in Newton was partially completed to include Nottage and New Well Lane, but the village proper was, so far, left as an open drain. The incomplete system discharged itself onto Underhill fields and originally emptied itself into a cavern alongside Glyn Cerrig (the doctor's home, in Newton Road). Other parts of the district drained into cesspools. The by-law for cementing the sides and bottoms of the cesspools had not been enforced.

Refuse. Ashpits, middens, and refuse heaps were cleared on appointed days. Caswell and Newton tipping ground was opposite the site for the New Church, and the Langland area put tippings in Thistleboon Lane. The soiled papers made an ugly mess on these neighbourhoods in dry and windy weather. Residents were encouraged to burn most of their litter.

Roads. The sweeping and cleaning by scavenger staff was alright in the winter, but in the summer it was a problem because of the great increase of trippers and dust. The public water supply was not constant and the air was filled with germ laden dust. Dr Lloyd Jones suggested the use of sea water. However, in Newton there was a pump and pistle so water was generally abundant.

The water supply

From early days there were several wells in Newton. There was one in Summerland Lane and a large well in the garden of Bryn Arden, the last house on the left hand side of Nottage Road. Many of the larger houses had their own wells. There was also the village pump at the top of New Well Lane but the water supply was often unreliable. Betty Siversten remembers as a child (early 1920s) playing in the gully which ran down the right hand side of the village from Picket Mead and disappeared into a culvert on the corner of Nottage Road

As the population rose there was a limited source of unpolluted water. However, in 1879 Major Morgan, who had bought land at Caswell Bay, purchased the water rights from a spring under his land from the Duke of Beaufort. Major Morgan formed a small, local private company with Mr Roger Beck and Sir John Jones Jenkins among others. This was the beginning of the public water supply at Mumbles. In 1881 the springs were tapped at the Freshwater Caves, in the western corner of Caswell Bay, and a windmill was built over the site to help the pump which was installed in an engine house at Caswell Bay. Water was pumped along a 5 inch pipe up into a small service reservoir at the top of Caswell Hill, at Kiln Green. This was 270 to 280 feet above sea level and from there it was to be linked to a system of mains. In 1882 it was actually supplying Mumbles with water as well as Newton but at first only the more wealthy residents could afford to be connected. In 1890 the Oystermouth Waterworks Co. Ltd. took it over and this contract lasted until 1918. By 1901 the windmill was no longer in use as the pumping station had been equipped with 2 oil engines which pumped about 12,000 gallons hourly up into the Kiln Green reservoir. It possessed no filter bed and supplies remained intermittent during the few hours each day it was in operation and

Postcard view of Caswell Bay showing the windmill on the hill, the pump station on the beach and Caswell Bay Hotel.

during droughts the reservoir failed to meet the local needs. The volume of water which emerged from the Freshwater Springs was tremendous, and this constant supply was increased directly after rainfall. However, at times of heavy flood it was often contaminated and at exceptional high tides it would taste salty. The windmill remained a landmark until it was destroyed by fire in 1930.

Unfortunately, the design of the reservoir was not efficient, so that much of the water collected there was stagnant. The reservoir was not covered, and so encouraged insect and vegetable life. Although frequent attempts were made to clear the reservoir, the water was not as clean as it might have been. There were occasional problems with the supply, as noted by Miss Ellen Howard, Mistress of Newton Village School. In September 1909 there had been no water in the tanks for 4 days. She reported it to the M.O.H., Dr Lloyd Jones. For one week the school had no water owing to damage to the waterworks caused by storms. In July 1911 the weather was very dry and there was no water in the lavatories – indeed, they had not been flushed for 2 weeks. Miss Howard had to send boys to Whetstone Pump to fetch water to dilute the disinfectant, which she found necessary to use every day during the shortage of water. Obviously the water supply was far from satisfactory.

The Post Office

The original Post Office was in the old off-licence next to the 'Rock and Fountain'. Before 1898 the Misses Potts were in charge. In 1898 Miss Gibbs, from Cardiff, became Post Mistress. She took up her duties at the tender age of 18.

The cottage in the photograph, by M. A. Clare, was demolished in the early 1900s to make room for the new Post Office. The village pump, and a gas lamp to light up Newton Road stand in front of the cottage. Note the open drainage along the left.

Miss Gibbs expanded her business in the new premises, selling items of clothing and newspapers, as well as carrying out the usual Post Office

M. A. Clare

business. The newspapers were brought to Mumbles on the old Mumbles steam train, and carried up to Newton by the paper boys. Miss Gibbs was an enthusiastic member of St Peter's Church choir, which presented her with an epergne, as a wedding gift, when in 1914 she married Mr Vosper Bevan of Mumbles. They

The newly built Post Office.
The gas lamp and pump may still be seen.

took up residence in the Post Office building. Their son, Denzil, was born there and later ran the paper shop with his wife, Valerie at the lower end of the village.

The Advent of Motorised Transport

Mrs Betty Sivertsen, a local resident since the 1920s, still remembers the horse-drawn carriages of Mr Abse Peachey waiting in Mumbles square.

She writes: *"He had an immaculate team and even to his dress, he charmed the ladies in the big houses in Newton who liked him."*

However, after the 1914-18 War, motorised vehicles became a more popular means of transport. Doubtless many of the occupants of the large houses around Newton invested in a motor car. Miss D. B. Fry, of Groves Avenue was thought to have been one of the first to own a vehicle.

Mr James Alfred Davies saw the need for a local garage, and shortly after the end of World War I he was in the business of repair and maintenance of motor vehicles. He continued with his business until his son Jim Davies, junior, took over in the 1930s, and improved the garage and continued in the business as a mechanic, as cars increased in number.

MAY, MAY 15, 1924

If you want
Comfortable & Roomy
Taxi Landaulettes
Ring up

BOND.

Mumbles 36.
Telegrams : Bond, Newton, Glam.

1924
Bond's Taxi Service was based
In Nottage Road, Newton next to
Newton School.
The advertisement for Bond's
Garage can be seen in the
photographs of the Football and
Hockey Teams. It was placed in
the window of the house which
is sideways on to the road, with
its front facing the school.

Bond's Taxi business was started in the 1920s based in Nottage Road, Newton, next to Newton School. It was owned by Mr Fred Bond. Taxis gave a more comfortable journey from Mumbles than the donkeys!

In 1957 John Ace took over the garage and again improved and extended it. The two cottages adjoining the garage were demolished, giving an extended area for additional petrol pumps and parking facilities.

The next owners were Mr and Mrs Greenslade who employed mechanics, whilst Sally Greenslade dealt with the business side of bills and accounts. Sadly, her life ended tragically. She was found dead in one of the vehicles with the engine running, by one of the mechanics.

The two chief mechanics, Stuart Smith and Robert Mills, bought the business and the garage, which started way back in the early 1900s and is still going strong today in the 21st century.

With the advent of the motor car, so came the buses. Again, Mrs Sivertsen remembers: *". . . there was a bus service to Caswell and Newton. People would catch it at [St Peter's] Church. It was always on time with kind, helpful drivers and conductors. They would look out for their regular customers and always connect with the Mumbles train both ways. In summer months the buses were always full. They would groan their way up Caswell Hill, often giving up half way. Then the passengers would get off and walk to the top of the hill and get back on the bus."*

Some interesting houses around Newton, many associated with some of the benefactors to St Peter's Church

The last thatched cottage. The house in Southward Lane, opposite the paper shop, was the last remaining thatched cottage in Newton. The thatch was replaced by a flat roof. Around the edge of the roof the stones were crenellated, so that they looked like battlements.

A man called Harry lived there with his wife and sister. They were rather odd so the house was known locally as "Mad Harry's Castle". The present

owner has had the flat roof replaced by a pitched roof. The walls are rendered and the house has been entirely modernised.

Rotherslade House was built in 1848 by John Jenkins near, what is now, the junction of Rotherslade Road with Langland Road, at Langland Corner. The house was described as being a two storeyed

Rotherslade House, circa 1920.

villa, with five or six bedrooms, the ground-floor had three bay windows facing the sea.

John J. Jenkins (1803-1868), a man of many talents, had a business as a clockmaker in Swansea. He was interested in astrology and was a member of the Royal Institution. His journeys to and from Swansea were as a passenger on the old horse-drawn Mumbles Train. At one time Dr A. Lloyd-Jones' family occupied the house, but it was demolished in the 1930s for road widening. At the time of building there were few houses in the vicinity.

A larger house close by, **Fairfield Villa**, was built by Crawshay Bailey (of the Merthyr iron-master family) as a summer cottage, and is now **2 Overland Road.**

Langland Road was not built until 1856. Previously, access to Langland corner was via Newton village and Southward Lane (Hart, R. J. 1997).

Osborne Cottage. In the 1850s, the photographer Attwell Francis' uncle built a cottage at Rotherslade, which was used later as a holiday cottage by the John Crow Richardson family. They were ship owners and dealt in the copper trade. The grandson, Ernald Edward, married Irene Caroline, née Burgess, also of a shipping family (see page 49).

After Mr Ernald Richardson died in 1909 at the age of 40 his widow, Mrs Irene Caroline Richardson moved to **Mentone**, further west along Langland Bay. She was a very religious lady. She re-named the house **Tawelfa** (house of peace) and it was there she founded the *Daisy League* for young children to learn Biblical stories (refer to page 127). She was also a generous benefactor to St Peter's Church. **Osborne Cottage** was described in the 1870 *Swansea Guide* as: *". . . perched on the cliff is a pleasant little bathing box of Messrs Richardson."* By 1880 it had been upgraded to a: *"charming marine residence . . ."* and was enlarged again in 1887 to become **The Osborne Hotel**.

Osborne Cottage.
(Atwell Francis album, Swansea Museum, SWASM. 1992. 26).

The Osborne Hotel started as a temperance hotel and in the C20th it was run, for awhile, by the Bassetts of the *Evening Post* and one time Mayor of Swansea. Alas, the building will see no more changes for it has been demolished and is now the site of luxury flats.

Rotherslade Bay has also seen many changes. The original rickety pathway, leading down the rocky face to the bay, gave way to a concrete edifice known locally as the "white elephant", until it was abandoned and for many years remained a derelict eyesore. After further deterioration, caused by wind and waves, it was demolished. Now, it has been landscaped with restructured steps and pathway leading to the bay.

Henry Crawshay's Marine Residence, 1864.
(Swansea Museum)

The Marine Residence of Henry Crawshay. This magnificent building with its tall tower has dominated Langland Bay since 1856, when it was built as a seaside retreat by Henry Crawshay, the ironmaster of Cyfartha. He was a great benefactor to the Parish of Oystermouth and in 1863 presented All Saints' Church with a memorial window after the death of his young daughter; and in 1873 he gave the church its first organ (Hart, 1994, *Gower*, 45).

The house was originally called *'Lan-y-llan'* and *The Cambrian* reports several fund-raising fêtes being held in the grounds.

After the death of Henry Crawshay's widow in 1887 the house was sold for a hotel. It was enlarged from designs by John Norton and later became the luxurious **Langland Bay Hotel**, with tennis courts, croquet grounds, and well-wooded, richly flowered, landscaped gardens (as seen on the postcard on page 212).

The hotel had bathrooms with fresh and sea water, hot and cold, on each bedroom floor. There were well-appointed drawing and billiard rooms, whilst from the top floor of the building was a fire escape bridge to the hill adjoining.

However, the hotel was never a financial success and it came up for sale several times in the early 1900s. It remained open during WW1 but in 1922 it was sold to the **Workingmen's Club and Institute Union** for a convalescent home. When it became the Convalescent Home, a new, non-residential Langland Bay Hotel was built alongside, converted from the stables and the grooms' living quarters, plus the billiard room of the original hotel. The new hotel had a restaurant with a ballroom and a grill room which had a tessellated floor and the walls lined with Indian tiles depicting game, such as partridges, hares and ducks.

A postcard of Langland Bay Hotel.

The new Langland Bay Hotel was run by Mrs Murison (mother of former parishioner, the late Kirsteen Foster), who had been employed in the original hotel. This later hotel was recently demolished and replaced by apartment residences known as Crawshay Court. The role of the grand old Crawshay buildings, as a Convalescent Home, also came to an end. The building was on the market for £3m, and in 2006 was sold and converted into modern flats.

Langland Bay House. On the death of Mrs Henry Crawshay the entire estate, which now included the area later covered by Langland Bay Golf Club, was sold to a syndicate. It eventually became the **New Langland Bay Co. Ltd.** in 1891 and the land was subdivided into plots 200 feet long by 100 feet wide.

At that time in 1900, the Langland Bay area had only 6 houses, 3 hotels and one farm. Plot 20 was bought by Mr Albert Mason, a builder, and plot 21 was bought by a local man called John Richardson of Llwynderw. On the 30th January, 1901, Arthur Gilbertson, a wealthy industrialist from Pontardawe bought plot 20 from Mrs Emma Mason for £425. Then on 23rd August he bought plot 21 from John Richardson for £425, in order to build a house (see pages 47-48). The house was completed in April 1910, with a carriage house and stables with stabling for two horses. There was also a tack room and the living quarters for the carriage driver/groom. In the roof of the carriage room was a trapdoor which led to the room in which he slept.

This was Arthur Gilbertson's marine residence until his death, in 1912, when his solicitor sold the house to a daughter-in-law, Ellen Christabel Gilbertson, for £3,000. On 13th December, 1921, David Harry, a mine owner from Llanelli, bought the house for his brother, Dr Walter Benjamin Harry, for his retirement. The present owners, Miles and Grace Thomas, have had family connection with the house since then.

Caswell Cottage. The large house was built in 1822 by William Tucker of Horton and by 1855 had been acquired by John Dillwyn Llewelyn, pioneer photographer and squire of Penllegaer, as his rather grand country cottage and marine residence. It stood at the entrance to Caswell Valley, facing beautiful Caswell Bay. The cottage was very isolated, for at that time, there were only two buildings between Caswell and Newton. They were Kiln Green and Kiln Cottage. The track which ran between Caswell and Newton is now Caswell Road (see page 60).

Caswell Cottage.
(Photograph courtesy of Dr D. Painting).

At the end of the 1800s John Dillwyn Llewelyn's daughter Miss Gwendoline Dillwyn Llewelyn occupied the house. She contributed greatly to the new church of St Peter's, with her fine embroidery of altar frontals, as well as by hosting many fund-raising functions in the fine grounds of her house.

Miss Dillwyn Llewelyn established an **Orphan Home** at the cottage. The girls attended Newton School as recorded in the School Log Book, by the Mistress, Miss Howard: on 20th January 1899 – *Admitted 2 little girls from Miss Dillwyn Llewelyn's "Home for Orphans" at Caswell;* 18th May 1903 – *Miss Dillwyn Llewelyn wrote a note stating that the children from the Orphan Home would be absent from School all day on Ascension Day, to attend services in church [All Saints in Oystermouth].*

In the *Oystermouth Parish Magazine*, August 1902, we read that a Pastoral Play was performed in the grounds of Miss Dillwyn Llewelyn's picturesque residence, in order to raise funds for the New Church at Newton. The house later became a boarding house and was eventually demolished for the site of the present car park at Caswell.

Havergal House, originally known as **Park Villa**. This house is situated on the Caswell Road at the end of Caswell Avenue. It was built after 1874 by John Tucker of Langland who had taken out a ninety-nine year lease on the land from John Woollacott, the farmer (see page 20).

In 1878 Frances Ridley Havergal, a well-known hymn-writer, came to stay there with her sister, for eight months up to her death. A memorial plaque to Frances was placed in the chancel at the New Church in Newton when the church was built. Her picture hangs inside Paraclete Chapel, and around 1913 the name of Park Villa was changed *to Havergal House*. Then, in July 1937, to mark the centenary of her birth, a memorial plaque was unveiled outside the house on the wall. Thus, there are four memorials in the village of Newton, where Frances Ridley Havergal spent the last eight months of her life.

Park Villa, where Frances Ridley Havergal resided with her sister and died in 1879.

Summerland House stood off Caswell Hill and was owned by Miss Davies. It had lovely grounds with a walled tropical garden on the left of the drive. Betty Sivertsen recalls: *"As children we adored it and thought it enchanted – we thought there were fairies there. If we went as far as the Black Rock, we could creep through the railings and wander around with magic dreams until we were caught."*

Llwyn-y-Môr House. This was the only really large house on the 1878 map of the area and was a well-built house on the Caswell Road. It stood 500 feet above sea level and overlooked the sea. It stood in extensive grounds. In 1932 it was sold to the **P.N.E.U. School** whose headmistress was Miss Brooke Gwynne, the sister of Bishop Gwynne of Cairo. The house has since been demolished and replaced by a number of flats.

Glynn Vivian Home, in Mary Twill Lane, was built from funds provided by Glynn Vivian, son of Lord Swansea, to be a residential home for the blind, as he also became blind later in life.

The Cliff [Source of information – John Isaac].
The Cliff is a lovely 28-room country house, built of local limestone, with sandstone mullioned windows. The foundation stone was laid in 1892 by Stella, the daughter of Harold William Williams, who built the property.

He was a wealthy jeweller, who had a shop in Swansea, which sold beautiful silver ware. In the 1901 census it is recorded that he had a wife and 2 sons and 2 daughters. Tragically, his second son died at a young age shortly after, and Mr Williams donated the font to the newly built St Peter's Church as a memorial to him (see page 47). Mr Williams took a great interest in the new St Peter's Church, becoming its first churchwarden for twenty years, and again later until his death in 1932. Also resident in the house was a cook, a housemaid and a nurse (for his 5-months-old daughter). Later, the old Swansea City Gates were acquired, from the old Guildhall, and brought to the gardens of the house, which were just under an acre in size. During the 1930s the property became a boarding school. Then during World War II it was taken over by American soldiers, who left their mark on the walls in the form of bathing belle graffiti. In the 1950s the property returned to private ownership. The lovely exterior was used in the Peter Seller's film *"Only Two Can Play"* starring Mai Zetterling. The house has also featured in commercials for Mercedes Benz.

The house was bought by the well-known interior decorators John Isaac and his wife and was beautifully restored throughout. They had the drawing room wall lined with ivory damask, depicting Aesop's Fables. The impressive dining room was given a ceiling copied from Balmoral. The property has now been sold on.

Nearby, in **Southward Lane**, there is a house which was built in 1900 and had wonderful views across Underhill Park. Its claim to fame is that it became the home, in 1957, of Dr Daniel Jones, the well known Welsh composer and one of the locally famous *"Kardomah Boys"*. His friends and contemporaries were Dylan Thomas, Fred Jones, Ceri Richards and also Wynford Vaughan Thomas who often met there.

The Manor House

The Manor House stood on the edge of the village, at the junction of the track to Murton and the old drovers' road to Highpool and the common. It was

built in 1861 for the Revd David Secretan Jones, the Vicar of Oystermouth, and his wife to be.

No expense was spared. It was built in the style of a French Chateau. The roof slates were imported from Belgium, the metal window furniture from France. French tradesmen built the house and lavishly decorated the interior. The wedding, however, did not take place, but Secretan Jones still took up residence and used it as his vicarage. In the 1901 Census, he was 66 years old and it is recorded that he lived there alone, with a live-in servant.

The Manor House still stands proudly looking down on the village – one of the unchanged old houses of Newton.

Glan-Y-Coed

[Source of information – Jonathan Clark, great grandson of Charles Gold]

The house was built in 1865 by Charles Gold, who came to Swansea to head the Swansea branch of Messrs Phillips and Sons of Swansea, Manchester and London, having married the daughter of Mr Thomas Phillips, tea merchant. They took up residence when it was completed around 1865.

It is an imposing residence, built of local limestone, probably from Colt's quarry. It is built in the castellated style, dressed with Bath stone facings, and

Mr Charles Gold with his horse and carriage.

approached by a carriage drive. The entrance hall is laid with Minton tiles, and the principal staircase and woodwork is polished pitch pine. There are very large rooms – a drawing room, dining room, breakfast or morning room, billiard room and eight large bedrooms. For the domestic staff, a large servant's hall, kitchen, scullery, butlers pantry, store rooms. Below was a larder fitted with slate counters, a lower hall and extensive cellarage, as well as a laundry with drying room opening out into a courtyard with coal and wood houses and other conveniences.

The stabling was built to conform with the house, and consisted of three large stalls, a double coach house, harness room, and all necessary conveniences above. It also had a turret clock and a stone balustrade to match the one in the grounds.

There were two lawns – the upper one laid out as an Italian garden with a stone balustrade 110 feet long. The lower lawn had an ornamental fishpond supplied by spring water from the hills. There was a large vinery and conservatory, both heated by hot water. The wall fruit from this sheltered situation was always abundant.

The house still stands overlooking Underhill Park. However, the land at the side has been sold and a large Georgian type house occupies what was once the Italian garden. The coach house has also been sold and converted very sympathetically into a house, having had a happy history of use by the local Brownies for their meetings for several years. It has been said that Charles Gold was responsible for building the Chapel of Rest in Oystermouth Cemetery. His son Sidney, who also lived at Glan y Coed, donated the elegant brass eagle lectern to St Peter's Church in memory of his daughter Noelle (refer to page 47).

North entrance to St Peter's Church.
(Drawn by the late Grahame Sutton).

References and Bibliography

Throughout the book relevant information has been extracted from the comprehensive collection of the *Oystermouth Church Magazines* (1889-1933) and the *Parish Magazines Newton* (1933-2009); *The Cambrian* (1901, 1903). The photographs from individual collections have been acknowledged in the text. The unnamed photographs of the furnishings were obtained from the excellent Inventory of St Peter's Church, carefully recorded by the late Mr Grahame Sutton, and his wife Anne. Their son David contributed to some of the photography. Several extractions have been taken from a number of the journals of the Gower Society, *Gower*, with the permission of the editor and authors where possible.

MANUSCRIPTS and RECORDS

ABERYSTWYTH	**National Library of Wales**. Church in Wales Records.
CARDIFF	The Church Representative Body, Llandaff, copies of Indenture of St. Peter' Church.
LONDON	**Lambeth Palace Library**. Incorporated Church Building Society Files. No. 10,255.
SWANSEA	**West Glamorgan Archive Service**. Tithe Map 1845; The Grove Estate; Oystermouth & Newton Parish Records.
SWANSEA	**Central Reference Library**. The Cambrian Index Project; The Royal Institution of South Wales for use of Guides, Photographs, Records; Kirkland Collection (SWASM-2000.7.3).

BOOKS and ARTICLES

Broady, M., 1996, 'An undervalued Welsh Art: "Celtic Studios" Stained Glass 1933-1992', *Minerva*, IV. Swansea Museum.

Building News, 1901, p. 417.

Cardy, B., 2000, 'The Kirkland Family', *Minerva*, VII. Swansea Museum.

Church Builder, 1901, 'Organ of the Incorporated Church Building Society, London, 1862-1915'.

Cowley, F. G., 2007, *A Centenary History of Clyne Chapel, Blackpill, Swansea 1907-2007*. The Vicar and churchwardens of Clyne Chapel.

Cowley, F. G, 2001, *The History of St Paul's Church, Sketty, Swansea*. The Vicar and churchwardens of St Paul's, Sketty, Swansea.

Crowle Advertiser, 1996, 'Special Supplement on John Wesley'.

Davies J. D., 1879, *Davies West Gower*, Part 1, H. W. Williams.

Davies, J. M., 1969, 'The Gilbertsons of Pontardawe', *Gower*, 20.

Davis, P. R., 1986, *Historic Gower*, Christopher Davies, Publishers, Ltd.

Gabb, G., 1999, *Jubilee Swansea II.* Private Publication.

Gabb, G., 1986, *The Story of the Village of Mumbles*, D. Brown and Sons.

Gregor, G., 1997, 'Devotion, Desire and Heart: Frances Ridley Havergal', *Gower*, 48.

Hart, R. J., 1994, 'The Crawshays of Langland', *Gower 45*.

Hart, R. J., 2001, 'The Richardsons Pretio Prudentia Praetat', *Minerva*, IX. Swansea Museum.

Hart, R. J., 1997, 'John Jenkins of Rotherslade', *Minerva*, V. Swansea Museum.

History and Guides: (1) *St Peter's Church, Newton.* Haines, J., editor); (2) *The Parish Church of St Teilo's.*

Howell, P., 2004, *Whess come from Boy?.* Private publication.

Hughes Jones, I., 1962, 'Lady Barham's Secretary – The Revd William Hammerton', *Gower*, XV.

Hughes, J. V., 1974, 'Emily Charlotte Talbot', *Transactions of the Port Talbot Historical Society*, vol. 3.

Hughes, K., 2004, *Meliville A. Clare.* Private publication.

Kelly's Directory, 1891.

Langly, D., date unknown., 'Notes on Shoemakers Martyred', Ideal Shoe Co.

Morgan, 1899, *Antiquarian Survey of East Gower Bishopston.*

Newman, J., 1995, *The Buildings of West Glamorgan.* Penguin Books.

Orrin, G. R. and Cowley, F. G., 1990, *A History of All Saints' Church Oystermouth*, Gomer Press, Llandysul.

Orrin, G. R., 1999, *Church Building and Restoration in Victorian Glamorgan, 1837-1901.* University of Wales, Lampeter.

Orrin, G. R., 1979, *The Gower Churches.* Swansea: The Rural Deanery of W. Gower.

Orrin, G. R., 1982, *A History of Bishopston.* Gomer Press, Landysul.

Orrin, G. R., 1990, 'The Revd Harold Stepney Williams', *Gower*, 41.

Painting, D., 1987, *Amy Dillwyn.* University of Wales Press, Cardiff.

Pearce, J. Jnr., date unknown, 'William Kirkland extracts from Clarks of Street 1825-1950, Memoirs of an Employee'.

Powell, C., 2002, Editor of *Mumbles Memories*, Vol 2.

Richards, H. J., 1967, *ABC of the Bible*, Chapman.

Taylor, R., 2003, *How to Read a Church*, Rider.

Thomas, N. L., 1978, *The Mumbles – Past and Present*, Gomer Press, Llandysul.

Thompson, A. G., date unknown, *Gower Journey.* The Author.

Williams, H. E., 2000, *The Parting Mist.* The Author.

Index

222